Bob Rees is one of our foremost Latter-day Saint scholars. For decades, his thoughtful, perceptive articles and essays on the teachings, principles, and practices of the restored church and gospel have enlightened and edified Latter-day Saint readers, including me. They are always suffused with Bob's personal humane aspirations and echo his exemplary pro-active discipleship. Rees's collection of essays on the Book of Mormon extend over half century of serious, meticulous scholarship that reflects the influence both of early mentors like Hugh Nibley, Truman Madsen, and Robert K. Thomas but also a generation of contemporary scholars who approach the book with new critical perspectives and tools. His work reflects his humanely profound appreciation of the sty-listic riches and narrative complexities of the Book of Mormon prophets and other record keepers, including their central focus on Jesus Christ. Rees responds to their personal lives and utterances with both his heart and his mind and persuades readers to do likewise. —Thomas F. Rogers, author of *Let Your Hearts and Minds Expand* and *Huebner*

a new witness to the world

for Johnny Johnson,
a family friend for over half
a century, with gratitude for
many fond remembrances of
you, your parents and your brothers.
I conclude this book with the
statement that the ultimate
message of the Book of Mormon
is love, something the world
needs to be reminded of.
   All good wishes,
         Bob Rees, 2022

By Common Consent Press is a non-profit publisher dedicated to producing affordable, high-quality books that help define and shape the Latter-day Saint experience. BCC Press publishes books that address all aspects of Mormon life. Our mission includes finding manuscripts that will contribute to the lives of thoughtful Latter-day Saints, mentoring authors and nurturing projects to completion, and distributing important books to the Mormon audience at the lowest possible cost.

a new witness to the world

ROBERT A REES

BCC PRESS

For information contact
By Common Consent Press
4062 S. Evelyn Dr.
Salt Lake City, UT 84124-2250

Cover art: "Joseph and The Seer Stone," Gary Ernest Smith, 48″ × 48″, oil on canvas
Cover design: D Christian Harrison
Book design: Andrew Heiss

www.bccpress.org
ISBN-13: 978-1-948218-35-1

10 9 8 7 6 5 4 3 2 1

To my father
Alvin Clayton Rees
(1913–1984)
who first taught me about love,
Jesus,
and the Restored Gospel;
and to all the teachers, scholars, and readers
who have enlightened my understanding
of the Book of Mormon.

Contents

Acknowledgements

In his poem "A Tuft of Flowers," Robert Frost speaks of coming to a field to stack the grass a mower had cut the day before. As he labors, he follows the flight of a butterfly who finds a tuft of flowers the mower had thoughtfully left for butterflies, and, ostensibly, for anyone who came after him to enjoy. "A message from the Dawn," Frost calls it. "A leaping tongue of bloom the scythe had spared." Acknowledging this unexpected gift, the speaker considers the mower

> . . . a spirit kindred to my own;
> So that henceforth I worked no more alone, . . .
>
> And dreaming, as it were, held brotherly speech
> With one whose thought I had not hoped to reach.
>
> 'Men work together,' I told him from the heart,
> 'Whether they work together or apart.'

Today we would say,

> "Men and women work together . . . from the heart,
> Whether they work together or apart."

Which expresses my sentiments for the many people who, in one way or another, have contributed to this volume. They are too numerous to mention here, but I would like to single out a few who have been especially helpful in inspiring, correcting, revising, and refining my thoughts and expressions. These include Ruth Stanfield Rees (1937–2012) with whom I read and studied the Book of Mormon for the fifty plus years of our married life; Gloria Gardner Rees, my current wife, whose good heart, mind, and spirit have encouraged and guided this collection; Dawn Hall Anderson, whose superb copyediting skills and sensitivities inspire awe and admiration; friends and Book of Mormon scholars Richard Dilworth Rust, Thomas Rogers, and Heather Hardy, all of whom have read the manuscript in its various stages of production and both saved me from potential embarrassment and provided many constructive suggestions for improvement. I single out Heather who, in my estimation, knows the Book of Mormon more extensively, fully, and deeply than anyone I know. She seems to know it by heart, which is the best way to know it.

A Note on the Text

This collection consists primarily of articles and essays I have published over the past nearly sixty years, beginning when I was in graduate school. As such, it includes a wide range of subjects relating to the Book of Mormon. Most of my study of the Book of Mormon has focused on the text itself because I feel it merits consideration over such scholarly matters as archaeology, geography, genetics, and other areas of scientific exploration. I don't dismiss these as unimportant or irrelevant by any means, only that to date most of the scientific research and publication on the world of the Nephites, Mulekites, and Jaredites has yielded little definitive evidence as to the book's origin and provenance. Nevertheless, as a scholar I remain open to any new developments on or discoveries of scientific matters relating to the book as well as to any information that challenges my own conclusions. After a lifetime of study of this most significant book, I feel "there are many great and important things" yet to be revealed and discovered, both in it and about it. To quote Thoreau, "Only that day dawns to which we are awake. There is more day to dawn. The sun is but a morning star."

"If we study all scriptures, certain fundamentals emerge clearly. One is the character of God. Over and over again in all four scriptures Jesus and the prophets bear witness that God is our Father—just, impartial, merciful, forgiving, law-abiding, creative, and intelligent. If we believe the scriptures, we can depend on God's integrity and love. I do not accept any interpretation of scriptural passages that portrays God as being partial, unforgiving, hateful, or revengeful. It is more important to uphold the character and will of God than it is to support every line of scripture."

—Lowell Bennion

"Learning How to Know Scriptures: Values and Limitations," The Best of Lowell L. Bennion: Selected Writings, 1928–1988, *ed. by Eugene England.*

It Has Opened My Heart Wider to Experience His Love

Note: The original of the following brief essay was written thirty years ago at the request of my friend Eugene England for inclusion in his edited collection, Converted to Christ through the Book of Mormon *(Deseret Book, 1989). Most of the scholarly work contained in* A New Witness to the World *was composed during the decades following this personal expression of the Book of Mormon's importance in my life .*

I am convinced that we can best obtain knowledge, understanding, and inspiration, as well as wisdom, through both mind and heart, thought and feeling, intellect and affect. That is, any serious study of the Book of Mormon must include an honest and open consideration and contemplation of the book's provenance and its textual perplexities as well as its spiritual richness. Scholarly and cognitive skills help us to see and weigh facts, evidence, and argument while intuition, imagery, and what might be called the intelligence of the heart help us to see beneath and beyond what is objectively apparent. It is the two in concert and conversation that gives us the greatest chance of reaching the truth, however elusive it sometimes may be.

"A person's life purpose is nothing more than to rediscover, through the detours of art or love or passionate work, those one or two images in the presence of which his heart first opened."

—*Camus*

I love the Book of Mormon. My heart first opened to it at the age of ten when my father, just returned from the Second World War, told me about it. Before going into the service, he had been miraculously converted to the gospel by virtue of a priesthood blessing that brought him back from the brink of death. Perhaps it was a combination of love for my father, a youthful openness, and the gift of faith, but whatever the reason, when I heard the story of the coming forth of the Book of Mormon, it struck my young untutored heart and mind as true.

That first impression has remained constant even though as a scholar and thinker I have studied the book seriously and wrestled with questions as to its authorship, provenance, and meaning, including its meaning for our time.

I love to read the Book of Mormon because it is an inviting book, one that rewards careful and thoughtful study. My experience with it over the years has been the same as with other books of world literature, including the Bible, Shakespeare, and great novels and poems: the more I read them, the more riches they yield and the more I see their relevance to my life. Thoughtful and sensitive reading of the Book of Mormon reveals the depth, complexity, and subtlety of this second testament of Christ. Each time I read it I see things I haven't seen on previous readings. One of the reasons for this is that I come back to the book a different person from the one I was on previous readings. Between readings, coming to terms with my own weaknesses and transgressions and facing the challenges of being a better husband, father, friend, and disciple, lead me back to the book, I hope as a more informed, sensitive, and perceptive reader. As Harold Bloom says, "One of the uses of reading is to prepare ourselves for change."[1] The Book of Mormon prepares us to change our minds and our hearts, to change our lives.

I love the Book of Mormon because in reading it I experience what might be called "the shock of recognition" that what I am reading is true. I have thought often as to why the Lord has commanded us to read the scriptures. I am convinced that as we read about the experiences of actual men and women and see how God acted in their lives, we are persuaded that he can act in our lives as well. Moreover, as the Spirit reveals to our hearts and minds the truth of what we are reading, we experience the love of God in a profound way. In fact, one might say that the whole purpose of the gospel and the Church is to provide us with opportunities to experience God's love personally and intimately and to share that love with others. In this way, we come to experience, as the angel testified to Nephi, "the love of God which sheddeth itself abroad in the hearts of the children of men [and women]" and to know that "it is most joyous to the soul" (1 Nephi 11:22–23). The revelation of that love and joy is available through reading the Book of Mormon.

I love to study the Book of Mormon. I make a distinction between reading and studying; generally, we read the Book of Mormon for inspiration and comfort, but we study it to gain understanding. Through serious, thoughtful study we are able to dive into the book's depths, explore its richness, and test its mettle. Reading the Book of Mormon in this way prepares us not only for further reading but for the essential work of discernment, of sifting and winnowing. As Sir Francis Bacon advised, "Read not to contradict and confute; not to believe and take for granted; not to find talk and discourse, but to weigh and consider."[2]

I first learned how to seriously and contemplatively study the Book of Mormon as a student at Brigham Young University under the tutelage of such great teachers as Robert Thomas, Truman Madsen, Hugh Nibley, and others. Thomas awakened me both intellectually and spiritually to the literary qualities of the Book of Mormon. He

---

1. *How to Read and Why* (New York: Simon & Schuster, 2000), 21.
2. "Of Studies," http://www.authorama.com/essays-of-francis-bacon-50.html.

had written his undergraduate thesis at Reed College on the parallels between biblical poetic style and that of the Book of Mormon; as a budding literary scholar I was intrigued by his insights. Hugh Nibley gave me respect for what he characterized as the book's toughness. He taught me how to consider its ancient roots and antecedents and how to discover its messages for our dispensation. Truman Madsen taught me how to connect the book's great messages with the rich philosophical, spiritual, and historical truths of other faith traditions. In Reid Bankhead's class, Jesus the Christ, I understood for the first time what the atonement of Christ meant for me personally. That experience was enhanced by Professor Bankhead's teaching me how the Book of Mormon testifies of and enlightens our understanding of the atonement. In Glenn Pearson's Book of Mormon class, I learned how this New World witness of Christ can bring others to Christ.

In graduate school, my studies of literary theory and criticism as well as exposure to the great literature of our culture gave me a new appreciation for the linguistic complexity and literary beauty of the Nephite record. The more I learned about the integrity of literary texts, the more convinced I was that that no one living in the 1820s could have written the Book of Mormon. In fact, after a lifetime studying of the Book of Mormon and the critical literature related to it, I am convinced that all the scholars and theologians in the world in 1830, working with all the known texts and reference materials, could not have written what was translated from the gold plates. The intricacies of the various literary styles and complex narratives, the journeyings and histories of previously unknown biblical peoples, the unfolding of new spiritual insights, and, especially, the wonderful revelation of the expansive mission of Jesus Christ all suggest a time and a people that neither Joseph Smith nor any of his contemporaries could have known or invented. It is in the details that any text has its greatest test and, time and again, it is in the details of the Book of Mormon where its authenticity rings true, and where I find intellectual and rational support for the spiritual witness the book inspires.

I love to teach the Book of Mormon. Over the years I have had many opportunities, both formally and informally of teaching it in various classrooms and contexts, including Sunday School, the Young Men's program, priesthood quorums, and in Seminary and Institute classes. For the past decade I have had the privilege of teaching the Book of Mormon at the undergraduate and graduate levels. The undergraduate class I taught at the University of California, Berkeley, to a group of Religious Studies majors (including Jews, Muslims, Mormons, Catholics, and a host of Protestant denominations as well as atheists and agnostics) I count as perhaps the best class I have taught over the nearly sixty years of my professional teaching career. Close behind are the graduate courses I have been teaching for the past decade at Graduate Theological Union, also in Berkeley. My students at GTU, most of whom are studying for the ministry in their respective religions, represent many faith traditions, and my delight in teaching and learning from them is enhanced both by their own experience with scripture and their committed devotion. One of the most insightful and inspirational graduate papers I have read over the years was an essay on King Benjamin's address written by one of my Jesuit students. It represents the kind of joy I regularly experience in teaching at GTU. Since I teach my GTU classes at the Berkeley Latter-day Saint Institute of Religion, Institute students often participate, enriching the experience.

As a father it has been my privilege to teach the Book of Mormon to my children and to testify of its truth to them. One of my greatest joys has been to see some of my children and grandchildren grow up with their own testimonies of the Book of Mormon and to see them share their testimonies with others through missionary work, teaching in the Church, and testifying to friends and acquaintances. In this way, the light of this great book is passed from generation to generation and to the wider world.

As Bishop of a singles ward in Los Angeles during the 1980s, I found teaching the truths of the Book of Mormon to my congregation to be a great resource for touching their lives and challenging them as well as myself to greater faithfulness. Often in ministering to members of my congregation, I found the Book of Mormon a rich resource for counseling and comfort. I remember a young man who had been involved in a series of sexual transgressions. He was not convinced that what he had done was particularly wrong or that it could have serious consequences in his life. As we conversed, I remembered Alma's words to his son Corianton. Opening the book, I read Alma's counsel to his son, including the following: "Behold, I say unto you, wickedness never was happiness" (Alma 41:10) and challenged this brother to consider whether he was really living his life according to the Plan of Happiness the gospel provides. I saw no evidence of any immediate change, but I was grateful to have Alma's counsel to pass along, perhaps as a seed that would take root in this young man's heart and mind.

I love to teach the Book of Mormon because it is a very teachable book, one that offers great lessons that can inspire faithfulness in confronting the fundamental problems of human relationships, the archetypal conflict between good and evil, and the eternal struggle between our wills and God's. Like all great literature, it allows us to relate imaginatively to the characters who inhabit its pages. Further, since it was written expressly for our day, we are able to gain insight from its stories and principles and apply them to our daily lives. Like Nephi, we are able "to liken all scriptures unto us, that it might be for our profit and learning" (1 Nephi 19:23).

I love to testify of the Book of Mormon. Knowing how much joy the book has brought me, I have sought for opportunities to tell others of its truths. When I was a young missionary, I thrilled to testify to people I met in cities and towns in the Midwest of the Lord's work among the ancient Americans. Nervously—to the very first person I taught on my first day of tracting in Kankakee, Illinois, a Mrs. Daggert—I testified to the truth of the Restoration, including the coming forth of the Book of Mormon. She received a witness through my very humble testimony that day. Since then I have testified to the truth of this second witness of Jesus Christ to thousands and have felt the exquisite joy that comes from being an instrument in bringing others to Christ. As Emily Dickinson said, "Truth is such a *rare* thing, it is a delight to tell it."[3]

Several of my many conversations with others about the Book of Mormon stand out in my mind. In the eighties, I had the privilege of working with the writer Norman Cousins in organizing a series of exchanges between writers from China and the United States, giving me a rare opportunity of becoming acquainted with distinguished writers, many of whose works I had taught in my literature courses at UCLA (e.g., Toni Morrison, Arthur Miller, Maxine Hong Kingston). At one conference in Los Angeles, I conversed with the fiction writer Kurt Vonnegut (*Cat's Cradle, Slaughterhouse-Five* and *Breakfast of Champions).* Upon discovering I was a Latter-day Saint, he asked if I really believed what the Church taught and specifically how I regarded the Book of Mormon. I replied that I considered it an authentic ancient record. He responded, "How can you believe something like that?" My response was the same as I have given to similar questions from students and colleagues in the various universities at which I have taught: "If I am both intellectually and spiritually honest with myself, I have to say that the spiritual and intellectual conviction I receive when reading the book is among my truest and most meaningful experiences."

I had a similar conversation in Suzhou, China, with the poet Allen Ginsberg (*Howl and Other Poems, Kaddish*) who had become a friend through these writers' exchanges. Our conversation one evening at a gathering of Chinese and American writers turned to religion. When Allen inquired about my religious beliefs, I briefly summarized our teachings, including those about the Book of Mormon. He asked incredulously, "This is actually believed?" I assured him that indeed it was and that I was one of the believers. Allen was a practicing Buddhist and had respect and tolerance for the beliefs of others, but this particular set of beliefs seemed to stretch the limits of his ecumenical spirit.

---

3. Sharon Leiter, *Critical Companion to Emily Dickinson: A Literary Reference to Her Life and Work* (New York: Facts on File, 2006), 181; http://archive.emilydickinson. org/correspondence/higginson/jnl342.html

I also told my Chinese friends about the Book of Mormon and included copies of it in collections of American literature our delegation gave to the Chinese Writers' Association libraries in Beijing and Shanghai. Later, on a trip to the Soviet Union for UCLA, I gave a copy of the book to a friend in Leningrad; in Moscow I had a conversation with a Russian associate who had been reading a copy given to him by my friend, Eugene Kovalenko. Later (1992–1996) as an Education and Humanitarian Service representative of the Church in the St. Petersburg, Russia and Baltic States Missions, I had many opportunities to teach and testify of the Book of Mormon. Over the decades, I have sent copies to acquaintances, friends, and associates. When the Family-to-Family Book of Mormon program began in the 1980s, our family participated by sending copies with our photograph and testimony pasted in the front to anonymous readers.

I love the Book of Mormon most of all because it has led me to a greater, deeper, and more expansive understanding of the life and mission of Jesus Christ—opening my heart wider to experience his love. The Book of Mormon testifies of Christ from the very beginning, declaring its intention to convince "Jew and Gentile that Jesus is the Christ, the eternal God, manifesting himself unto all nations" (Preface). That intention is evident from the very first chapter where the prophet Lehi has a vision of "One descending out of the midst of heaven [whose] luster was above that of the sun at noon-day" (1 Nephi 1:9) to the very last chapter where Moroni says, "If ye by the grace of God are perfect in Christ, and deny not his power, then are ye sanctified in Christ by the grace of God, through the shedding of the blood of Christ, which is in the covenant of the Father unto the remission of your sins, that ye become holy, without spot" (Moroni 10:33). Through the many testimonies of the Book of Mormon prophets and through Christ's own testimony to the Nephites and through them to future generations, including those of us living in this day, I have come to exclaim, as does Nephi,

I glory in plainness;
I glory in truth;
I glory in *my Jesus*,
For he has redeemed my soul from hell.

(2 Nephi 33:6, emphasis added)

I love the Book of Mormon. And I love the Lord for sending it to bless our lives.

Introduction

Carrying Water
on Both Shoulders

*"I am committed both to religious faith and
idealism and to the best critical thinking of
men [and women]. The reason for this dual
commitment is that each has greatly enriched
my life. I can deny neither at this point."*
—*Lowell Bennion*[1]

How are we to regard the Book of Mormon and how are we to read it?
How we read it to a large extent depends on how we regard it. Even
before it was published, the Book of Mormon generated controversy
about its origins, and immediately after it was published, theories about
its composition began to abound. Some said that Smith must be the
author and others countered that he was too ignorant and provincial to
have written any book, let alone the Book of Mormon. Since that time,

---

1. "Carrying Water on Both Shoulders," *Dialogue* 6:1, 110–112., Hereinafter Bennion.

there have been numerous theories about the authorship of the book. These range from it being a tale told by an idiot, devoid of either sound or fury and signifying nothing very important, being inspired by the devil, written by or plagiarized from other writers, and penned by a genius who was inspired by God.

Louis Midgley summarized the various attempts to explain the book into four categories: 1) "Joseph Smith wrote the book as a conscious fraud"; 2) "Joseph Smith wrote the book under the influence of some sort of paranoia or demonic possession or dissociative illusion"; 3) "Joseph Smith had the help of someone like Sidney Rigdon in creating the book"; and 4) "Joseph Smith wrote the book while under some sort of religious inspiration."[2] A more modern theory is that the book is a product of automatic writing (See Chapter 8, "The Book of Mormon and Automatic Writing"). Taken together, these explanations show Joseph Smith variously as a country bumpkin and a brilliant sophisticate, a simple self-delusionist and a conspirator, a plagiarizer and an originator, an idiot and a genius, and as devil-inspired and God-inspired.

Assessments of the Book of Mormon itself are no less extreme. Early views included seeing it as "the result of gross imposition, and a grosser superstition,"[3] the ramblings of a digger for treasure, and a compilation of "every error and almost every truth discussed in N[ew] York during the ten years before its publication."[4] Others accused Smith of stealing the basic plot and much of the substantive content from Ethan Smith's *View of the Hebrews* or a fictional narrative written by Solomon

---

2. "Who Really Wrote the Book of Mormon? The Critics and Their Theories," in Noel B. Reynolds, ed., *Book of Mormon Authorship Revisited: The Evidence for Ancient Origins* (Provo, UT: Foundation for Ancient Research and Mormon Studies, 1997), 104. Hereinafter BMAR.

3. Francis W. Kirkham, *A New Witness for Christ in America: The Book of Mormon*, Vol. 1 (Independence, Mo: Zion's Publishing, 1959), 149.

4. Alexander Campbell, *Delusions: An Analysis of the Book of Mormon . . .* (Boston: Benjamin H. Greene, 1832), 13, as quoted in Richard Bushman, "The Book of Mormon and the American Revolution." *BYU Studies* (17:1), 20.

Spaulding. In his *Comprehensive History of the Church*, B. H. Roberts catalogues some of the early anti-Mormon assessments: Governor Ford of Illinois saw it as "the fumes of an enthusiastic and fanatical imagination"; for Lily Dougal it was "the work of a genuinely deluded . . . but undisciplined brain"; and, according to I. Woodbridge Riley, it was the product of "subjective hallucination, induced by hypnotic suggestion."[5] Mark Twain, who considered the book boring, opined, "If Joseph Smith composed this book, the act was a miracle—keeping awake while he did it was, at any rate. If he, according to tradition, merely translated it from certain ancient and mysteriously-engraved plates of copper, which he declares he found under a stone, in an out-of-the-way locality, the work of translation was equally a miracle, for the same reason."[6]

In the eighteenth century there was a controversy over the authenticity of a collection of prose poems called *The Poems of Ossian*, which James Macpherson had written but tried to pass off as the work of a third-century, blind epic poet named Ossian. The book was extremely popular in both America and Europe and most people considered it authentic. The venerable Samuel Johnson, upon being asked whether he thought the work could have been written by a modern man, replied, "Yes, Sir, many men, many women, and many children."[7] Sometimes I get the impression that some critics have the same opinion of the Book of Mormon—that not only could many men, women, and possibly even children have written it, but that any fool could have and that one particular fool named Joseph Smith certainly did write it.

While nineteenth century estimates tended to see the book as the product of a deluded or demonic mind, twentieth and twenty-first century evaluations have tended to be more sophisticated, if at times no more reasonable. Bernard DeVoto postulated that Smith wrote the book under

---

5. *Comprehensive History of the Church of Jesus Christ of Latter-day Saints*, Vol. 1 (Provo, UT: Brigham Young University Press, 1965), 150–51.
6. *Roughing It*, ed., Harriet Elinor Smith and Edgar M. Branch (Berkeley: University of California Press, 1993), 107.
7. James Boswell, *The Life of Samuel Johnson, LLD* (London: Bickers and Son, 1874), 492.

the spell of epileptic seizures, producing "a yeasty fermentation, formless, aimless, and inconceivably absurd . . . ."[8] After the advent of Freud it was inevitable that someone would try to explain the Book of Mormon in strictly psychological terms. The first significant attempt was Fawn Brodie's *No Man Knows My History* (1954; revised, 1971) which argued that the book was nothing more than a playing out of Joseph Smith's fantasies and the Smith family's psychological history.[9] Robert Anderson's *Inside the Mind of Joseph Smith* (1999) attempts a detailed argument for the book as a psychological roadmap of the lives of Joseph Smith and his family. Unfortunately, because Anderson relies so slavishly on Freudian analysis and so heavily on Brodie's book, he is even less successful in finding the true Joseph Smith or the Book of Mormon than was Brodie.

As a literary critic I am aware of the multiple ways of looking at a book or a blackbird. Sometimes when I teach a text, the students and I examine it from the perspectives of various critical approaches— new critical, historical, biographical, Freudian, Marxist, feminist, deconstructionist, reader response, etc. All of these might be considered legitimate approaches to a text as long as they acknowledge their respective biases and limitations and don't become too extreme or doctrinaire, which they often do. Reading contemporary criticism of the Book of Mormon reminds one of Emerson's statement, "If I know your sect, I anticipate your argument."[10] That is, critics who do not believe in angels, miracles, or communication from beyond the veil that separates the living from the dead, must locate the Book of Mormon someplace within the early nineteenth century. Other critics (e.g., Evangelicals) who do believe in angels and miracles but do not consider Joseph Smith a prophet also posit a naturalistic or even demonic explanation of the

8. "The Centennial of Mormonism," *American Mercury*, 19:5 (Jan 1930), 5, as quoted in Louis Midgley, "Who Really Wrote the Book of Mormon?" BMAR, 105.

9. *No Man Knows My History: The Life of Joseph Smith, the Mormon Prophet*, 2nd ed., revised and enlarged (New York: Knopf, 1971), 43, 413–17.

10. "Self Reliance," in *Essays by Ralph Waldo Emerson*, ed. Edna H.L. Turpin (New York: Charles E. Merrill Co., 1907), 79–116; https://archive.vcu.edu/english/engweb/transcendentalism/authors/emerson/essays/selfreliance.html.

book's authorship and setting. Only those who consider the possibility of spiritual or supernatural phenomena and consider Joseph Smith a prophet are open to the possibility of an ancient origin for the book.

Over the years as I have read the opinions, analyses, examinations, and theories of various Book of Mormon scholars, I have been intrigued by the chasm that tends to divide the believers/apologists from the non-believers/naturalists, those who consider the book an authentic, divinely inspired ancient text from those who consider it a product of a modern mind, experience, and imagination. One of the things that characterizes the relationship between these two camps (I call it a relationship since for the most part "dialogue" doesn't accurately describe their discourse) is the tendency of each to dismiss and negatively label the other. Since I have been labeled both an apologist and a naturalist critic, sometimes in pejorative terms, I have watched this exchange with interest.

I am grateful for anyone who has sincerely tried to come to terms with the Book of Mormon. Those who have challenged the traditional explanation of the book by exploring its nineteenth-century origins and setting have often raised important issues, some of which apologists tend to dismiss too easily; on the other hand, naturalist critics often dismiss the findings of scholars who likewise have raised important issues and have deepened and broadened understanding of the text and its possible connection to its purported ancient setting.

It is fascinating that one group finds parallels only in the late eighteenth and early nineteenth centuries which convince them that the book is a product of a modern American mind, while the other group finds parallels within the ancient world and concludes that the book could only have originated from ancient peoples. Since the parallels (or at least some of them) that each group finds are or seem to be legitimate or at least worth considering, what are we to conclude? One feels that this discourse often is reduced to, "My parallel arguments are better, more authentic, and more persuasive than yours!"[11] Since everyone uses parallel arguments, and since no parallel argument is likely to be absolutely conclusive, the questions we have to ask are: "How legitimate is the parallel?"; "How many points of correspondence exist between the two things being compared?"; and, "How unique is the comparison?" The more general the parallel and the more widely it can be found in a particular culture, the less convincing it is likely to be. Gordon C. Thomasson argues that parallels that can be found outside of "the information environment" of Joseph Smith and the period of the publication of the Book of Mormon have "a different apologetic weight than something which was known" to be in that environment. To emphasize this difference, Thomasson states, "For example, the Dead Sea Scrolls (including biblical variants) were not part of Joseph Smith's or anyone else's information environment in 1830, whereas, for example, the writings of Ixlilxochitl were known or knowable."[12]

Since the latter decades of the twentieth century, a new group of scholars has staked out territory somewhat between the apologist and naturalist positions. These scholars, of whom Anthony A. Hutchinson and David P. Wright are representative, consider Joseph Smith a prophet (although not in the same sense the Judeo-Christian world considers Moses and Daniel prophets) and the Book of Mormon inspired, but do not consider it an ancient text. They argue that the speakers of the Book of Mormon have important things to say even though they are fictional characters. For example, Hutchinson feels "The Book of Mormon should be seen as authoritative scripture." He adds, "God remains the author of the Book of Mormon viewed as the

---

11. For a discussion of the use of parallel arguments, see Douglas F. Salmon, "Parallelomania and the Study of Latter-day Saint Scripture: Confirmation, Coincidence, or the Collective Unconscious?" *Dialogue* 33:2 (Summer 2000), 129–156). For a rejoinder to Salmon, see Gordon C. Thomasson's "Personal Parallel Perspectives on Parallelomania," unpublished paper in my possession.

12. Ibid., 4, 3.

word of God, but Joseph Smith, in this construct, would be the book's inspired human author rather than its inspired translator."[13]

Such a position raises ultimate questions about the Book of Mormon. For example, if Alma is a fictional rather than an historical character, and if the Jesus who speaks in 3 Nephi is really Joseph Smith trying to imagine what Jesus would have said had he visited ancient America, and if the central purpose of the text is to provide a guide for moral behavior rather than a second testament of Jesus Christ, it radically alters the way we read and find meaning in the text. Such reading tends to make irrelevant or diminish the importance of such questions as to whether the text enlightens our understanding of how God acts in history and whether Jesus is the literal Son of God who atoned for the sins of all Adam and Eve's children.

A related approach is offered by Mark Thomas in his *Digging in Cumorah: Reclaiming Book of Mormon Narratives*. Thomas, who wrote in hope that his work would mark the beginning of "a foundation for a new tradition in Book of Mormon studies," states, "In the end, a book's authority lies less in its origin than in its messages." Thomas attempts to stake out a critical perspective somewhere between the apologist and naturalist positions. For example, he states, "We will never find the book's real value or message until we set aside the apologetic issues of authorship, at least temporarily. . . ." Later he states, "Biblical scholarship has faced similar interpretive problems with apologetic interests

---

13. The full text of Hutchinson's argument reveals his thoughtful if nuanced position: "The Book of Mormon should be seen as authoritative scripture, part of a larger canon, reliable in conveying the truth of the restored gospel when read and used in faith and repentance and doctrinally construed in light of all scripture and revelation, past, present, and future. In terms of general interpretation of the book's themes and stories, our overall approach should not be substantially changed by abandoning insistence on the book's ancient origin. What would be changed though is our general use of the book as an apologetic argument or a sign of the uniqueness of Mormonism and warrant of its authority and truthfulness. "The Word of God is Enough: The Book of Mormon as Nineteenth-Century Scripture," in *New Approaches, to the Book of Mormon* (Salt Lake City: Signature, 1993), 1, 2; hereinafter *New Approaches*.

interfering with interpretation."[14] However, it can be equally argued (likely with Thomas's affirmation) that a balanced position would be as demanding of naturalist issues of authorship and acknowledge that rationalist interests at times also interfere with interpretation. I agree with Thomas's view of the primacy of the book's message but also argue that how one deciphers and understands that message depends to some extent on how one views the book's provenance.

Grant Hardy does a masterful job of bracketing issues of historicity and scholarly approaches in his *Understanding the Book of Mormon*. Also, Hardy's *Readers' Book of Mormon* has made the text accessible in ways it hasn't been before. I believe both Hardy's text and his scholarship are factors in encouraging more non-Mormon scholars to take the book seriously, as is the following from his "Afterward" inviting: "There is much more to discover in terms of narrative techniques, connections between various people and events, thematic development, and specific language employed by different speakers. The key to reading the Book of Mormon well is to start with the organizing principle of the text—the fact that it presents itself as the work of narrators with distinct voices and perspectives."[15]

It is important to acknowledge that the Book of Mormon represents a unique challenge with regard to its provenance because of its own "history-like narrative" which so emphatically asserts its own historicity. One need only consider the detailed internal chronology and geography and repeated references to actual plates, records, and artifacts, to say nothing of Moroni's role as its closing figure as well as the angel who very tangibly presented himself on numerous occasions to Joseph Smith. It is also important to acknowledge such naturalistic evidence as literary and historical anachronism as well as the absence of evidence regarding DNA analysis and New World archaeological remains. What I personally find inexplicable is dismissing the book

---

14. (Salt Lake City: Signature, 2000), 1. Hereinafter, *Digging in Cumorah*.
15. *Understanding the Book of Mormon: A Reader's Guide* (Oxford: Oxford University Press, 2010), 268.

because of the absence of such things as Semitic DNA among Amerind peoples or archeological evidence of Lehite or Jaredite cultures while ignoring the evidence of the text.

That is, while there is much historical and scientific evidence about the Book of Mormon that is absent or incomplete, what we do have is the evidence in the text itself, and that is the most essential thing. As the theologian Hans Frei argues, "I am persuaded that historical inquiry is a useful and necessary procedure but that theological reading is the reading of a *text*, and not the reading of a *source*, which is how historians read it. Historical inquiry, while telling us many useful things, does not tell us how we are to understand the text as texts."[16]

Editors Elisabeth Fenton and Jared Hicks tackle the historicity issue head on in their Introduction to *Americanist Approaches to the Book of Mormon* (Oxford: Oxford University Press, 2019): "*The Book of Mormon* has been deemed by many Americanist scholars as either too hot to handle or unworthy of handling with care." They state further, "Because of [the] particulars of the text's publication and dissemination, *The Book of Mormon* has tended to neatly demarcate 'religious' and 'secularist' interpretive positions along a temporal axis." The consequence of such dualism "has tended to transform all discussants of the text into either debunkers or defenders of the Mormon faith."[17] What this has created in my view is a situation in which some scholars politely or at least carefully bracket matters of provenance and historicity due to concern over their scholarship being dismissed because it and they will be labeled apologetic/believer or naturalist/critical.

While the text is paramount, questions about its origin are hardly irrelevant, although I am willing to concede that some such discussion may be irrelevant, and some certainly misguided. Were Mormon a fictional character in a historical novel written by Joseph Smith, I think I would still find his discourse on charity (Moroni 7:44–48) and his invitation to come unto Christ (10:32–33) inspiring, but they have more

---

16. *Types of Christian Theology* (New Haven: Yale Univ. Press, 1994), 11.
17. (Oxford: Oxford University Press, 2019), 2, 3.

meaning and have a more profound impact if I consider that these are the words of an actual man who walked the earth and who struggled with his soul and its relation to his Savior, just as I do. Personally, I don't believe such narrative elements are a product of Joseph Smith's experience or creation, even though they may be expressed in his language.

Two Critical Cultures

In relation to Book of Mormon scholarship, the heart of the problem as I see it is that those on each side of the argument seem to be talking past one another or, to use Paul's words, to be "speaking into the air" (1 Cor. 14:9). Thus, at the end of his essay, "'A Record in the Language of My Father': Evidence of Ancient Egyptian and Hebrew in the Book of Mormon," Edward Ashment, former coordinator of Church Translations Services, comments, "Unfortunately there is no direct evidence to support the historical claims of the Book of Mormon—nothing archeological, nothing philological. As a result, those for whom Truth is the product of spiritual witness, not empirical inquiry, resort to developing analogies and parallels to defend the book's historic claims. That is the apologetic historical methodology."[18] It is interesting that this charge is similar to that leveled against the naturalist critics by apologists, who see such critics as ignoring compelling empirical historical, textual, and philological evidence and developing analogies and parallels to attack the book's historicity. Ashment does not seem to see the possibility that truth can be the product of *both* spiritual witness and empirical inquiry. I argue that it is the two in concert that have the best chance of leading us to truth. This is what Lowell Bennion called "carrying water on both shoulders."[19]

I contend that both sides of the Book of Mormon scholarly divide suffer from what Peter Enns calls "the sin of certainty," which leads

---

18. *New Approaches*, 374.
19. Bennion, 111.

them to distrust or discount the scholarship of those who do not believe (or disbelieve) as they do. As Enns argues, "None of us rises above our place in the human drama and grasps God with pure clarity, without our own baggage coming along for the ride. We all bring our broken and limited selves into how we think of God. . . . We can't help but think of God in broken and limited ways, as creatures limited by time and space." He adds that "God is okay with our humanity"[20]; the problem is that we are not okay with the humanity of those who differ from us.

Perhaps there is reason for each side to be skeptical of the other because each side has been, in my judgment, too quick to dismiss the methods and observations of the other, too quick to question the methodology and scholarship of their opponents, and too quick to rush to judgment about one another's discoveries as well as motives. John Stuart Mill observes, "For while everyone well knows himself to be fallible, few think it necessary to take any precautions against their own fallibility, or admit the supposition that any opinion, of which they feel very certain, may be one of the examples of the error to which they acknowledge themselves to be liable." Mill also states, "It is only by the collision of adverse opinions that the . . . truth has any chance of being supplied,"[21] an observation that echoes Joseph Smith's dictum, "by proving contraries, truth is made manifest."[22]

We need to recognize that as extremes each position is limited. Those who defend the Book of Mormon primarily with their testimonies tend not to be open to some of the challenging questions the book presents in its claim to be a translation of an ancient text. They need to acknowledge that some questions raised by those who do not consider the book of divine origin and influence are worthy of consideration and examination. Not everyone who questions Joseph Smith's account of

20. *The Sin of Certainty: Why God Deserves Our Trust More Than Our "Correct" Beliefs* (HarperCollins, 2016).

21. *On Liberty*, ed., David Spitz (New York: Norton, 1975), 54, 82.

22. Joseph Smith to L. Daniel Rupp, 5 June 1844, (*Documentary History of the Church* (Salt Lake City: Deseret Book, 1948) 6:428.

the book's origins is an enemy of the truth or the Church. Responding to such issues merely by testifying or invoking spiritual authority tends to close off dialogue.

On the other hand, those who refute the divine origin of the book tend not to respect the spiritual experience of believers or to be open to evidence that suggests that the book has an ancient source. They also need to acknowledge the challenges that face their scholarship if they contend that Joseph Smith or some other nineteenth-century American was the author of the book. The believers/apologists need to be less pious and judgmental and the non-believers/naturalists/empiricists need to be a little more honest and humble about the limitations of what they consider empirical proof. If one believes in the possibility of supernatural influences and events (for example that prayers can be answered, God and angels can communicate with humans, and dead bodies be resurrected), then one's range of possible explanations for something like the composition of the Book of Mormon is larger than those who do not.

In an article titled, "Suspending Disbelief," Linda Stone, a contemporary visionary thinker, says, "Everything we know, our strongly held beliefs, and in some cases, even what we consider to be 'factual,' creates the lens through which we see and experience the world, and can contribute to a critical, reactive orientation. This can serve us well. For example: Fire is hot; it can burn me if I touch it. [However,]These strongly held beliefs can also compromise our ability to observe and to think in an expansive, generative way."[23]

Stone then cites the examples of three scientists—Barbara McClintock, Stanley Pruisner and Barry Marshall—all of whom made important scientific discoveries which were rejected by their respective scholarly communities in spite of the evidence supporting them. According to Stone, McClintock, who discovered "jumping genes," "was ignored and ridiculed, by the scientific community for thirty-two years before winning" the Nobel Prize in 1984. Prusiner was also widely

---

23. http://lindastone.net/2011/02/06/suspending-disbelief/.

criticized and ridiculed for his prion theory years before he won the Nobel Prize for it in 1982. Marshall, who theorized that stomach ulcers were caused by bacteria rather than acid and stress (the prevailing theory), lamented, "Everyone was against me."[24] In making a distinction between projective as opposed to reactive thinking, Stone says, "Progress in medicine was delayed while these 'projective thinkers' persisted, albeit on a slower and lonelier course."[25] What Stone seems to be suggesting is that in both truly trying to weigh and measure evidence as well as openly consider opinion and surmise, it may be necessary at times to suspend both belief and disbelief, to be willing to question one's conclusions as well as assert one's findings.

Until the Enlightenment, academics and religionists alike tended to see the world through two lenses—*logos* and *mythos*—and considered each essential in seeking and living by truth. As Karen Armstrong argues in *The Battle for God*, "The *mythos* of a society provided people with a context and made sense of their day-to-day lives; it directed their attention to the eternal and the universal. It was also rooted in what we call the unconscious mind." She adds, "*Logos* was equally important. *Logos* was the rational, pragmatic, and scientific thought that enabled men and women to function well in the world. . . . In the pre-modern world, both *mythos* and *logos* were regarded as indispensable. Each would be impoverished without the other."[26]

I believe we need to recapture this older way of looking for truth, to recognize that *logos*, with its emphasis on cognitive processes and empirical proof, ultimately may be no more reliable nor less essential than *mythos*, with its emphasis on ritual and mysticism. It is the dialogue between the two, the respect for what they each can teach us, which should inform our quest for both temporary and ultimate meaning, for what our brains can help us discover from empirical evidence and what our hearts can help us discern of what lies beneath and

---

24. Ibid.
25. Ibid.
26. (New York: Random House, 2000), xv, xvi-xvii.

beyond such evidence. In other words, God speaks to us from his heart and his mind, speaks in prophecy, poetry, and prose to reveal truth and the wonders of creation. I believe he also expects us to speak from and listen with *our minds and hearts*, to be open to what we see and hear but also to what we intuit and imagine.

In a dialogue with Earl Wunderli over my review of his *An Imperfect Book: What the Book of Mormon Tells Us about Itself* (Salt Lake City: Signature Books, 2013), the premise of which is that the Book of Mormon is entirely the product of Joseph Smith's mind and imagination, I offered the following: "If someone were to find a MS in the Library of Congress or the British Museum dating from the sixteenth century that included a history of Ancient Americans who came from the Near East and included characters named Nephi, Moroni and Ether, I would have to seriously re-examine my position [that the book is of ancient origin]. I would hope that if some stele were uncovered in Guatemala that contained similar names, confirmed naturalist critics would be open to doing the same."[27]

A Tentative Theory

> *"Words may be a thick and darksome veil of mystery between the soul and the truth which it seeks."*
>
> —*Nathaniel Hawthorne to Sophia Peabody, 19 May 1840*

It appears that those who hold strict naturalist or apologetic critical positions in regard to the Book of Mormon are caught in a seemingly hopeless and endless dialectic. Each side has dug in for the long battle and each uses whatever weapons in its arsenal it feels necessary to defend its position. But what if neither side were completely right or

---

27. "An Imperfect Book," Review of Earl M. Wunderli's *An Imperfect Book: What the Book of Mormon Tells Us about Itself* (Salt Lake City: Signature Books, 2013), 389 pp. *Interpreter: A Journal of Mormon Scripture* 12 (2014), 33–47.

completely wrong? In other words, what if there were a third option? I doubt that such an option would be tenable to either side because it would mean retreating from their certain, strongly held, and passionately defended positions. As I have read the Book of Mormon over a lifetime, I have been committed to thoroughly and thoughtfully considering all the evidence and arguments put forth by scholars, believers, and skeptics as to the book's claims. In doing so, I have tried to employ my best scholarly and analytical skills while being open to intuitive and imaginative perceptions--and appraising and pondering my spiritual experiences with the book (which have been consistent over a lifetime). Through this process, I have come to the conclusion that the Book of Mormon may genuinely be both an ancient and a modern text. By this I mean I believe that there were real people named Nephi, Alma, Moroni, and Mormon who came from the Middle East and who lived and wrote on the American continent. The records they kept were like the records kept by other ancient peoples in that they contain a chronicle of their cultural experience and religious history, and were expressed in the forms and styles of their literary tradition. But what thoughts and feelings they hoped to pass on to future generations were "translated" or expressed in Joseph Smith's American-English language and through the experience of his nineteenth-century mind and culture.[28] As Lowell Bennion has argued, "Revelation is of God and is authoritative for the believer, but it is given in man's language and weakness, in his own thinking and understanding (D&C 1:24–28)."[29]

This would explain why one finds examples in the Book of Mormon of expressions and verbal coloring that most likely were not in the original source. For example, I think David Wright argues convincingly that in his expression of ideas found in Alma 12–13, Joseph Smith

---

28. At least some of the translation/compositional process by which Joseph Smith produced the Book of Mormon may be related to that which he employed in his revision of the Bible and in his production of the books of Moses and Abraham. In each instance, Joseph created new or revised existing texts either with an actual text in hand or through some other process.

29. *Understanding The Scriptures* (Salt Lake City, Utah: Deseret Book, 1981), 23.

"transformed" the Letter to the Hebrews rather than, as some apologist critics argue, there was an ancient prototype that served as a source for both Alma and Hebrews.[30] While Wright's argument is persuasive, I don't agree with him when he states, "It goes almost without saying that this conclusion means further that the rest of the Book of Mormon was composed by" Joseph Smith.[31]

The position I am arguing for here is similar to that which Blake Ostler articulates in his *Dialogue* article, "The Book of Mormon as an Expansion of an Ancient Source." Ostler makes a convincing case for the possibility of both an ancient source and a modern transformation of that source so that the book presents "a modern world view and theological understanding superimposed on the Book of Mormon text from the plates."[32] Although somewhat parallel, my argument is more conservative than Ostler's. That is, it seems to me that one has to do too many intellectual and spiritual gymnastics either to see the Book of Mormon as a perfectly literal translation of an ancient text source, or to see it as entirely a product of a nineteenth-century mind. On the one hand (as I argue in Chapter 9), there are simply too many things in the book that neither Joseph Smith nor any of his known contemporaries could possibly have known; too many complexities, subtleties, and intricacies in the text that were beyond his or any of his contemporaries' intellectual capabilities; too many examples of spiritual depth and profound expression that were certainly beyond his cognitive or expressive abilities when the Book of Mormon was written. I believe that the integrity of the text requires us to look for the source of all these things outside Joseph Smith and beyond the nineteenth century.

On the other hand, there are matters of composition, style, and subject matter in the book that require us to have a more liberal, open concept of translation to include transformation, expansion, extrapolation, and perhaps even invention or midrash. That is, it would not

---

30. *New Approaches*, 165–229.
31. *New Approaches*, 207.
32. *Dialogue: A Journal of Mormon Thought* 20:1 (Spring 1987), 39, 66.

be surprising that, as he was translating, Smith came to prophecies concerning our day in which he took the basic idea presented by an ancient author and through inspiration expanded on it or, as likely is the case of Alma 12–13, turned or was guided to a scripture with which he was familiar in order to find a fuller expression of a concept in the original source. In some instances, perhaps because of the difficulty of translation or simply for convenience, Smith copied the King James text, even when, as we now know, that text was corrupt. This seems to be the case with the Sermon on the Mount. As Stan Larson argues, when one compares Christ's sermon in 3 Nephi 12 with the King James Version and the earliest extant Greek texts, "where the KJV mistranslates [a phrase] . . . the Book of Mormon simply follows this mistranslation."[33] In my estimation, it does not invalidate the text as scripture to see it in such terms.

One of the points some critics neglect or choose not to address is Joseph Smith's motivation. At age seventeen (if one marks the first visit of Moroni), if he was indeed intent on deluding people and perpetuating a fraud, one has to ask why he would have done so, especially after the hostile response to his claimed theophany and angelic visits. Even if obtaining riches had been his aim, with so much resulting persecution, it would seem more likely for him to have admitted his scheme or simply let it fade from public memory rather than insisting on it and, ultimately, dying for it. Further, if somehow he was driven to persist (either from intent or delusion), one faces the fact that his intended outcome (given the content of the book he supposedly intended to palm off on the public) was to produce a 500 page book whose primary purpose was to convince "the Jew and the Gentile that Jesus is the Christ, the Eternal God, manifesting himself to all nations" and to produce a surprisingly coherent and prescient Voice of Warning for modern readers.

---

33. *New Approaches*, 121.

Hearts and Minds

As I said earlier, I believe the Book of Mormon is best approached through a combination of rational and spiritual methods. Those who are skeptical of cognitive approaches to the book's origin and meaning tend to forget, as Sir Thomas More says in Robert Bolt's *A Man for All Seasons*, that "God made the angels to show him splendor. . . . But Man he made to serve him wittily in the tangle of his mind,"[34] or as an Episcopalian ad puts it, "Christ came to take away our sins, not our minds." We are not simply to testify of the hope that is in us, but, as Peter said, to give a reason for it. (1 Peter 3:15)

But if believers need to be reminded, so to speak, that God expects us to think, non-believers and skeptics need to remember that we have hearts as well as minds and that both are essential for seeking truth as well as meaning. Increasingly, scientists are speaking of what they call "heart intelligence" and "emotional intelligence," ways of knowing that are different from but complementary to cognitive intelligence.[35] As Hamlet says to Horatio, "There are more things in heaven and earth than are dreamt of in your philosophy" (Act 1, scene 5).

It is by thinking *and* feeling, by intuition *and* inspiration, by study *and* contemplation that we may have the best chance of arriving at the truth, keeping in mind that neither heart nor mind nor the two in concert are infallible. Eugene England has argued that this is the only way to understand Joseph Smith himself: "If we are better to know him, better to know his history, which he said we would never know until the judgment day, we must know both his heart and his mind, much better than we have."[36] As William Blake postulated: "If it were not for the Poetic or Prophetic character the Philosophic & Experimental

---

34. *A Man for All Seasons: A Play in Two Acts* (New York: Random House, 1962), 126.
35. For a summary of this research see *Science of the Heart: Exploring the Role of the Heart in Human Performance* (Boulder Creek, CA: Institute of HeartMath, 2001).
36. "How Joseph Smith Resolved the Dilemmas of American Romanticism," in Bryan Waterman, ed. *The Prophet Puzzle* (Salt Lake City: Signature Books, 1999), 181.

would soon be at the ratio of all things, & stand still unable to do other than repeat the same dull round over again. Therefore God becomes as we are, that we may be as he is."[37]

The danger of our age is it that we have become too intoxicated with reason, too slavishly dependent on strictly empirical and cognitive processes. In his important book, *Voltaire's Bastards: The Dictatorship of Reason in the West,* John Ralston Saul chronicles the extent to which we have exaggerated the importance of reason since the Enlightenment. The price we have paid for this over-reliance on the mind is that we have become an increasingly scientific, technological, and mechanistic society. As Saul says, with the Enlightenment, "Reason began, abruptly, to separate itself from and to outdistance the other more or less recognized human characteristics—spirit, appetite, faith and emotion, but also intuition, will and, most important, experience."[38]

In *Life is a Miracle: An Essay Against Modern Superstition,* Wendell Berry speaks of the current scientific reductionism that sees the world and everything in it as if they were mechanical and predictable. Like Saul, Berry deplores what he sees as "the preeminence of the mind," and the "academic hubris" that thinks it can understand the world when it has "no ability to confront mystery (or even the unknown) as such, and therefore has learned none of the lessons that humans have always learned when they have confronted the mystery." According to Berry, when we accept the non-rational or mysterious "as empirically or rationally solvable," we never find them.[39]

Thus, we can be so locked in our minds and so locked out of our hearts that we can become, as the Book of Mormon warns, "past feeling" (1 Nephi 17:45) so that like Laman and Lemuel we cannot "feel words." Mormon uses the same phrase in his letter to his son Moroni claiming

---

37. *There Is No Natural Religion* (1788). https://en.wikisource.org/wiki/There_is_no_natural_religion#/media/File:There_is_No_Natural_Religion_copyG_c1794_a1.jpg.
38. (New York: Vintage, 1992), 51.
39. (Washington, D.C.: Counterpoint, 2000), 15, 27

that his people are "past feeling" (Moroni 9:20). But it is also true that we can become so captive of our emotions, so imprisoned by our feelings of certitude and self-righteousness that we can become past thinking.

Mark Thomas in *Digging in Cumorah* says, "This visionary book speaks to us—children of the Enlightenment—of the nonrational, spiritual world."[40] I believe this is so, but I also believe it speaks to us of the rational world, of the analytical and discursive processes of the mind. We need both, in concert with one another, in approaching so rich and challenging a text as the Book of Mormon.

Some Analogies

I have tried to think of an analogy which fits the idea of Joseph Smith writing the Book of Mormon. To me it would be as if a frontier craftsman who was a maker of rag rugs were suddenly to produce an oriental carpet that required a knowledge of the ancient tradition of weaving, dyes, and fabrics and then weave a carpet of such complexity that only in the twentieth century was someone able to discern and decipher its intricate figures and patterns. Or it would be like a frontiersman who could pluck out a few bars of "Yankee Doodle Dandy" on a banjo being able to compose and dictate an elaborate fugue or a symphony for full chorus and orchestra. Perhaps Hugh Nibley provided the best analogy, one characteristic of his wit: "To put it facetiously but not unfairly, the artist [who set out to create such a work as the Book of Mormon] must not only balance a bowl of goldfish and three lighted candles on the end of a broomstick while fighting off a swarm of gadflies, but he must at the same time be carving an immortal piece of statuary from a lump of solid diorite."[41]

---

40. *Digging in Cumorah*, 2.
41. *Since Cumorah: The Book of Mormon in the Modern World* (Salt Lake City: Deseret Book, 1970), 159.

I Nephi:
Reading Nephi Closely

All stories have a beginning. How an author chooses to commense his or her narrative gives us a clue as to how we are to read it. Some beginnings are particularly memorable: "It was the best of times, it was the worst of times . . . " (*Tale of Two Cities*); "Call me Ishmael" (*Moby Dick*); "All happy families are alike; each unhappy family is unhappy in its own way" (*Anna Karenina*); "You better not never tell nobody but God" (*The Color Purple*). The opening words of the Book of Mormon are "I, Nephi, having been born of goodly parents . . ."

Just as each story has a unique beginning, each is also told from a particular narrative point of view, the vantage point from which an author tells his or her story. Unlike the infinite variety of plots, settings, and characters that are at an author's disposal, the number of available narrative points of view are few: first person, second person, and third person, with the latter further divided into objective, limited, and omniscient.[1]

---

1. "A Narrative Approach to the Joseph Smith Translation of the Synoptic Gospels," *BYU Studies* 54:2, https://byustudies.byu.edu/journal-issue-ids/journal-542.

Nephi's story is clearly told from a first-person narrative point of view. Critical analysis that focuses on the author of a text is sometimes referred to as "author-centered criticism." In other words, in reading Nephi's story, we need to keep in mind that, like all memorialists, he is an author with a particular history, including—especially in Nephi's case—a family history and also a unique personality and way of seeing the world. Any author is furthermore a story teller possessed of his own unique compositional strategy, rhetorical style, and expressive gifts and talents. Understanding Nephi can help us understand his text. As Jared Ludlow says, by looking closely at the narrator, "We can examine how [he] guides the reader to perceive characters and events."[2] It is clear, as I hope to show, that Nephi is indeed guiding our reading in a way that meets his own design, objectives, and purposes.

By his opening declaration, "I Nephi," we know the narrative of First and Second Nephi will unfold through the mind, memory, and experience of a particular Israelite who leaves the city of Jerusalem not long before the Babylonian captivity and travels with his family on an unknown journey. From the very beginning, Nephi signals his intention to tell his own story from his own point of view rather than, say, the point of view of his father or older brothers or that of an editor like Mormon, who, except when he is speaking about his own experience, writes as a chronicler or historian.

In both fiction and non-fiction, as in real life, first-person narrators can be unreliable storytellers. It isn't that they consciously are deceptive or dishonest (although that possibility always exists), but rather that, like everyone, they have their individual motivations, objectives, prejudices, and limitations in the way they see and make sense of the world, including their own and other's experiences. Invariably, if we read closely, such narrators may tell us more than they intend to, including about themselves. For example, while most readers of the Book of Mormon likely consider Nephi a reliable and unbiased recorder of the history of his people, like everyone who tells a story or writes

---

2. *Ibid.*

a history, he is anything but a neutral historian. In other words, his narrative point of view is slanted, both consciously and unconsciously, as can be seen through the details he chooses to include (as well as exclude) and the way in which he arranges them. Thus, Nephi makes choices in his narrative that reveal not just what he has experienced, but also who he is, what he *thinks* and how he *feels*.

One of the most important details about Nephi is that he is a younger brother. His whole life unfolds in relation to this central fact and it informs his writing at every turn. We cannot understand the text of his narrative without understanding the sibling rivalry between him and Laman and Lemuel. The story he tells and his perspective on it are heavily influenced by this fact. Such conflict within his own family would have been familiar to Nephi from his familiarity with younger son "chosenness" in numerous biblical narratives.

We might pause here to note that in the beginning of this narrative, it is understandable if some readers identify more with Laman and Lemuel than with Nephi, in spite of the fact that that is the last thing Nephi intends. As Grant Hardy notes, "From the beginning, he [Nephi] structures his narrative in such a way as to prevent readers sympathizing with his older brothers." He adds, "Nephi, writing from the spiritual and political needs of thirty years later, takes care to present his brothers in the worst light possible."[3] For readers who have had a precocious, super-righteous younger sibling or who are in relationship with someone who is always both right and righteous, Nephi might come off as a bit insufferable, at least in the beginning. He doesn't intend for us to see him in this way, but it is understandable if we do. Few older siblings like to hear from a parent, let alone an angel, "Know ye not that the Lord hath chosen him to ruler over you?" Such a question is particularly difficult in reference to a younger sibling who describes himself as being not just young, but "exceeding young" (1 Ne. 2:16).

---

3. *Understanding the Book of Mormon: A Reader's Guide* (Oxford: Oxford University Press, 2010), 34, 37.

We see Nephi's youthfulness most clearly when, not long after he leaves his brothers to get the brass plates, he encounters his kinsman, Laban, lying drunk with his sword beside him. When he sees Laban's sword, for a moment Nephi forgets why he is there. His total focus is on the sword, with an amazement and curiosity similar to that of, say, a fifteen-year-old frontier boy coming upon a drunken cowboy with pearl-handled six-shooter. Note Nephi's wonderment: "I beheld his sword." But he doesn't just behold it: "I drew it forth from the sheath thereof; and the hilt thereof was of pure gold, and the workmanship thereof was exceeding fine, and I saw that the blade thereof was of the most precious steel" (1 Nephi 4:9). In other words, this is the most amazing sword he has ever seen. Every teenage boy of Israel dreamed of holding such a sword, and he has one in his hands! The detail he reveals in recounting the experience over thirty years later shows how fresh the image of that sword in his hand still is.

But note another telling (and surprising) detail: A very short time later, after he has slain Laban with this very sword—without question the most difficult thing he will ever have to do—Nephi says, "And now I, Nephi, *being a man*, large in stature, . . ." (4:31, emphasis added). He tells us this, I believe, because in retrospect it is the turning point of his life. Nephi presenting himself as evolving in just minutes from being "*exceeding young, . . .* large in stature"(2:16) to "*being a man*, large in stature," would not have been lost on ancient readers of this text.

This episode reflects the "coming-of-age" motif familiar to world literature and is characteristic of Hebrew literature portraying a person of seemingly ordinary capabilities dramatically changed by his or her willingness to be obedient to God in an extremely challenging situation. (One thinks for instance of Abraham who is shown early in the Genesis narrative as a person who lacks faith that God will bless the barren Sarah to have a child but who later is willing to sacrifice that very child out of obedience to God.) If nothing else, this evidences that Nephi was also likely influenced in telling or framing his own story by reading Old Testament narratives in the brass plates.

If we identify with Laman and Lemuel in the beginning of Nephi's narrative, his presentation of them as persistently bullying, hostile, and rebellious causes us to shift whatever sympathies we may have had for them to Nephi. One of the ways in which Nephi consciously influences such a shift is the manner by which he highlights certain details of his experience with his brothers. For example, of all the details he could have chosen to include from the family's eight-year journey from Jerusalem to Bountiful, one might wonder why Nephi recounts the blessings their father Lehi gives to Laman in naming a river after him ("O that thou mightiest be like unto this river, continually running into the fountain of righteousness") and to Lemuel in naming a valley after him ("O that thou mightiest be like unto this valley, firm and steadfast, and immovable in keeping the commandments of the Lord!") (1 Nephi 2:3–10). By selecting such detail, Nephi wants us to understand that although he was not the recipient of such an honor and blessing (or else he most assuredly would have recorded it), yet it is he rather than his brothers who has been like the river running into the fountain of righteousness and like a valley steadfast in keeping God's commandments. Thus, Nephi foreshadows himself inheriting the birthright blessings that normally would have gone to his older brothers had they been faithful. While there is no evidence that he gloats over this, the very fact that he selected this experience three decades later when he begins his history is telling. It is also telling that later in this same chapter Nephi records a blessing from the Lord to him that is far superior to those of his brothers (see vv. 19–24).

We likely forget that Nephi is not relating the story as it unfolds like a travelogue or a personal journal, but rather decades after his family has left Jerusalem and arrived in the Promised Land. Further, like many recorders of scriptural narrative (including Mormon and Moroni), he is recounting it as a broken-hearted prophet. His older brothers have tried to thwart him at every juncture since the family left Jerusalem: returning to get the brass plates, traveling through the Arabian desert, building a ship at Bountiful, setting forth upon the high seas, and in multiple ways since arriving in the Promised Land. In other words, the fraternal conflict that manifests itself early in the narrative with the rebellion of his older brothers grows in intensity until it breaks out in attempts at both patricide and fratricide and ultimately bloody conflict and civil war. As Nephi summarizes a decade after beginning his narration, "It sufficeth me to say that forty years had passed away, and we had already had wars and contentions with our brethren" (2 Ne 5:34). The murderous intent of his brothers toward Nephi clearly colors his portrayal of them—and of himself—as the story unfolds.

At the time he commences his history, Nephi's calling as prophet-leader of his people has been fraught with difficulties and challenges, with his brothers and their followers fighting against him and their New World civilization in peril. Thus, in the first verses of this first chapter, Nephi's intent is to establish his *bona fides* as the rightful inheritor of his father's mantle as prophet and family patriarch. He has seen in vision the sad ending of his people's history and hopes perhaps that through his writing he can forestall such an end by convincing his brothers and their offspring to recognize his prophetic calling and position. At the very least, he may hope to persuade future readers of his history that he was the prophet called to succeed his father as leader.

We see Nephi's strategy in establishing his identity and leadership in the very first sentence of his history when he tells us he was "born of goodly parents" and in his frequent use of first-person personal pronouns (e.g., "*I* was taught," "*I* make a record," "*I* know"; and "*my* days," "*my* own hand," "*my* knowledge" [emphasis added here and with other scriptural citations in this chapter]). All told, in the first chapter alone, Nephi uses "I" eighteen times, "my" sixteen times, and "mine" three times, for a grand total of thirty-seven uses of the personal pronoun in twenty verses, or nearly two per verse.

Nephi shows us how he has become the prophet-leader and record keeper by reporting in detail how each of his callings came directly from the Lord (1 Nephi 2:18–24; 9:3–5; 19:1). Nephi also builds a case for his leadership by highlighting his trials, his virtues, and his accomplishments. In the very first verse he shows himself as "having seen many afflictions" and also being "highly favored of God"—not just favored but "highly favored." He also reports that he possesses "great knowledge of the goodness and the mysteries of God." Only when his credentials are firmly established does he tell us, "I make a record of *my* proceedings in *my* days." Not *"our* proceedings in *our* days" (1 Nephi 1:1, 17). In other words, in these first verses, Nephi is staking claim to his role as leader and establishing his authority to a group of people, some of whom, including the followers of his brothers in the New World, recognize neither.

What else does Nephi reveal about himself in these first verses?

- That his record is true;
- That he is educated in "the learning of the Jews and the language of the Egyptians";
- That he is skilled in metallurgy (twice he tells us he made the metal plates on which he is writing "with mine own hand"—no small feat);
- That he has edited ("abridged") his father Lehi's record;
- That he is acting in his prophetic role.

Having established his calling and accomplishments, Nephi next does something that is both intentional and subtle—he makes an indisputable link between himself and his father Lehi. Repetition in a text is always an indication that, as readers, we should pay particular attention. And writers of Hebrew literature are masters of repetition. Note how almost every verse of the first chapter of Genesis opens with "And God" and ends with "and it was good." As my Bible as Literature teacher said, "If all you got from that chapter is that God did something and it was good," the writer would have been pleased that he got his point across. Note that Nephi employs repetition to great effect throughout his narrative, but especially in the first chapters. For example, he uses the phrases, *my father* or *my father, Lehi,* a dozen times in this opening chapter. In addition, he refers to his father by using the pronouns *he, his,* and *him* 46 times in the same space! All in all, in the first six chapters of his first book, Nephi uses the phrase "my father" a staggering total of eighty-nine times! It is as if he's saying, "My father Lehi—I'm with him!"

He also frequently emphasizes his father's status as a prophet. Thus, Nephi references Lehi praying to God, seeing dreams and visions (including of Christ), being instructed by an angel to read out of a book, prophesying (including to his own children), recording his prophesies, calling people to repentance, and testifying against their wickedness. These details are significant because basically they are the same things Nephi himself has been doing, especially following his father's death. The effect of his repetition and use of parallel experiences between Nephi and his father are clearly intended to establish his—rather than his brothers'—identity with their father, thus undermining any claim to authority they have tried or may try to assert.

In these verses, Nephi takes pains to make an indelible connection between the prophet whom God called out of Jerusalem (his father) and the prophet God called to lead his people in the Promised Land (Nephi himself) because he knows that many of his father's descendants do not recognize him as prophet and, not incidentally, some are trying to kill him. Thus, through the deliberate and systematic linking of himself with his father, Nephi asserts his role in continuing the prophetic tradition of Hebrew prophets from Abraham and Moses to Jeremiah and from his father to himself.

In Chapter 2, Nephi further strengthens the case for his father as a prophet called of God, thereby strengthening his own role as prophet. He does this directly when he writes, "*I and my father* had kept the commandments wherewith the Lord had commanded *us*" (5:20). Note that he puts himself first in this pairing. He also strengthens the link between himself and his father by the repetition of "Blessed art thou Lehi . . . because thou hast been faithful" (2:1) and "Blessed art thou Nephi because of thy faith" (2:19) and by recounting his father's and his parallel visions (see 1 Nephi 8, 10 and 11–14). I believe Nephi includes his father's vision to remind Laman and Lemuel of Lehi's dream of the tree laden with white fruit, the iron rod that leads to it, and the large and spacious building in which, by inference, his brothers have chosen to live. And he does more than this, linking himself not only with his father but also with his mother ("and also my mother, Sariah, was exceeding glad, for she truly had mourned because of us," 5:1), his fore-fathers, *"my fathers"* (6:1). and then specifically with the father-prophets of Israel, including Moses (4:2,15), Joseph (5:16), and the three great Israelite prophets, Abraham, Isaac, and Jacob (6:4). He knows that Laman and Lemuel and their followers cannot easily dismiss such associations or unlink him from them.

Nephi next does something that is both subtle and rhetorically powerful: knowing how much his brothers' anger toward their father and toward him is related to the riches the family left behind as they fled into the desert, and which the brothers have been claiming as their own inheritance since, Nephi says of Lehi, "And *he* left *his* house, and the land of *his* inheritance, and *his* gold, and *his* silver, and *his* precious things, and took nothing with *him* save it were *his* family, and provisions, and tents, and departed into the wilderness." Nephi's emphasis here is to counter his brothers' claim, which we soon hear, that Lehi's leaving Jerusalem deprived *them* "of *their* inheritance, and *their* gold, and *their* silver, and *their* precious things to perish in the wilderness" (2:11). The purpose of such a careful parallel construction is to present a case to his brothers and their followers that the riches they continue to claim Nephi has stolen from them (a complaint that will last for generations) were not theirs at all and therefore their accusation and grievances are without merit. I feel that this confirms Hardy's argument "that parallels and allusions in the Book of Mormon are deliberate and meaningful rather than coincidental."[4]

Having taken considerable pains to place himself on the side of his father (and in the prophetic tradition) and place his brothers in an opposing position, Nephi does something unexpected: When he hopes for his brothers' cooperation in obtaining the precious plates containing their religious heritage, he shifts from referring to Lehi as "my father" to speaking of him as "our father" (3:15–16) and speaking of the family riches as their collective possessions: "And it came to pass that we went down to the land of *our* inheritance, and we did gather

---

4. Hardy xvii.

together *our* gold, and *our* silver, and *our* precious things" (3:22, 24, emphasis added). When, shortly thereafter, Laman and Lemuel express anger toward Nephi and Lehi (to whom Nephi once again refers as "my father") and begin to beat Nephi and their younger brother Sam, perhaps in an attempt to heal the fraternal rift between them, Nephi uses first-person pronouns to include his brothers as he pleads with them to join him in getting the records: "Let *us* be strong like unto Moses, for he truly spake unto the waters of the Red Sea and they divided hither and thither, and *our fathers* came through, out of captivity, on dry ground . . . ." (4:2–3). While some of the change in pronouns might be explained by the difference between Nephi's addressing his future audience and his direct address to his brothers, some such expression, whether conscious or not, reveals a sophisticated use of language.

In other words, in the midst of the internecine conflict that is wrenching his people apart, Nephi gives evidence of the mature and sensitive spirituality that will be required of him as he progressively takes on the mantle of a prophet, a role of importance not only for his contemporaries but for future generations who will read his record. He does this aware of what must have been a devastating revelation—that ultimately his people the Nephites will be destroyed and that those who remain will be the descendants of these same brothers who complicate his life with their persistent hostility toward him.

Another example of Nephi's intention to disarm and verbally counter his brothers can be seen in his subtle and sophisticated manipulation of word choice to overthrow their arguments. As with earlier and later episodes of fraternal conflict in the book, this one is about power, but it is also about epistemology, about what one knows and doesn't know. The irony one finds in this episode is actually set up earlier in 1 Nephi 3 where Nephi tells his brothers that their father "*knew* that Jerusalem must be destroyed" (3:17). Lehi knows this of course because it has been revealed to him, just as Nephi knows by revelation that his own people, the Nephites, will ultimately be destroyed.

In Chapter 4, Nephi tries to inspire his rebellious and recalcitrant older brothers to go up to Jerusalem and get the Brass Plates by cleverly reminding them of a truth they cannot deny—God's deliverance of Moses and the Children of Israel from Egyptian bondage through the Red Sea—the great miracle in Israelite history: "Now let us be strong like unto Moses, for he truly spake unto the waters of the Red Sea and they departed hither and thither, and our fathers came through out of captivity . . . . Now behold *ye know* that this is true; and *ye also know* that an angel hath spoken unto you; wherefore can ye doubt?" (4:2–3). His linking God delivering Moses and the Israelites from bondage with God delivering Laban into their hands is intended to disarm their hatred and persuade them that he, their younger brother, has been chosen to lead his people, including them, out of bondage.

Knowing how much their hearts are set upon the riches the family left in Jerusalem and perhaps of their wish to stay and reclaim them, in Chapter 7, Nephi testifies to his brothers of something they do not know now but soon will know—the destruction of the city: "And *ye shall know* at some future period that the word of the Lord shall be fulfilled concerning the destruction of Jerusalem" (7:13). All this is a prelude to the episode in chapters 16 and 17 where the words "knew" and "know" are repeated numerous times. For example, in 1 Nephi 16:38, Laman and Lemuel state declaratively, "*We know* he lies" of Nephi's claims that the Lord has spoken to him. Later, when Nephi tries to engage their help in building a ship, they verbally attack him by saying, "*We knew* that you could not construct a ship, for *we knew* that ye were lacking in judgment" (17:19).

Laman and Lemuel blame Nephi for their suffering in the wilderness and complain that had they stayed in Jerusalem, "we might have enjoyed *our* possessions and the land of *our* inheritance; yea, and we might have been happy" (17:20), which, given their continual complaints throughout the narrative, is highly doubtful. The older brothers next state as knowledge something they know is false: "And *we know* that the people who were in the land of Jerusalem were a righteous people; for they kept the statues and judgments of the Lord, and all his commandments, according to the law of Moses; wherefore, *we know* that they are a righteous people" (17:22). Since they have invoked the name of Israel's great leader, Nephi recounts the story of Moses leading the children of Israel out of Egypt (as he had previously done when they went to retrieve the plates) to confront his brothers with their usage of the word "know." He does this with a highly sophisticated use of verbal irony. That is, he states what he knows they cannot deny in order to show that what they say they know is false[5]:

> Now *ye know* that the children of Israel were in bond-age; and *ye know* that they were laden with tasks, which were grievous to be borne; wherefore, *ye know* that it must needs be a good thing for them, that they should be brought out of bondage. Now *ye know* that Moses was commanded of the Lord to do that great work; and *ye know* that by his word the waters of the Red Sea were divided hither and thither, and they passed through on dry ground. But *ye know* that the Egyptians were drowned in the Red Sea, who were the armies of Pharaoh. And *ye also know* that they were fed with manna in the wilderness. Yea, and *ye also know* that Moses, by his word according to the power of God which was in him, smote the rock, and there came forth water, that the children of Israel might quench their thirst. . . . And they did harden their hearts from time to time, and they did revile against Moses, and also against God; nevertheless, *ye know* that they were led forth by his matchless power

---

5. One could argue that what they claim may be technically right but morally wrong. That is, the inhabitants of Jerusalem may indeed have been keeping the letter of the Law of Moses and still be considered unrighteous, which seems to be the case. Or, it may be that they increased in wickedness, for Nephi says, "And now, after all these things, the time has come that they [i.e., the Jews at Jerusalem] have become wicked, yea, nearly unto ripeness and I know not but they are at this day about to be destroyed; for I know that the day must surely come that they must be destroyed" (17:43)."

> into the land of promise. . . . And *ye also know* that
> by the power of his almighty word he can cause the
> earth that it shall pass away; yea, and *ye know* that by
> his word he can cause the rough places to be made
> smooth, and smooth places shall be broken up. O,
> then, why is it, that ye can be so hard in your hearts?"
> (17:25–29, 42, 46)

In this passage, Nephi uses their word "know" eleven times. But significantly, he uses the phrase "I know" with regard to himself only twice:
"And now, after all these things, the time has come that they [i.e., the
Jews at Jerusalem] have become wicked, yea, nearly unto ripeness; and *I
know not* but they are at this day about to be destroyed; for *I know* that
the day must surely come that they must be destroyed" (17:43). Note
that Nephi states the negative before the positive, showing that, unlike
his brothers, he does not claim knowledge that he does not possess, but
also that the knowledge he does possess is based on revelation. In this
same episode, the Lord tells Nephi that he *"shall know"* things which
God promises will happen. Later, Nephi learns from his father's vision
that Jerusalem has indeed been destroyed (2 Nephi 1:4).

This episode ends on another point of irony in their debate over
what they know and don't know. For a brief period, Nephi has such
power that his brothers realize that he could disable them merely by
touching them—the kind of power every young man fantasizes having!
The Lord then commands Nephi to stretch forth his hand and shock
them, which he does. (One can imagine that psychologically this is the
easiest commandment for Nephi to keep!) Laman and Lemuel, having
been jolted by their brother's power right before his eyes, then use the
word "know" honestly for the first time, "*We know* of a surety that the
Lord is with thee, for *we know* that it is the power of the Lord that has
shaken us" (17:55). After this experience, one in which their knowledge
is not just cognitive but also physical, a further irony is that their honesty lasts such a short time.

What Nephi is doing, of course, is confronting his brothers with truth that no Israelite could deny, the miraculous deliverance of the children of Israel from the Egyptians through the Red Sea, their rebellion against God, and Moses leading them to the Promised Land. He then uses this great defining moment in Israelite history to parallel their family's deliverance from spiritual and impending physical bondage, their sojourn across the Arabian desert, and their subsequent voyage to their own promised land. By using the words "know/knew" twenty-two times in this short space, Nephi dramatically demonstrates the difference between the ways he and his brothers operate in the world—they posture and dissemble, while he always acts with integrity. They claim as knowledge things they know are false and deny things they know are true, whereas he always speaks the truth.[6]

The truth he speaks, however, undergoes a spiritual sea change. It is fascinating to see the shift in Nephi's attitude toward "his brethren," Laman and Lemuel and their descendants, from the first part of his narrative as compared to the last chapters in his second book. The memory of his conflict with them is so fresh in the early part of the story that he is only capable of seeing them as arch enemies. As we re-experience something traumatic in our past, the amygdala, that part of our brain that holds the emotional strength and depth of memories, brings them into the present as if they were still with us. Although it is many years after these early experiences, as Nephi recalls them, his pain and anguish are experienced anew, which makes him incapable of seeing his brothers as other than caricatures of evil. Not once in these early chapters does he refer to them as "my beloved brethren." He is simply too close to the pain of their relationship to have such

---

6. This small episode foreshadows several later episodes in which there is a contest between a righteous man who testifies of what he truly knows and a false testifier who says he knows things that he doesn't (see especially the conflicts between Gideon and Nehor, Alma and Korihor, Amulek and Zeezrom, and Alma and Amlici—all in the book of Alma, discussed in Chapter 2).

sentiments. As the narrative unfolds, however, we see Nephi's attitude toward his brothers shifting to a more charitable stance.

The prelude to Nephi's first use of "my beloved brethren," which doesn't come until 2 Nephi 26, is what happens in 2 Nephi 25 where he interprets the words of Isaiah concerning the Messiah, which leads to his declaration of his people's Christ-centered theology: "For we labor diligently to write to persuade our children, and also our brethren, to believe in Christ, and to be reconciled to God" (25:23); "And we talk of Christ, we rejoice in Christ, we preach of Christ, we prophesy of Christ, and we write according to our prophesies, that our children may know to what source they may look for a remission of their sins" (25:26). In other words, it is only after his heart is touched by a remembrance of his own personal experience with the Savior, to whom he refers later as "*my* Jesus" (33:6), and his awareness of Christ's love for his people, that Nephi is able to use the words, not just "my brethren" but "my beloved brethren."

I speculate that Nephi is influenced in using this phrase because he likely heard it in the sermon of his younger brother, Jacob, to the Nephites (2 Nephi 6–10), where it appears for the first time in the Book of Mormon. In fact, Jacob uses the term "my beloved brethren" thirteen times in his brief record. Note that Jacob does not begin his chronicle with "I Jacob" but rather "Behold, my beloved brethren, I Jacob, . . ." (2 Nephi 6:1). In other words, it is Jacob's brothers (and sisters) rather than himself who is the focus of his narrative.

Nephi was also likely influenced in seeing his brothers and their descendants as "beloved" by his reading the chapters of Isaiah he includes in his narrative, particularly Chapter 15, which includes "The Song of the Vineyard" from Isaiah 5, the opening verses of which are:

> And then will I sing to my well-beloved a song of my
> beloved, touching his vineyard: My well-beloved hath
> a vineyard in a very fruitful hill.

Nephi understands that Isaiah's "well-beloved" refers to Christ (as with so much of the rest of the Isaiah text Nephi includes in his personal record). That understanding, along with his personal experience with and witness of Christ, are what I believe cause him to begin using this phrase in the concluding chapters of his narrative. We can witness him therein interweaving both phrasing and arguments from his prior extended quotations from both Jacob and Isaiah. Of course, it should be noted that Nephi is addressing an imagined future audience but one he is aware includes the descendants of his brothers. Once he begins using this phase, "my beloved brethren," one is struck by how frequently he uses it—sixteen times in these closing chapters, including eight times in the chapter that focuses so specifically on what Nephi calls "the doctrine of Christ" (31).

Such observations help us to see the internal processes at work in Nephi's heart and mind, to see how he develops as a writer of his own experience and a recorder of his people's history. Part of my intention in focusing on some of the detail in these first chapters is to demonstrate the book's substantiality, its importance and its artistry, to affirm Grant Hardy's observation, "If we keep our focus squarely on the narrative, it turns out there *is* an organizing principle at work, but it is fairly subtle." And his declaration that "the Book of Mormon is an extraordinarily rich text . . . , [one that] appears to be a carefully constructed artifact."[7] Indeed, it is.

---

7. Hardy, xiv, xii, xiv.

2

To Sing the Song of Redeeming Love: The Book of Alma

As recounted in my personal essay at the beginning of this collection, I first heard the story of the coming forth of the Book of Mormon when I was ten years old. My father had just come home from the Second World War and one of the first things he did was to tell me about the Book of Mormon, which he had recently discovered. I had had no religious upbringing and had never been to church except for a few times when my mother sent my brother and me to a small Latter-day Saint branch in Durango, Colorado, while our father was in the South Pacific. She sent us there because our father, from whom she had been divorced for some years, wrote to her from the ship he was on asking her to do so. He had been converted to the gospel through a miraculous priesthood healing, and as he witnessed the devastation of war, he must have felt some urgency to get his sons connected to something more hopeful than the carnage he saw all around him. Of course, as I was later to discover, the Book of Mormon included plenty of carnage itself.

The Book of Mormon first came alive for me in classes I took as an undergraduate at BYU. As an openhearted teenager, its messages sank deep into my soul. I remember reading the fifth chapter of Alma and being struck by the question as to whether I had received God's image in my countenance. I wanted his image to be in mine, and for the first time in my life, I understood what it meant to "sing the song of redeeming love" (Alma 5:26). Singing that song has inspired me to read and understand the Book of Mormon and to tell others of its message.

"Go Ye Into All the World"

It is that burning desire to share the gospel that informs nearly every page of the book of Alma. In fact, Alma could be seen as a primer on the Great Commission, the term most Christians use for Jesus' admonition to his disciples to go into all the world to preach his gospel. From beginning to end, Alma is a compendium of evangelizing. If Paul's letters remain the greatest narrative of a single missionary, Alma's record provides the greatest variety and the most compelling stories of those who have a "fire shut up in [their] bones" (Jeremiah 20:9). Everyone in the book, it seems, tries to persuade others either to believe or disbelieve. Those who try to lead people away from the Church are no less passionate and zealous than those who try to bring converts and reconverts to it. The entire book is a great tug-of-war for the souls of Lehi's children.

Alma the Younger is to the Book of Mormon what Saul of Tarsus is to the New Testament. From his miraculous conversion until his mysterious disappearance at the end of his life, Alma's life is defined by his missionary experiences. Even after his lengthy ministry, he cannot refrain from evangelizing. Alma is like Tennyson's Ulysses, who, restless among the mundane household gods at Ithaca after returning from Troy and his adventurous odyssey, sets sail on one last voyage.

> Death closes all. But something ere the end,
> Some work of noble note, may yet be done,
> Not unbecoming men who strove with Gods.[1]

Like Ulysses, Alma "could not rest, and he also went forth" on a last mission, this time with the Sons of Mosiah (43:1).

A Perilous Mission

The story of Alma and his companions is the material of myth, romance, and epic. These sons of temporal and spiritual royalty are engaged in destroying the work of their fathers, thereby imperiling the civic and religious life of their nation. Later, in recounting his youthful activities to his son Helaman, Alma does not soften the seriousness of his mayhem: "I had murdered many of [God's] children, or rather led them away unto destruction" (36:14). Judging by how effective Alma is in preaching to the Nephites, and the Sons of Mosiah are in converting the Lamanites, one can imagine the degree to which these young men were successful in leading people astray.

As they go about their work of destruction, these young rebels are confronted by an angel who speaks to them with a voice of thunder. This is a sobering experience, to say the least. So grateful are these young men for their deliverance from spiritual bondage that they give up position and power to preach the word of God. Alma surrenders the chief judgeship to preach to the people in Zarahemla and other cities, and the sons of Mosiah give up kingship to preach to their archenemies the Lamanites who, according to a report from the time of Enos several hundred years earlier, had become a "wild, and ferocious, and a blood-thirsty people, full of idolatry and filthiness; feeding upon beasts of prey; dwelling in tents, and wandering about in the wilderness with a short skin girdle about their loins and their heads shaven" (Enos 1:20).

---

1. Alfred Tennyson, "Ulysses"; https://www.poetryfoundation.org/poems/45392/ulysses.

The mission to such people by the sons of Mosiah was considered by their friends so ridiculous and foolhardy that they "laughed them to scorn" (Alma 26:23–25), thinking it better to kill Lamanites than convert them.

The mission turned out to be perilous, for when Ammon meets his brothers later, he is struck by their suffering: "for behold they were naked, and their skins were worn exceedingly because of being bound with strong cords. And they also had suffered hunger, thirst, and all kinds of afflictions" (20:29). Later Ammon says, "We have suffered every privation. . . . We have been cast out, and mocked, and spit upon, and smote upon our cheeks; and we have been stoned and taken and bound with strong cords, and cast into prison" (26:28–29). All of this "that perhaps we might be the means of saving some soul" (26:30).

A Cosmic Conflict

The Book of Alma is a microcosm of the archetypical conflict between the forces of good and evil. The stage is set in the very first chapter when two men on opposite sides claim to preach the word of God. Nehor introduces priestcraft for the first time among the Nephites, preaching "that which he termed to be the word of God" (1:3) and testifying that "all men should have eternal life" (1:4). Immediately, Nehor is confronted by the righteous Gideon. "Because Gideon withstood him with the words of God" (1:9), Nehor killed him with his sword. The conflict in Alma between word and sword thus begins. And while in the beginning the victor in this conflict may seem in doubt, Alma later assures us that "the preaching of the word had a . . . more powerful effect upon the minds of the people than the sword" (Alma 31:5).

The contest for the souls of the people ensues over the entire sixty-three chapters of Alma, with Alma, the Sons of Mosiah, and their companions "bearing down in pure testimony" (4:19) against the Nephites, Lamanites, Amulonites, Amalakites, and Zoramites, and with such figures as Nehor, Amlici, Zeezrom, and Korihor attempting to undermine their work at every step. The dramatic struggle plays out as powerful men fight one another with words and with weapons of war.

A War of Words

It is notable the degree to which the conflict in the book of Alma is a contest of words. Alma, who is described as "a man of many words" (Mosiah 27:8), has impressive persuasive powers, as do the Sons of Mosiah. Ammon is said to catch King Lamoni "with guile," although his motive for doing so is honorable. Those who oppose these missionaries are also sophisticated in their use of language. One after another, they lead people astray by their sophistry. These language merchants are best exemplified by the lawyers among them, who "were learned in all the arts and cunning of the people; and this was to enable them that they might be skilful in their profession" (10:15). By the use of intellectual argument, cross-examination, contradiction, and verbal deception these men try to undermine the work of the Lord's servants. When Korihor appears before Alma, for example, we are told "he did rise up in great swelling words" (30:31), a powerful image of someone overinflated with his own importance.

That this contest between good and evil is waged with words is seen in the way the term "word" is used in Alma's narrative. Nearly half of the uses of "word" in the entire Book of Mormon are found in this one book, including such phrases as "the word," "the Word of God," "the Word of the Lord," "the Words of Christ," to list a few examples. Together, they constitute a leitmotif running throughout the narrative. "The word" is used so frequently and in such a variety of ways and contexts that it begins to take on powerful symbolic significance. By the end of the book "the word" has become "The Word," the tree that bears the ripe round fruit of God's love.

As a young missionary in the Northern States Mission (1955–58) I saw this same war of words played out on the streets of Chicago, Milwaukee, Dubuque, and Omaha as well as in a number of smaller cities and towns. Later, as a senior missionary and member of the Baltic States' mission presidency (1992–96), I witnessed and participated in similar encounters in Vilnius and Kaunas, Lithuania; Riga, Latvia; Tallinn and Tartu, Estonia; and Kaliningrad. Since the beginning of the Restoration, all over the world, Latter-day Saint missionaries, generally unsophisticated but nevertheless sincere and earnest, have engaged in gospel conversations with other believers as well as with nonbelievers, agnostics, and atheists. Many fulfilling the "Great Commission" to preach the gospel find courage and inspiration from the example of Alma and the Sons of Mosiah.

The Power of Silence

For all the verbal sparring, for all the contests of words, and for all the preaching and teaching in the Book of Alma, some of the most dramatic events happen as a result of silence. For example, in recounting his conversion to his son Helaman, Alma tells how he was struck dumb (Mosiah 27:19), and when Alma and Amulek are interrogated in prison by the followers of Nehor, knowing that no answer will suffice, like Jesus before Pilate, they "answered them nothing" (14:18).

The most dramatic example of silence is when, in seeking for a sign, Korihor is struck dumb. Ironically, as he once led people away from the church by his words, he now inadvertently leads them back by his silence, for when all the people "who had believed in the words of Korihor" (30:57) see him wordless in Zarahemla, "they [are] all converted again unto the Lord" (30:58). The irony is compounded when Korihor, a once powerful man who used his rhetorical skills to elevate himself above others, is reduced to begging and again when we realize he may have been killed because he couldn't use his voice to cry out when a carriage approached, for he was "run upon and trodden down, even until he was dead" (30:59).

The Evocative Silence of Women

One wonders about the silence of women in the Book of Alma, as with most of the books in the record of the Lehites. An exception is Abish, one of the two non-family female descendants of Lehi in the Book of Alma who are given names (the other is Isabel). A secret convert among the Lamanites "on account of a remarkable vision of her father" (19:16), for years Abish hasn't told a soul about what must have been the most meaningful experience in her life, her conversion to Christ. However, when the opportunity finally presents itself, she also proves to be a zealous missionary, running "forth from house to house, making it known unto the people" (19:17) that God was working among them.

Besides Abish, the only other individual women mentioned in Alma are: the princess offered to Ammon as a wife; Mary and Eve, archetypal mothers; Isabel, a harlot; Morianton's maid servant; and the queens of Kings Lamoni and Limhi, who, unlike their husbands, are identified only by their royal title. One of these women, the wife of King Limhi, is shown by what in the book is an uncharacteristic glimpse into an individual and unique personality. When her servants tell her that her husband "is dead and that he stinketh, and that he ought to be placed in the sepulchre, she states, "As for myself, to me he doth not stink" (19:5). The other nameless women in Alma include the Anti-Nephi-Lehite women who were slain rather than take up arms against their enemies and the survivors of this slaughter whose sons became Helaman's stripling warriors (24–27).

In the Book of Mormon there are allusions or references to faithful, courageous, and righteous women as well as to ordinary women— women who bore children under harsh conditions, women who had visions and who received angelic visitations, women who buried their weapons and were slain because they would not take them up again, women who were kidnapped and taken captive by their enemies, and women who went down to the sea in ships with the explorer Hagoth and were never heard of again. Undoubtedly, there were women who loved their husbands and begged them not to go to war and who wept when they were carried home on their shields or left to rot on some desolate battlefield; women who passed on the traditions of weaving, of making beautiful vessels, of telling stories; women who danced and sang the songs of Israel in their new land; women who taught their children how to cook and sew, how to be brave, how to know the scriptures, and above all else, how to love God and others.

What we have of these women is not individual lives but generic types: we are told that the "Ishmaelitish women" were among those on whom God set a curse (3:7), that "many women" were caused to "commit whoredoms" (30:18), and that "Amulek saw the pains of the women and children who were consuming in the fire" (14:10). Ironically, the blessings which Alma conveys to the male members of the church include "all that you *possess*, your women and your children . . ." (7:27, emphasis added). We hear of women, mothers, sisters, wives, daughters, and widows, but rarely of individual women.

Where are the women of the Book of Mormon? We know Alma, but what of Alma's wife and mother? We know he had sons, but did he also have daughters? And what of the sisters, wives, and daughters of Mosiah's sons? Were we to have a full account of their history, I am certain there would be moving narratives of women who were like Hannah, Jael, Rebecca, and Esther or like Mary, Martha, Junia, and Priscilla. Undoubtedly, in some sealed Book of Mormon records, there are stories of women who performed heroic deeds, who sacrificed their lives for what they believed, who persuaded men to lay down their weapons and to listen to still small voices. We know that some Book of Mormon women had remarkable spiritual experiences, for Alma tells us that God "imparteth his word by angels unto men, yea, not only men but women also" (32:23). I long for the day when the rest of the Book of Mormon is unsealed and the tongues of the New World daughters of Israel are unloosed.

Vain Repetitions upon Rameumptom

One of the strangest uses of words in Alma is seen among the Zoramites who live in the land of Antionum. Here it isn't the eloquence of language or its subtleties that is striking but the repetitious, formulaic language of the Zoramite prayers. When Alma and his companions go to preach to the Zoramites, they are amazed to find them worshiping "after a manner which Alma and his brethren had never beheld" (31:12). This strange order of worship consisted of individual Zoramites reciting a memorized prayer on top of a tower called Rameumptom, which had been "built up in the center of their synagogue, a place for standing, which was high above the head, and the top thereof would only admit one person." The prayer they offer is almost a parody of self-worship since its essential message is, "Holy God, . . . Thou has elected us that we shall be saved, whilst all around us are elected to be cast by thy wrath down to hell. . . . We thank thee, O God, that we are a chosen and a holy people" (31:15–16). Since the Zoramites offer this prayer one person at a time on top of a tower, it symbolizes the way in which language can be used, not to unify worshipers with one another or with the heavens, but to isolate them from both. Alma and his co-missionaries are "astonished beyond all measure" (31:19) by this practice which they consider "gross wickedness" (31:26). Rameumpton, this isolated "holy stand," thus becomes a sort of one-person Tower of Babel. As a solitary sanctuary of self-worship, it is as apt a display and symbol of hubris as one could imagine.

The Traditions of the Fathers

The Book of Mormon can be seen as the lengthened shadow of the original sibling rivalry between Nephi and his older brothers, although it is important to remember that all we know of Laman and Lemuel comes from Nephi. As in most families, where hurts are kept alive like smoldering coals, Laman and Lemuel continue to fuel their resentments and burn over what they perceive as the injustices and indignities suffered at the hands of their younger brother, including losing their inheritance of gold, silver, and jewels, which they feel Nephi had foolishly bartered for the brass plates. Century after century, their grievances are repeated and imprinted anew on the hearts of successive generations.

In Alma's narrative, this rivalry based on family memories continues to play out, often with disastrous results. It is the strength of their ancient enmity as well as their superior numbers that make the Lamanites so dangerous. When King Lamoni's father, who is also a "king over all the [Lamanite] land" (Alma 20:8), encounters his son Lamoni travelling with Ammon, he rebukes him, "Whither art thou going with this Nephite, who is one of the children of a liar? . . . Behold, he *robbed our fathers*; and now his children are also come amongst us that they may, by their cunning and their lyings, deceive us, that they again may rob us of our property" (20:10, 13, italics added). So angry is the king that he takes out his sword and tries to kill Ammon. Thus, we see that the remembrance of family treasures left at Jerusalem still has the power to enrage the descendents of Laman and Lemuel hundreds of years later. The loss of property and imagined injustices suffered by their progenitors are as fresh as if they had just happened.

What is surprising about the Lamanites' selective cultural memory, at least as it is reported by Nephite narrators, is how vividly they remember the injustices originally proclaimed by Laman and Lemuel and how little else they seem to retain of their culture and history. In this, with some exceptions (see Alma 23–24 and 53:17), they repeat the pattern of their forefathers, for both Lehi and Nephi felt compelled to remind Laman and Lemuel of "the great things the Lord had done for them in bringing them out of the land of Jerusalem, . . . the mercies of God in sparing their lives" and bringing them to the promised land (2 Nephi 1:1–3).

Thus, by and large, the Lamanites keep alive the idea of the Nephites lying to them and stealing from them and lose memory of nearly everything positive, including a remembrance of their Hebrew traditions and the very rudiments of their religious and cultural heritage. This is seen when Ammon comes among the Lamanites and some mistake him for God or "the Great Spirit," others see him as a man with supernatural powers, and still others regard him as "a monster, who had been sent from the Nephites to torment them" (19:25–26). King Lamoni tells him, "I know that thou art more powerful than all [my armies]" (18:21).

So erased is their cultural and spiritual memory that many of the Lamanites aren't even certain of the existence of God. As King Lamoni's father says in his prayer, "O God, Aaron hath told me that there is a God; and if there is a God, and if thou art God, will thou make thyself known unto me?" (Alma 22:18) When Ammon prepares King Lamoni to receive the gospel, he has to explain to him what heaven is, who Adam and Eve are, what the Fall means, and "the records and the holy scriptures of the people, which had been spoken by the prophets, even down to the time that their father, Lehi, left Jerusalem" (18:37). He even has to educate him about the history of their experience in the New World and "the rebellions of Laman and Lemuel, and the sons of Ishmael" (18:38). Since they had retained no written record, "he expounded unto them all the records and scriptures from the time Lehi left Jerusalem down unto the present time" (18:38). All this must have been an astonishing revelation to someone who had no prior knowledge of his rich heritage.

If nothing else, the Book of Mormon illustrates the tragedy of the erasure of cultural memory. In doing so, it validates the significance of the book's first dramatic episode—the importance of returning to Jerusalem to rescue the brass plates, which contained the family's sacred history and genealogy. What happens with the Lamanites over the centuries confirms what the angel tells Nephi about the consequences of his people not having their scriptures: "they should dwindle and perish in unbelief" (1 Nephi 4:13). The late BYU Professor of History, LeGrand Baker, reminds us of what an apt word "dwindle" is. After citing the definition found in the Oxford English Dictionary ("to become smaller and smaller; to shrink, waste away, decline; to decline in quality, value, or estimation; to degenerate; to reduce gradually in size, cause to shrink into small dimensions"), Baker observes,

"So dwindling in unbelief is not a static state of apostasy. Rather, it is a state of ever diminishing understanding of what is truth."[2]

What Laman, Lemuel, and their descendants lose is "the traditions of their fathers [and mothers]," which, as their history reveals, is just about everything.

Remember the Red Sea!

Among the traditions lost to the Lamanites is their nation's most memorable act of providence—the deliverance of the Israelites from the Egyptians by the parting of the Red Sea. As recounted in Chapter 1, the importance of this deliverance is seen at the very beginning of the Book of Mormon when Nephi tries to persuade his brothers to return to Jerusalem: "Therefore let us go up; let us be strong like unto Moses; for he truly spake unto the waters of the Red Sea and they divided hither and thither, and our fathers came through, out of captivity, on dry ground, and the armies of Pharaoh did follow and were drowned in the waters of the Red Sea" (1 Nephi 4:2). Along with invoking the names of "Abraham, Isaac, and Jacob," the call to "remember the Red Sea!" had been the national rallying cry of ancient Israel, and so it is not surprising to find it holding the same prominence for those transplanted New World Israelites who had not rejected their spiritual heritage.

When Alma prepares his son Helaman to take his place, he uses all of these events to impress on him the solemnity of his calling: "I would that ye should do as I have done, in remembering the captivity of our fathers; for they were in bondage, and none could deliver them except it was the God of Abraham, and the God of Isaac, and the God of Jacob; and he surely did deliver them in their afflictions. . . . And I will praise him forever, for he has brought our fathers out of Egypt and he has swallowed up the Egyptians in the Red Sea; and he led them by

---

2. http://www.legrandlbaker.org/2014/02/12/1-nephi-1011-legrand-baker-to-dwindle-in-unbelief/

his power into the promised land; yea, and he has delivered them out of bondage and captivity from time to time" (36:1, 28). Alma's use of the present perfect tense is designed to make this epochal experience more immediate, to awaken his son's memory of the significance of this great and miraculous delivery. It is also likely that he intends for him to connect it to their own people's deliverance from impending bondage at the time their forefather Lehi was led by God to bring them out of Jerusalem.

His Own House

Three times during his missionary labors Alma returns to Zarahemla "to his own house . . . to rest himself from the labors which he had performed" (8:1, 15:18, and 27:20). This is an intriguing bit of information that tantalizes for what it suggests. If Alma had a house in Zarahemla, what was it like? What did his family do and how were they supported during the years he was in the mission field? Did he or his sons make repairs to "his own house" or was he independently wealthy? It is the absence of such details of daily life that for some prevents the Book of Mormon from being a more engaging and compelling narrative. For all we do know of the Nephites and Lamanites (and all the other "ites" in the book), we know practically nothing of their domestic life. How did they live? What were the routines of their daily lives? How did they educate their children? What of their marriage customs? What songs did they sing? As we look into the distant mirror of their lives, hardly anything concrete is reflected back to us. A generation ago we knew practically nothing of the Vietnamese except that we were killing them with "the fury of aerial bombardment."[3] In her poem about the people of Vietnam and their lives before the American invasion titled "What Were They Like?" Denise Levertov asks:

---

3. Richard Eberhard, "The Fury of Aerial Bombardment" https://www.poetryfoundation.org/poems/42979/the-fury-of-aerial-bombardment

Did the people of Viet Nam
    use lanterns of stone?
    Did they hold ceremonies
    to reverence the opening of buds?
    Were they inclined to quiet laughter?
    Did they use bone and ivory,
    jade and silver, for ornament?
    Had they an epic poem?
    Did they distinguish between speech and
    singing? . . .

There is an echo yet
    of their speech which was like a song.
    It was reported their singing resembled
    the flight of moths in moonlight.
    Who can say? It is silent now.[4]

The answers to similar questions would help us know the Nephites more intimately than do all the accounts of their battles and doctrinal expositions. It is such everyday details in the lives of Lehi and Sariah's children for which we long.

Besides this, hints of omitted events also leave us wishing there had been room for more on the plates. Many unusual and even strange details are merely mentioned in the book of Alma: the destruction of Ammonihah and all its inhabitants, King Lamoni's servants carrying the limbs of the bandits Ammon had severed, the pacifism of the Anti-Nephi-Lehies, the cataclysmic shifts between righteousness and wickedness, an explanation of the Liahona, the disappearance of Alma (who was either "taken up by the Spirit, or buried by the hand of the Lord, even as Moses" ([5:19]), and the sea voyages of the "exceedingly curious" Hagoth (63:4–8). There are also references to the previously mentioned but unknown Old Testament prophets, Zenos and Zenock (1 Nephi 19 and Jacob 5), whose words are invoked by Alma in his great sermon on faith (Alma

---

4. http://www.americanpoems.com/poets/Denise-Levertov/15411.

33:17). These and many other elements of the narrative suggest that the original record of Alma's life was full of rich and wonderful events and stories, the details of which we can only now imagine.

And So Forth

Sometimes I find things in the Book of Alma (and the Book of Mormon) that surprise me. For example, the conjunction "and so forth" occurs several times in Alma. Generally, this use is conventional, as in "and all their sufferings with hunger and thirst, and their travail, and so forth" (18:37), but in one instance its use seems irreverent: "And since man had fallen he could not merit anything of himself; but the sufferings and death of Christ atone for their sins, through faith and repentance, and so forth" (22:14). Never have the first principles and ordinances of the gospel been so summarily reduced! The use of such a phrase seems to me an evidence of the authenticity of the Book of Mormon, for it is highly unlikely that anyone trying to perpetuate a deception would include such a phrase in such a place. It seems more likely an artifact from a very different language and culture.

At times, one wishes that the Book of Mormon narrators had used "and so forth" more frequently, especially when it comes to details about battles! There might have been room for narratives about domestic life or stories about women had Mormon in his synopsis said at the beginning, "They had many wars and much bloodshed, and so forth," and left it at that!

The Seed Becomes the Fruitful Tree

Among the most important contributions of the book of Alma is Alma's extended metaphor on the Word of God as a seed that one sows in one's heart. Alma speaks to the Zoramites of faith as an empirical experiment, using such horticultural language as planting, establishing roots, sprouting, nourishing, and bearing fruit as evidence that what has been planted is good. Mormon, in reporting on the Zoramites' response to Alma's sermon reveals that they understood that "the seed, or the word . . . must be planted *in their hearts*" (33:1; emphasis added); in other words, the tree will not grow from seeds planted in the mind!

Alma's discourse on faith offers readers not a theoretical but an experimental approach to spiritual discovery. As a treatise on religious epistemology, it is without parallel in sacred literature (although Moroni's admonition [in Moroni 10:4–5] comes close). All that is required, Alma states, is not profound inquiry or dramatic miracles, but a willingness to "experiment upon my words, and exercise a particle of faith" (32:27). And even if such a particle is lacking, desire alone is sufficient. Alma's promise is that the heart will know a good seed from a bad. It is remarkable that Alma's formula for discovering truth postulates that the experiment on faith will be experienced in a holistic manner—the seed planted in the heart causes not only a swelling in our hearts but also in our bodies, souls and minds: "it will begin to swell within your breasts"; "the word hath swelled your souls"; "your understanding doth begin to be enlightened, and your mind doth begin to expand" (32:28–35). How different such swelling words are from those of Korihor! (30:31)

Alma's formula for growing from desire to knowledge is validated by contemporary theories of epistemology which recognize various kinds of intelligence—emotional, social, spiritual, and cognitive—that complement, correct, and sustain one another. Such knowledge is not imaginary but real, as Alma says, "because it is light; and whatsoever is light is good, because it is *discernible*, therefore ye must know that it is good" (32:35, emphasis added).

In a marvelous way, Alma's metaphor is connected to the dreams of Lehi and Nephi in which they see a tree covered with white fruit. Alma says, "Behold, by and by ye shall pluck the fruit thereof, which is most precious, which is sweet above all that is sweet, and which is white above all that is white, yea, and pure above all that is pure; and ye shall feast upon this fruit even until ye are filled, that ye hunger not, neither shall ye thirst" (32:42). Later, Amulek identifies the seed as Jesus Christ himself: "The word [you plant in your hearts] is in Christ unto salvation" (34:5–6). Alma ends his sermon on the seed by saying, "And now, my brethren, I desire that ye shall plant this word in your hearts, and as it beginneth to swell even so nourish it by your faith. And behold, it will become a tree, springing up in you unto everlasting life" (33:23). As with the tree in Lehi's vision, the word of God becomes the Word made flesh, Christ as an evergreen tree, the balm or balsam tree of Gilead that heals the sin-sick soul.

Over the course of my eighty plus years, I have given nearly a tithe of my life to missionary work: first as a young missionary serving in the American Midwest; as a ward missionary in various stakes in which I have lived; and then, along with my wife, as an education and human-itarian service missionary in the Saint Petersburg Russia and Baltic States Missions (lasting nearly four years). In addition, I have taught the gospel in many settings: in the Army, in various organizations in which I have worked, when I have traveled abroad, and in many instances when I was simply attempting to fulfill the Lord's call to share the gos-pel with others. In all these missionary endeavors, I have been inspired by the experiences of Alma and his missionary companions.

During the first two months of my first mission, to the Northern States, I had the privilege of teaching the gospel to three young cou-ples who lived in Kankakee, Illinois: Rick and Donna Scharp, Neil and Helen Talbert, and Bob and Bobbye Talbert. We have remained friends over the years. In spite of the fact that the baptism of these three cou-ples took place in winter, there was a "fire shut up in my bones" that day (Jeremiah 20:9). I was excited to be part of such a meaningful culmina-tion of our teaching. I have a photograph of the three couples standing together, their hair wet, their faces radiant, their joy overflowing. At the fiftieth anniversary of their baptism, I took another picture. While some of these friends have since passed, others, who are still here have faces seasoned by age and bodies reshaped by the decades, but the light in their eyes and the joy in their hearts have only increased in depth and richness over the years. On a recnt visit to Bob and Bobbye

Talbert's home, my wife and I saw a map of the world showing the thirty-six missions they, their children and grandchildren and their children's spouses have served, totaling more that fifty years of missionary service! Along with others with whom I have had the privilege of sharing the message of the Restoration, they have made possible the "great joy" that the Doctrine and Covenants promises those who are instrumental in bringing others to Christ and which Alma says was what motivated his own missionary labor: "That I might bring them to taste of the exceeding joy of which I did taste" (36:24).

That seed of faith planted by my father nearly seventy-five years ago has indeed proven to be a good seed, springing up into a tree that has flowered in my heart and whose fruit has blessed my life. That tree and its fruit, as the angel said to Nephi, has a beauty "far beyond, yea, exceeding of all beauty; and the whiteness thereof . . . exceed[ing] the whiteness of the driven snow; . . . [It is a] tree which is precious above all" because its fruit represents "the love of God, which sheddeth itself abroad in the hearts of the children of men; wherefore, it is the most desirable above all things . . . and the most joyous to the soul" (1 Nephi 11:8–9, 22–23).

Like Lehi, I have found the pure white fruit hanging from that tree "most sweet, above all that I ever before tasted," and it has "filled my soul with exceeding great joy" (1 Nephi 8:11–12). And like Lehi, Nephi, and Alma, I have sought to invite others partake of this fruit that they might taste what I have tasted, that they too might sing the song of redeeming love.

3

Ammon:
The Hero's Journey

The story of Ammon is one of the most heroic in scriptural literature. From a disobedient and dissentious prince, one of "the very vilest of sinners" (Mosiah 28:4), rebelling against his father Mosiah and fighting against the church of God in his father's kingdom, Ammon undergoes a transcendent conversion and undertakes an odyssey that has many similarities to the monomyth or hero's journey as popularized by Joseph Campbell in his influential study, *The Hero With a Thousand Faces* (1949).

Alma's recounting Ammon's journey from rebellious prince to high priest suggests that he recognized that such a story, with its examples of great faith, repentance, courage, and love, would well support the expressed purpose of the Book of Mormon: "Which is to show unto the remnant of the House of Israel what great things the Lord hath done for their fathers; and that they may know the covenants of the Lord, that they are not cast off forever" (Title Page). The power of this story, with its compelling similarity to other epic heroic journeys, may be one of the reasons Mormon, faced with choosing among a repository of narratives, chose to include it in his abridgement.

Our first encounter with Ammon finds him trying to destroy the church. With his brothers and with Alma the Younger, he rebelled not only against the commandments of God but also against the proclamations of his father, King Mosiah, who had established a law prohibiting persecution of the believers. What is said of Alma undoubtedly was also true of Ammon: "He became a great hinderment to the prosperity of the church of God; stealing away the hearts of the people; causing much dissension among the people; giving a chance for the enemy of God to exercise his power over them" (Mosiah 27:9). Later, in recounting this period of their lives to his brothers, Ammon said, "Behold, we went forth even in wrath, with mighty threatenings to destroy his [God's] church" (Alma 26:18).

Alma the Elder was so troubled by the rebellion of his son Alma that he prayed "with great faith" that the Lord would show him the error of his ways (Mosiah 16:14). In response, the Lord sent an angel, who appeared to Alma and to Ammon and his brothers, speaking "with a voice of thunder, which caused the earth to shake" beneath them (Mosiah 27:11). Like Paul, who had a similar experience on the road to Damascus, Ammon and his companions were astonished and frightened, for they recognized this as a demonstration of the power of God, which they had been denying. Following the angel's departure, they fell to the earth, doubtless overpowered by a realization of their perilous position before the Lord. In this state they began to repent, and the Lord, in Ammon's words, "snatched us from our awful, sinful, and polluted state. . . . In his great mercy [he] hath brought us over that everlasting gulf of death and misery, even to the salvation of our souls" (Alma 26:17, 20).

So grateful were these young men for being redeemed from their iniquity that Ammon, his brothers, and Alma set out to make restitution for the wrongs they had done, "zealously striving to repair all the injuries which they had done to the church, confessing all their sins, and publishing all the things which they had seen, and explaining the prophecies and the scriptures to all who desired to hear them" (Mosiah 27:35). Note how the totality of their conversion is emphasized by the repetition of "all" in this sentence. In spite of being persecuted and abused by nonbelievers, they "did impart much consolation to the church" (Mosiah 27:33) and brought many to a knowledge of Christ.

Not content simply to rectify the wrongs they had done among their own people, Ammon and his brothers were so grateful for the mercies of the Lord that they each declined an invitation to succeed their father as king of the land of Zarahemla (Alma 17:6). They relinquished a worldly kingdom to labor for the kingdom of God, devoting their lives to preaching the gospel to the Lamanites, "for they could not bear that any human soul should perish; yea, even the very thoughts that any soul should endure endless torment did cause them to quake and tremble" (Mosiah 28:3).

The faith, courage, and especially the love that this mission to the Lamanites required are a testament to their devotion. Their fellow Nephites did not believe they could succeed and, in Ammon's words, "laughed [them] to scorn" for even contemplating such an mission (Alma 26:23). Not only that, but the Nephites also proposed to Ammon that they all take up arms to annihilate the Lamanites, for they greatly feared them (Alma 26:24–25). And they had good reason for that fear, for, as Alma says, Ammon and his brothers "had undertaken to preach the word of God to a wild and a hardened and a ferocious people; a people who delighted in murdering the Nephites, and robbing and plundering them" (Alma 17:14).

As discussed in Chapter 2, the Lamanites were not only hostile and hardened, but they had also lost almost all understanding of God from their faded ancestral memory. King Lamoni, to whom Ammon first preached the gospel, didn't even have an understanding of the words *God* and *heaven* (Alma 18:24–32). In fact, he mistook Ammon for "the Great Spirit" (Alma 18:2, 4, 11, 18). The record further indicates that "notwithstanding they believed in a Great Spirit," their moral system was such that "they supposed that whatsoever they did was right" (Alma 18:5). And the traditions of their fathers, Laman and Lemuel, still held sway over their beliefs. King Lamoni's father, who was king over all the land of the Lamanites, called Ammon "one of the children of a liar [Nephi]," who "robbed our fathers [evidently referring to the sacred records and, certainly, the family treasures left in Jerusalem—compare Mosiah 10:11–17]; and now his children are also come amongst us that they may, by their cunning and their lyings, deceive us, that they again may rob us of our property" (Alma 20:10, 13).

In the face of this deeply ingrained enmity, Ammon and his companions set out to teach the gospel to "their brethren," the Lamanites. After journeying into the wilderness, and perhaps sensing for the first time the difficulty of their undertaking, they become discouraged and disheartened. Ammon reports, "Our hearts were depressed, and we were about to turn back." At this moment the Lord comforts them, saying, "Go amongst thy brethren, the Lamanites, and bear with patience thine afflictions, and I will give unto you success" (Alma 26:27).

Emboldened by this witness, they set out to accomplish their mission, going their separate ways into the various areas of the land inhabited by the Lamanites. Before doing so, Ammon administers to each of his brothers, blessing them and giving them their instructions from the Lord. It is interesting to note that while Ammon apparently was not the eldest of Mosiah's sons (the kingship was first offered to Aaron; see Mosiah 29:1–3), he was "chief among them," possibly because of his great faith and leadership (Alma 17:18).

Of Ammon's fourteen-year sojourn among the Lamanites, Mormon chose to give us a detailed account of only one experience, Ammon's visit to the land of Ishmael. Why he chose this one out of what must have been a rich and varied record we can only surmise, but it is hard to imagine a more dramatic example of a person accomplishing great things by putting his complete trust in God. Indeed, the conversion of King Lamoni and his people, which the Lord brought about through Ammon, ranks among the most arresting stories of faith and daring in the scriptures. Ammon is like David going against Goliath, like Joseph in the court of Pharaoh, or like Nephi going up to Jerusalem to get the brass plates. He is the archetypal devoted servant of God courageously facing great obstacles and seemingly insurmountable odds that he might accomplish a righteous task.

As he enters the land of Ishmael, Ammon is bound and taken before the king to be interrogated, "as was the custom," and his fate determined, ranging from execution or imprisonment to servitude of some sort (Alma 17:20). When the king questions his motives for entering their lands, Ammon replies simply, "I desire to dwell among this people for a time; yea, and perhaps until the day I die" (Alma 17:23). During the interview King Lamoni is "much pleased" with Ammon, so much so that, as often happens in a hero's journey, the king offers him one of his daughter's hand in marriage (v. 24)—an extraordinary gesture considering that Ammon is a Nephite intruder among a people who traditionally had "an eternal hatred towards the children of Nephi" (Mosiah 10:17). What could have prompted King Lamoni to invite Ammon to be part of the royal family? Perhaps he recognized in Ammon's regal bearing his quiet self-confidence and his eagerness to serve, the attributes of an extraordinary person, one rare in any kingdom. Perhaps the Spirit even took part in prompting this unusual offer. But Ammon, having already forsaken one position of royalty, declines the offer, saying, "Nay, but I will be thy servant" (Alma 17:25).

As a servant, Ammon is given the task of helping to watch the king's flocks and feed his "horses."[1] When a band of Lamanite herdsmen

---

1. Archeologists contend that there were no horses in the Americas contemporaneous with Book of Mormon peoples. Therefore, this is likely a reference to some other four-legged animal, perhaps similar to a horse in appearance, but not necessarily so. This frequently occurs when people new to a region apply familiar names to unfamiliar species. For instance, the ancient Greeks gave the name *hippopotamos* (river horse) to a big, barrel-shaped animal they saw in Africa, which scarcely even resembles a horse. *Hippopotamos* is a combination of the Greek words *hippos*, meaning *"horse,"* and *potamos*, meaning "river." In fact, the hippopotamus is more closely related to the hog than to the horse. http://word-central.com/cgi-bin/student?hippopotamus. A readable and engaging discussion of this subject can be found under the heading, "Horses in the Book of Mormon," online at fairmormon.org. https://www.fairmormon.org/archive/publications/horses-in-the-book-of-mormon.

scatter the flocks in hopes of stealing some of the strays for themselves (see 18:7), Lamoni's servants fear that the king will put them to death as previously he had other servants (Alma 17:28); but Ammon rejoices, for he sees this as an opportunity to demonstrate the power of God to his "fellow-servants," thus winning their hearts and making it possible for them to believe his words (Alma 17:29). Ammon urges the other servants to find the scattered animals and gather them together. Once the flock is contained, he tells them to guard it while he goes out to find and "contend" with the robbers, who were waiting nearby the watering place to again scatter the flock (17:33).

Again, consider what happens in relation to the hero's journey, which often pits a lone man of courage against a formidable enemy: alone, with only a sling and a sword, Ammon defends the king's flocks against a sizable number of the enemy. Single-handedly he slays six with his sling and with his sword kills the enemy leader and cuts off the arms of "not a few" of those who raise their swords against him (Alma 17:33–38). Such a heroic display of courage and strength so impresses the other servants that they feel Ammon has supernatural powers that prevent him from being slain. King Lamoni, on hearing of Ammon's feats, says, "Surely this is more than a man. Behold, is this not the Great Spirit?" (Alma 18:2) The servants, who later call Ammon "Rabbanah," meaning "powerful or great king" (Alma 18:13), reply that they do not know whether Ammon is a man or the Great Spirit, but they do know he is "a friend to the king" (Alma 18:3).

While his heroic deeds are being recounted with enthusiasm and wonder at court, Ammon is off feeding the king's "horses." The king, astonished by this faithful service as by the account of Ammon's physical prowess, exclaims, "Surely there has not been any servant among all my servants that has been so faithful as this man" (Alma 18:10), an exuberant compliment that echoes the extravagant praise often associated with the feats of mythological heroes.

As Ammon had hoped, his faithfulness results in an opportunity to teach the gospel to the king. Starting with the Creation, Ammon recounts to Lamoni the scriptural history from Adam to Lehi and from

Lehi down to their own time (18:38). When Ammon then tells Lamoni of the plan of redemption, Lamoni cries to the Lord for forgiveness and falls to the earth as though dead (Alma 18:39–43). Carried by his servants to his bed where he is mourned over by his wife and children for two days, Lamoni lies unconscious (Alma 18:39–43). And then, symbolic of spiritual resurrection, he rises on the third day to exclaim, "Blessed be the name of God. . . . Behold, I have seen my Redeemer" (Alma 19:12–13). His joy is so full that he is again overcome by the Spirit, and his testimony is so powerful that not only his wife, but also our hero Ammon and the king's servants all fall to the earth overcome. While they are in this state, one of Lamoni's servants, Abish, a secret believer among the Lamanites who had been converted "on account of a remarkable vision of her father," sees her opportunity to help others "believe in the power of God" (Alma 19:16–17) and runs from house to house calling the people to witness what has happened. (This is an example of how a seemingly small piece of information in the text reveals something highly significant: genuine visions were possible to someone open to receiving them, even among a morally backward and superstitious people like the Lamanites).

Through Abish's efforts a "multitude" is present when Ammon, the king, and his household arise and to the astonished and perplexed citizens of Lamoni's kingdom exclaim that "their hearts had been changed; that they had no more desire to do evil" (Alma 19:33). As a result, many believe and are converted. Thus, beginning with the powerful conversion of King Lamoni, the church is established among the Lamanites for the first time in more than four hundred years. So significant is Lamoni's conversion that it leads not only to the establishment of the church in the land of Ishmael but also, through its influence on his father, the high king of the Lamanites in all the Land of Nephi.

Like his son, Lamoni's father is spiritually awakened by "the generosity and the greatness of the words of . . . Ammon" (Alma 22:3). Upon hearing the gospel from Ammon's brother Aaron, the king declares, "I will give up all that I possess, yea, I will forsake my kingdom, that I may receive this great joy" (Alma 22:15). When Aaron invites him to ask the Lord for forgiveness, the king prays to God, "I will give away all my sins to know thee" (Alma 22:18). Because of the king's testimony, the entire royal household is converted, and the king sends a proclamation throughout his land that Ammon and his brothers are permitted to teach the word of God unmolested.

With the support of the Lamanite king, Ammon and his brothers are able to convert thousands of the Lamanites to the gospel. But what is more remarkable, "as many of the Lamanites as believed in their preaching, and were converted unto the Lord, *never did fall away*" (Alma 23:6, emphasis added). So total is the conversion of the previously wicked and murderous Lamanites who accept the gospel that they covenant that they would never again take up weapons of war, even to defend their own lives. The forgiveness of their sins includes the miraculous further blessing of having "taken away the guilt from [their] hearts." So grateful are they that they choose to suffer death, if necessary, rather than risk sinning again (Alma 24:10, 5–16) Later, when their enemies come against them, many of these new converts are slain, but "more than a thousand" of the enemy are so moved by their deep faith and astonishing courage in facing certain death that they throw down their weapons, repent, and are themselves converted to Christ (Alma 24:27).

The extent to which Ammon's influence on the lives of these Lamanites is recognized is seen in the fact that shortly afterward, when they move into the Nephites' land of Jershon, they call themselves "the people of Ammon" (Alma 27:26). Worried for their safety and moved by "the pity and the exceeding love which Ammon and his brethren" have for the people, they bring these converted Lamanites down to the land of Zarahemla where they can be protected by the Nephites (Alma 53:11).

It is fitting that Ammon becomes a high priest over the Ammonites. Having forsaken a throne to be a servant in the household of King Lamoni and having declared that he desired to live among these people "perhaps until the day I die," Ammon continues to serve them, presumably until the end of his life. Thus, again echoing the hero's journey, Ammon moves from tending the animals of his archenemy to the highest position of spiritual leadership in that part of the land.

Near the end of their missionary journey, Ammon and his brothers are reunited. On one occasion, Ammon summarizes their experiences and rejoices in their blessings, celebrating their great success among the Lamanites:

> My brothers and my brethren, behold I say unto you, how great reason have we to rejoice; for could we have supposed when we started from the land of Zarahemla that God would have granted unto us such great blessings? . . . Behold, . . . our brethren, the Lamanites, were in darkness, yea, even in the darkest abyss, but behold, how many of them are brought to behold the marvelous light of God! And this is the blessing which hath been bestowed upon us, that we have been made instruments in the hands of God to bring about this great work. Behold, thousands of them do rejoice, and have been brought into the fold of God. . . . Blessed be the name of our God; let us sing to his praise, yea, let us give thanks to his holy name, for he doth work righteousness forever.
>
> (Alma 26: 1–9)

Ammon's focus differs from classical heroic figures in that his focus is not on his own heroic journey and action but rather on God as hero. C. S. Lewis says the image we get of the great epic poets is "the picture of a venerable figure, a king, a great warrior, or a poet inspired by the Muse, seated and chanting to the harp a poem on high matters [usually of his own heroism] before an assembly."[2] Typically, the epic poet or the poet's vaunted hero made a boast of his own prowess in battle or of his great deeds, but Ammon exults in the Lord. His brother Aaron, misunderstanding Ammon's rejoicing at the things they have

---

2. Preface to *Paradise Lost* (Oxford: Oxford University Press, 1968).

accomplished rebukes him: "Ammon, I fear that thy joy doth carry thee away unto boasting" (Alma 26:10), but Ammon replies that he was not vaunting his own strength and wisdom but the Lord's: "Therefore I will not boast of myself, but I will boast of my God, for in his strength I can do all things" (Alma 26:12). After reviewing their successes among the Lamanites and praising God for his goodness and mercy, Ammon reiterates that he was glorying in the Lord: "Now if this is boasting, even so will I boast; for this is my life and my light, my joy and my salvation, and my redemption from everlasting wo. Yea, blessed is the name of God" (Alma 26:36). Ammon's paean is similar to the hymns of Moses and Deborah in the Old Testament (see Exodus 15; Judges 5), the Magnificat in the New Testament (Luke 2:46–55), and Nephi's "psalm" in the Book of Mormon (2 Nephi 4:15–34). It is an outpouring of joy and rejoicing, an extended song of praise to God.

The story of Ammon speaks to those of us in Christ's kingdom today. It reminds us that repentance takes courage and sacrifice; it inspires us to share the gospel with others, no matter how hardened their hearts or foreign their way of life; it teaches us that heroism inspired of God is possible for all and that with faith we can perform great miracles. The way is not easy, as Ammon continually reminds us, but the joy is unspeakable and the peace past understanding. Finally, Ammon reminds us that those who have tasted of the love of the Father and the Son should praise him. Again and again, Ammon expresses his love to the Lord in paeans of praise and thanksgiving. Those who, like Alma and Ammon, have "felt to sing the song of redeeming love" (Alma 5:26) could well take Ammon's concluding expression as their own: "Now this is my joy, and my great thanksgiving; yea, I will give thanks unto my God forever. Amen" (Alma 26:37).

Finally, Ammon's hero's journey is patterned after that of Christ, who undertook the ultimate hero's journey by giving up his heavenly and earthly throne to become the savior and servant of all by descending below all things (D&C 122:8), by conquering sin and death, by triumphing over all his enemies, and by becoming the great High Priest of humanity.

4

Alma the Younger's Seminal Sermon at Zarahemla

History has sometimes turned on the power of a great speech, oration or sermon. Think, for instance, of Queen Elizabeth's speech to the Troops at Tilbury or of Patrick Henry's "Give me liberty or give me death" speech in 1775. Abraham Lincoln's "Gettysburg Address," Winston Churchill's "We shall fight on the beaches" at the beginning of World War II, Mohandas Gandhi's "Quit India" speech in 1942, and Martin Luther King's "I Have a Dream" speech in 1963 were all pivotal moments in history. I would place Alma the Younger's sermon to the inhabitants of Zarahemla in the company of such history-turning addresses.

Alma the Younger is the greatest spiritual orator in the Book of Mormon. We are blessed to have five of his sermons:

- To the members of the Church and potential converts at Zarahemla (Alma 5),
- To the people in Gideon (Alma 7),

- To those in Ammonihah (Alma 9:8–30),
- His additions to Amulek's sermon to Zeezrom (Alma 12:3–13:30), which "were heard by the people round about; for the multitude was great" (12:2), and
- His address on faith to the Nephite colony of Zoramites (Alma 32:8–33:23).

The first of these—the sermon at Zarahemla—took place not long after the people of Limhi, a Nephite colony now returned to Zarahemla, had passed through a crisis that nearly destroyed their society. The wickedness of King Noah and his corrupt priests resulted in a political, cultural, and spiritual crisis that, had it not been for Alma's father, might have descended into total chaos.

At the Waters of Mormon, Alma the Elder began a small and ultimately triumphant transformation of Nephite society in the colony by establishing ecclesiastical authority and social coherence. The peoples of Limhi and of Alma ultimately escape situations of bondage in the Land of Nephi, dominated by Lamanites, and are reunited with the people of Mosiah at Zarahemla in the north.[1] Although Alma the Younger was blessed to live during this more positive and peaceful social time at Zarahemla, he and the Sons of Mosiah rebelled against their fathers and "went about . . . seeking to destroy the church of God" (Alma 36:6; see Mosiah 27:10).

As the formerly sinful son of a high priest, in addressing the people at Zarahemla, Alma knows of the societal dangers of discord, for he and the Sons of Mosiah had personally been responsible for fomenting them. More significantly, he knows the personal price that must be paid by those who rebel against God, for, as he later recalls to his own son, Helaman, "I was racked with eternal torment, for my soul was harrowed up to the greatest degree and racked with all my sin. . . . I

---

1. For locations and dating of events taking place during this time period in the Land of Zarahemla to the north and the Land of Nephi to the south, see *The Book of Mormon: A Reader's Edition*, edited by Grant Hardy (University of Illinois Press, 2003), Appendix 7, pp. 676–77. I can't recommend this valuable resource too highly.

was racked, even with the pains of a damned soul" (Alma 36:12, 16). The use of such language reveals the degree and depth of Alma's suffering: "harrow" means to "wound the feelings, distress greatly" or "to ravage, plunder; seize, capture"; "racked" (repeated three times in this short passage) means "to torture on the rack."[2]

After repenting—and upon the death of his father—Alma becomes the high priest, which puts him "in charge concerning all the affairs of the church" (Mosiah 29:42). He is also appointed chief judge and thus inaugurates the reign of the judges among the Nephites. Immediately, Alma has to deal with political dissent, treason, social unrest, ecclesiastical divisiveness, and armed conflict with the rebellious Amlicites who have joined forces with the Lamanites. Although Alma is successful in defeating his enemies, the war exacts a great cost to the Nephites: "Now the number of the slain were not numbered, because of the greatness of their number. . . . Now many women and children had been slain with the sword, and also many of their fields of grain were destroyed, for they were trodden down by the hosts of men" (Alma 3:1–2). The result of these losses produces a brief period of retrenchment during which thousands join the church, leading to social stability. This stability, however, quickly begins to erode when the wealthier members of the church begin setting themselves above and persecuting their poorer brothers and sisters. These prideful members infect not only the church, but "lead those who were unbelievers on from one piece of iniquity to another, thus bringing on the destruction of the people" (Alma 4:11). The vivid characterization of iniquity as progressing in "pieces," one type of immorality after another, makes it much more threatening than to characterize it generally.

It is against this backdrop of recently subdued external threat and internal discord that Alma surrenders his position as chief judge and, retaining his office of high priest, goes "forth among his people . . . that he might preach the word of God unto them, to stir them up to remembrance of their duty, and that he might pull down, by the word

---

2. On-Line Etymology, etymonline.com

of God, all the pride and craftiness and all the contentions which were
among his people, seeing no way that he might reclaim them save it
were in bearing down in pure testimony against them" (Alma 4:19).
Note the implications of the verb, "pull down," not only suggesting the
pride that lifted the people into wickedness but evoking the image of
Alma's vigorous efforts to bring it to an end.

Alma's sermon to the church members in Zarahemla as recounted
in Alma chapter 5 is a skillful blending of various rhetorical devices,
making it an exceptional achievement, a virtual sermonic tour de force.
These include parallelism, allusion, repetition, imagery, symbolism,
contrasting pairs, rhetorical questions. and more. Suggesting his skill
and power with language, Alma was described even before his conversion as "a man of many words." At that point in his life his verbal skills
were being employed to entice "many of the people to do after the
manner of his iniquities" (Mosiah 27:8). He now is in a position both
politically and spiritually to turn those gifts to righteous uses.

Alma begins his sermon with a statement of his identity and authority similar to Nephi's (1 Nephi 1:1) and Jacob's (2 Nephi 6:2): "I Alma,
having been consecrated by my father, Alma, to be a high priest over
the church of God" (3).[3] In beginning this way, he reminds his hearers
of the deliverance of their ancestors from the destruction at Jerusalem
and their blessings in being brought to a land of promise. By invoking
his father, he reminds them of the dramatic turn in Nephite history
brought about by his father's faith and courage: "He [Alma the Elder]
having power and authority from God to do these things, behold, I say
unto you that he began to establish a church in the land which was in
the borders of Nephi; yea and he did baptize his brethren in the waters
of Mormon" (3). By alluding to the baptisms at the Waters of Mormon,
Alma is hoping his hearers remember the dramatic contrast between
life under the wicked King Noah and that under Alma the Elder and
King Mosiah. He skillfully brackets his sermon by invoking the baptis-
mal covenant at the Waters of Mormon at the beginning of his sermon

---

3. All references to the sermon in Chapter 5 are cited by the verse number only.

and returning to it at the end when, alluding also to Nephi's powerful dream, he invites his hearers to "Come and be baptized unto repentance, that ye also may be partakers of the fruit of the tree of life" (62).

To emphasize the significance of his father's establishment of the church after the wickedness of King Noah, and his own personal rescue from "the pains of hell" (36:13), Alma introduces the first of his central themes (also central to the Book of Mormon and the Bible): the contrast between captivity/bondage and deliverance/liberation. In doing so, he reminds his listeners of the social and spiritual bondage the people (their parents and grandparents) suffered under King Noah and the physical bondage and captivity they endured at the hands of the Lamanites: "Behold I say unto you, they were delivered out of the hands of the people of king Noah by the mercy and power of God. . . . They were brought in bondage by the hands of the Lamanites, . . . yea . . . they were in captivity, and again the Lord delivered them out of bondage" (4–5). Alma here is also echoing Mosiah who, just before Alma the Elder was chosen as leader, told the people: "Yea, remember King Noah. . . . Behold what great destruction did come upon them [the people]; and also because of their iniquities they were brought into bondage" (Mosiah 29:18).

Just as Jews have been admonished to remember the captivity and subsequent deliverance of their forbearers in Egypt (see Alma 36:28), so Alma asks, "Have you sufficiently retained in remembrance the captivity of your fathers? Yea, and have you sufficiently retained in remembrance his mercy and long-suffering towards them? And moreover, have ye sufficiently retained in remembrance that he has delivered their souls from hell?" (6) (Note the accumulating force of the repeated question, "Have ye sufficiently retained in remembrance . . . ?") Captivity and deliverance is just one of the themes Alma will continue to weave throughout his sermon. Referring to a matrix of deliverances—physical and spiritual, individual and collective, and mortal and immortal—Alma employs various images and symbols to dramatize the contrast between freedom and bondage, the most powerful of which are "bands of death" and "chains of hell," both of which can be "loosed" as people repent and turn to God (9). His use of such imagery undoubtedly is related to his own personal spiritual captivity, for he speaks of himself being bound by and then freed from the chains of iniquity.

To signify their spiritual captivity, Alma employs images relating to encircling bands and chains: "they were encircled about by the bands of death, and the chains of hell" (7). Alma increases the force of these images through repetition. Having introduced them in verse 7, he asks, "Were the bands of death broken, and the chains of hell which encircled them about, were they loosed?" (9) He then asks how they could have been loosed: "What is the cause of their being loosed from the bands of death, and also the chains of hell?" (10)

In this sermon Alma, like Lehi before him, presents his hearers with a series of contrasting pairs that throw into bold relief the choice before them of choosing "liberty and eternal life" or "captivity and death" (see 2 Nephi 2:27–29 & 10:23). These include: God/Devil, birth and life/death, light/dark, white/stained, pure/filthy, truth/lies, awake/ sleep, saved/damned or destroyed, rejoice/mourn and wail, accept/ deny, righteous/wicked, faithful/unfaithful, faith/doubt, belief/unbelief, remember/forget, harken/ignore (not listen), humility/pride, rich/ poor, guilty/guiltless, good shepherd/bad shepherd, and sheep/wolves. Alma employs such a long catalogue of opposites not only to demonstrate that his listeners have been making the wrong choices at the peril of their souls but also to remind them that they have the agency and the power to choose which way they will live, to undertake a change of heart, beginning on the very day he addresses them: "Can ye feel so *now?*" (26, emphasis added)

One of Alma's chief rhetorical devices is repetition. Not only does he repeatedly present contrasting choices, but he continually repeats words and phrases for emphasis. In fact, one gets the impression that nearly every word or phrase in the sermon is repeated at least once. One of the most important of these repeated phrases is, "I say unto you," which is found an amazing thirty-five times in this sermon (this might seem somewhat extreme until we see its rhetorical purpose). The effect of such repetition not only affirms Alma's authority but also shows the depth of his personal witness. That is, he is speaking to his auidience both as high priest-leader of the church and as a reformed sinner ("a very wicked and an idolatrous man" [Mosiah 27:8]). He thus speaks with ecclesiastical as well as personal authority.

Toward the end of the sermon as he continues to use this phrase, Alma cleverly expands it from "I say unto you" to "thus saith the Spirit" (50), "the Spirit saith unto me" (51), and "the Spirit saith" (52), extending the authority of his words to that of the Holy Spirit and ultimately to Christ: "I say unto you, all you that are desirous to follow the voice of the good shepherd" (57). Then, adroitly, he shifts the burden to *them*: "What have ye to say against this?" (58) The accumulated force of his multiple uses of "I say unto you" and his one "What have ye to say?" would, one would guess, leave his hearers speechless. What could they say against such a barrage of appeal and testimony?

Counterbalanced by the declarative "I say unto you" are a series of thirty-five rhetorical questions, most at the beginning of his sermon. The majority of these questions take the form, "I ask" or "I ask of you." These are often interwoven with "I say unto you," as in the following example:

> And now *I ask of you*, my brethren, were they destroyed? *Behold I say unto you,* Nay, they were not. And *again I ask*, were the bands of death broken, and the chains of hell which encircled them about, were they loosed? *I say unto you*, Yea, they were loosed, and their souls did expand, and they did sing redeeming love. And *I say unto you* that they are saved" (8–9, emphasis added).

At times Alma's use of "I say unto you" is followed by a question, which is then followed by another "I say unto you," as in the following example:

> "I say unto you, . . . can ye imagine yourselves brought before the tribunal of God with your souls filled with guilt and remorse,

having a remembrance of all your guilt,
yea, a perfect remembrance of all your wickedness,
yea, a remembrance that ye have set at defiance the
        commandments of God?
I say unto you . . . "

(16–19, lines divided to highlight
strategic repetition of the
word *remembrance* as well)

This constant saying and questioning creates a powerful accumulation of emotional logic, especially as Alma brings it to the present moment. He knows he is speaking to members of the church who are aware of the teachings and practices that once were but no longer are a part of their spiritual lives. Thus, as noted above, he asks, "If ye have experienced a change of heart, . . . can ye feel so now?" (26)

Not satisfied with asking, "Have ye spiritually been born of God?" (14), a general call to repentance that might allow his hearers to excuse certain sinful behaviors, Alma zeros in on their specific transgressions: Have "ye been sufficiently humble?" (27); "Behold, are ye stripped of pride?" (28); "Is there one among you who is not stripped of envy?" (29); "Is there one among you that doth make a mock of his brother, or that heapeth upon him persecutions?" (30). Such questions suggest a newer, more spiritually elevated gospel standard of behavior.

That Alma is concerned with an inner sanctification and not just an outward show of obedience can be seen in his most penetrating series of questions, ones that cut to the hearts of his listeners: "And now behold, I ask of you, my brethren of the church, have ye spiritually been born of God? Have ye received his image in your countenances? Have ye experienced this mighty change in your hearts?" (14) Alma here is suggesting, as did the American Puritans, that one's spiritual repentance and renewal can be visible but, as he makes clear, they must also be internal.

Alma asks his hearers not simply to consider changing their lives but also to use their imaginations in doing so: "Can you *imagine* to

yourselves that ye hear the voice of the Lord?" "Do ye *imagine* to yourselves that ye can lie to the Lord?" "Can ye *imagine* yourselves brought
before the tribunal of God?" (16–18; emphasis added) By inviting his
hearers to focus their imaginations on a future time when they will
stand before the Lord to give a full accounting of their discipleship,
Alma hopes to inspire a *present* devotion consisting of feeling, doing
and thinking: "Can ye look up to God at that day with a *pure heart* and
clean hands? . . . Can ye *think* of being saved?" (19–20, emphasis added).

Alma also introduces images having to do with purity and impu-
rity. Besides asking, "Can ye look up to God at that day with a pure
heart and clean hands?" (19), he even more pointedly demands, "How
will any of you feel, if ye shall stand before the bar of God, having your
garments stained with blood and all manner of filthiness?" (22). In contrast with the image of filthy, blood-stained garments, Alma speaks of
the cleansing and purification that come through the blood of Christ:
"For there can no man be saved except his garments are washed white;
yea, his garments must be purified until they are cleansed from all
stain, through the blood of him of whom it has been spoken by our
fathers, who should come to redeem his people from their sins" (21).
The unclean to whom Alma addresses his remarks are set against "all
the holy prophets whose garments are cleansed and are spotless, pure
and white" (24).

Another clever strategy Alma employs to call his hearers to repentance is to invoke the fathers, that is, ancient prophets and patriarchs
of Israel, but he does so by moving from the personal "my father Alma"
(3, 11) and "your fathers" (6, 13) to the collective, "our fathers" (21), and
then specifically to the three great fathers of Israel: "Behold, my brethren, do ye suppose that such an one [i.e., an unrepentant sinner] can
have a place to sit down in the kingdom of God, with Abraham, with
Isaac, and with Jacob?" (24) Invoking the names of the great patriarchs
of Israel is designed to remind his hearers (who include the Mulekite
majority of Zarahemla who surely know of the patriarchal fathers),
of the great figures with whom God established Israel by covenant:
"I am commanded to stand and testify unto this people the things

which have been spoken by our fathers concerning the things which are to come" (44); "And moreover, I say unto you that it has thus been revealed unto me, that the words which have been spoken by our fathers are true" (47).

This invocation of the Fathers was deeply engrained in the consciousness of every father and mother in Israel, who were expected to teach their children to remember these first patriarchs. Later in speaking to his son, Helaman, Alma says, "I would that ye should do as I have done, in remembering the captivity of our fathers; for they were in bondage, and none could deliver them except it was the God of Abraham, and the God of Isaac, and the God of Jacob" (36:2, 28–29).

Alma also calls to mind the first fathers of the Book of Mormon, Lehi and Nephi, by using the central image of their remarkable shared vision of the Tree of Life "Yea, he [the Lord God] saith: Come unto me and ye shall partake of the fruit of the tree of life; yea, ye shall eat and drink of the bread and the waters of life freely" (34; see also Alma 42:27). By referring to these earlier Book of Mormon symbolic events, Alma may be reminding his hearers of the contrasting choices made by Lehi's sons—those who chose righteousness and those who chose wickedness and of the unfolding of their respective histories from these choices.

Another archetypal image used by Alma in this sermon is that of the shepherd and his sheep. Emphasizing the role of the caring and beneficent shepherd, Alma uses the term "good shepherd" seven times, most instances coming at the end of his sermon.

Echoing Isaiah (53:6), he speaks to those who "are not the sheep of the good shepherd" (38) but rather those that "have gone astray, as sheep having no shepherd, notwithstanding a shepherd hath called after you and is still calling after you, but ye will not hearken unto his voice!" (37) Instead of listening to the voice of the Good Shepherd, some of these Nephites have chosen "the devil [as their] shepherd" (39).

Alma's attitude toward his hearers is seen in his frequent reference to them as "my brethren," an appellation which occurs seven times in the beginning and middle of the sermon. At the end of the sermon when the logic of his argument reaches its climax, that is, when he hopes that his words have caused his hearers "to sing the song of redeeming love," Alma shifts to the more endearing "my beloved brethren," which he repeats three times. This is similar to the way Alma ends his sermon to the people at Ammonihah: "And now, my beloved brethren, for ye are my brethren, and ye ought to be beloved" (9:30).[4] Thus, not only does Alma remind his hearers of their kinship and spiritual relationship, but he reveals the charity he feels toward them in spite of his strong language condemning their recalcitrant obedience. It is important to note that such language choice is not accidental but deliberate. That is, Alma carefully chooses his words and expressions for their fullest effect.

There is a definite shift in the middle of the sermon when Alma begins to modulate his bolder, more confrontational language with the softer invitation to accept Christ: "Behold, he sendeth an invitation unto all men, for the arms of his mercy are extended towards them, and he saith: Repent, and I will receive you. Yea, he saith, Come unto me" (33–34). Christ is the "good shepherd [who] doth call you; yea, and in his own name he doth call you" (38).

The ultimate power of Alma's sermon is seen not only in the logic of his argument, his many rhetorical devices, and his personal persuasiveness ("I speak in the energy of my soul" [43]), but because of his being called to this task: "Behold I testify unto you that I do know that these things whereof I have spoken are true. . . . Behold, I say unto you they are made known unto me by the Holy Spirit of God" (45–46). Further, he wants his hearers to know of his personal desire to know the truth of what he has said to them: "Behold, I have fasted and prayed many days that I might know these things of myself. And now I do know of myself that they are true; for the Lord God hath made them manifest unto me by his Holy Spirit; and this is the spirit of revelation which is in me" (46).

---

4. As discussed in Chapter 1, we see a similar change in Nephi's attitude and language in addressing his brothers and their descendants who become the Lamanites. They also become "my beloved brethren" (2 Nephi 2:26).

Despite his gentle and heartfelt invitation to them to come to Christ, followed by his testimony of a divine mandate to issue that call, Alma clearly fears the pride and stubbornness of his hearers will win out. He expresses that fear through his repetition of "persist": "*Will ye still persist* in the wearing of costly apparel and setting your hearts upon the vain things of the world, upon your riches? Yea, *will ye persist* in supposing that ye are better one than another; yea, *will ye persist* in the persecution of your brethren . . . Yea, and *will you persist* in turning your backs upon the poor, and the needy, and in withholding your substance from them?" Perhaps sensing that his hearers are inclined to answer in the affirmative, Alma shifts from rhetorical questions to a declarative statement: "And finally, all *ye that will persist* in your wickedness, I say unto you that these are they who shall be hewn down and cast into the fire except they speedily repent" (53–56).

Alma is aware that the people to whom he speaks know the spiritual trajectory of his life. As the notorious son of a famous father, his life is a dramatic example of someone who rebelled and then, through repentance, rose through the mercy of Christ to the preeminent position in his society. His audience likely heard him testify on previous occasions that "after wading through much tribulation, repenting nigh unto death, the Lord in mercy saw fit to snatch me out of an everlasting burning, and I am born of God. . . . I was in the darkest abyss; but now I behold the marvelous light of God" (Mosiah 27:28–29).

Everything in Alma's sermon at Zarahemla—his invitation to his hearers to repent of their sins, to break their bonds of iniquity, to cleanse their garments, to remember God's longsuffering and mercy toward them—is designed to bring his hearers to Christ so that they might repent of their sins and gain salvation. This includes the rhetorical devices he uses: the images, repetition of words and phrases, rhetorical questions, declarative statements, references to scripture, use of symbolism, and the invocation (by direct reference or by implication) of Nephite and Israelite history (specifically of Lehi, Nephi, Mosiah, and Alma the Elder, and of Abraham, Isaac and Jacob). The language he uses indicates that he sees this as an ultimate decision.

That is, he expects his hearers to make an ultimate commitment, not merely to make an outward show of their devotion, but to undergo a total conversion, one involving "a mighty change" of their hearts that would result in God's image being engraved on their countenances and cause them "to sing the song of redeeming love" (12–14).

Alma ends his sermon at Zarahemla by making a distinction between those who are members of the church and those who are not. To the former he says, "I speak by way of command," and to the latter he says, "I speak by way of invitation, saying: Come and be baptized unto repentance, that ye also may be partakers of the fruit of the tree of life" (62).

The effect of Alma's sermon is immediate, both for those who accept his message and for those who reject it. As soon as he finished his address, "he ordained priests and elders, by the laying on his hands according to the order of God, to preside and watch over the church. . . . And thus they began to establish the order of the church in the city of Zarahemla" (6:1, 4). Those who refused to repent "were rejected, and their names were blotted out, that their names were not numbered among those of the righteous" (6:3). Having fully succeeded in cleansing and reforming the church, Alma departs for Gideon to continue his ministry.

In his subsequent sermons, Alma uses many of the same devices he employs in his great sermon at Zarahemla, but in none does he do so as extensively or as impressively as in his first sermon. And none reflects the extent of intellect, learning, complexity, and sophistication that we see in this one. It is as if Alma, in his impassioned plea to the peoples of Zarahemla, senses the pivotal role he will play in Nephite history for the next two decades and therefore wants to make as certain and as strong a statement as possible at the outset of his ministry. In a way, this sermon can be seen as his inaugural address. And it can be seen as defining his spiritual calling. The themes he introduces here are those he will continue to emphasize throughout his ministry, and the rhetorical devices he employs with such skill and sophistication here will continue to echo throughout his life in his role as chief priest. All in all, it is one of the most brilliant sermons in sacred literature.

5

The Heart in Alma 12–13

"Before mankind knew anything about itself, it knew it had a heart."
—*Louisa Young,* The Book of the Heart[1]

"The only whole heart is a broken one."
—*Menachem Mendel Morgenstern*[2]

The heart is one of the most potent and prevalent symbols in human culture and is central to the traditions and sacred texts of the world's major religions.[3] The word "heart" or "hearts" appears more than a

---

1. Louisa Young, *The Book of the Heart,* (New York: Doubleday, 2003), xxiii.

2. As quoted by David Wolpe, *The Healer of Shattered Hearts: A Jewish View of God* (New York: Henry Holt and Co., 1990), 45.

3. This chapter is based on a paper developed in the Book of Mormon Seminar held at Graduate Theological Union in Berkeley, California, June 2016, and published along with other seminar papers in *A Preparatory Redemption: Reading Alma 12–13,* ed. Matthew Bowman and Rosemary Demos (Provo, UT: Maxwell Institute, 2018). The text for the seminar was confined to Alma 12:19-Alma 13:20.

thousand times in the Bible and figures prominently in the Koran, the Upanishads, the Tao Te Ching, and other sacred texts, including the Book of Mormon, where it appears nearly seven hundred times. This chapter examines the symbolism of the heart in Alma 12:19–13:20 with insights drawn from ancient spiritual traditions as well as new scientific discoveries about the heart in psychology, physiology, and neurocardiology.

The heart was seen anciently as the locus of the mind and the soul—and in some traditions even of being itself. Central to the consciousness of the Israelites, for instance, was the association of the heart with volition (the will), cognition (thought and understanding), and memory. Old Testament scholar, R. C. Dentan observes, "Because of its concrete character, the Hebrew language can hardly express the idea 'to think' except by the phrase 'to say in the heart.'"[4] Many Old Testament scriptures bear this out. For example, in Proverbs we read, "apply thine heart to understanding" (2:2) and "As he thinketh in his heart, so is he" (23:7). Note in this last proverb that understanding and emotion unite in the heart and define the person: "so is he."

Furthermore, in the Old Testament the defining character, not just of an individual but of the people as a whole, rests in the heart. As Gail Godwin, author of *Heart: A Personal Journey through Its Myths and Meanings*, explains, "For the ancient Hebrews, heart, *lev,* meant the seat of wisdom and understanding, the inner personality, the whole gamut of emotional life, as well as *the collective mind, or mind-set, of the people*, the mental as well as the fleshly heart"[5] (emphasis added).

In addition, according to influential philosopher of religion Mircea Eliade, for the Hebrews, "the heart is the locus not only of the whole

---

4. *Preface to Old Testament Theology* (1962), 550, as cited in Glen H. Elder, Jr., *The Body, An Encyclopedia of Archetypical Symbolism*, vol. 2 (Boston: Shambhala, 1996), 288.
5. Gail Godwin, *Heart: A Personal Journey through Its Myths and Meanings* (New York: William Morrow, 2001), 35. "Godwin's explorations and meditations brilliantly track themes of the heart in life, legend, and in art: from the first drawing of the 'heart-shaped' heart to the first valentine, from Gilgamesh to Confucius, from the heart of darkness to wearing one's heart on one's sleeve" (inside back coverflap).

psychological and intellectual life but also of moral life."[6] Various scriptures suggest that just as God wrote the Ten Commandments on stone tablets, so he writes his word on people's hearts (e.g., Jeremiah 31:33, a scripture quoted in Hebrews 8:10). Alma 12:7 speaks of "the thoughts and intents" of the heart, and in Alma we read: "And there was no inequality among them [for] the Lord did pour out his Spirit on all the face of the land to prepare the minds of the children of men, or to prepare their hearts to receive the word which should be taught among them at the time of his coming, that they might not be hardened against the word, that they might not be unbelieving and go on to destruction, but that they might receive the word with joy" (16:16–17)—or in other words God poured out his spirit that his New World children might feel his love in their hearts, what the Persian philosopher-poet Rumi called "the deep ear inside the chest."[7]

The ancients understood truths and mysteries about the heart that are being validated by modern science. According to one 2017 report, "Scientific research has established the existence of complex, highly sophisticated neural pathways that connect the human heart and brain, confirming that the activity of the heart directly influences the activity of higher brain centers involved in perceptual and cognitive processing and in the creation of emotional experience."[8] Thus science confirms and explains what we so often experience: heart and mind interact and affect one another. What we feel affects what we think and vice versa. Beyond this, a more startling discovery of modern science is the evidence of the heart having its own mind, so to speak: "The heart's

---

6. Mircea Eliade, ed., *The Encyclopedia of Religion* (New York: Macmillan, 1987), 234 (emphasis added).

7. Rumi, "Listening," *The Glance: Songs of Soul Meeting,* Trans. Coleman Barks (New York: Penguin Compass, 1999), n.p.

8. Rollin McCraty and Robert A. Rees, "New Perspectives on the Role of the Heart in Positive Emotions, Intuition and Social Coherence," *Handbook of Positive Psychology*, 3rd edition, ed. C. R. Snyder et al. (Oxford: Oxford University Press, 2017).

intrinsic nervous system is a sophisticated information-encoding and processing center that operates independently of the brain."[9]

The rich, deep, and multi-faceted understanding of the heart found in Hebrew scriptures was carried by the people of Lehi as they crossed the Arabian Desert and the great ocean to reach their new home in the Promised Land. It was embedded not only in the brass plates but also in their hearts and minds.

The use of the heart in the Book of Mormon, including in chapters 12 and 13 of Alma, is rooted in the rich cultures and languages of ancient Near Eastern peoples. There are sixteen references to the heart in Alma 12 and 13, more than in any two contiguous chapters in the Book of Mormon. Of the sixteen references, twelve include the figure of a hardened heart, an image that is found some eighty-four times among the multiple references to "heart" in the Book of Mormon. "Hardness of heart" is also a figure found in the Bible, although far less frequently than in the history of the Lehites. Of the 1,075 mentions of the heart in the Old and New Testaments, only nine refer to a hardened heart and all nine are in scriptural texts that would have been found on the Brass Plates and therefore represent a possible source for the writers of the Book of Mormon, something one speculates would have been completely unknown to Joseph Smith.

The idea of a hard or hardened heart among the people of the Book of Mormon is introduced in the second chapter of 1 Nephi where Nephi tells us, "Having great desires to know of the mysteries of God . . . I did cry unto the Lord; And behold, he did visit me, and did soften my heart" (1 Nephi 2:16). That is, for all his greatness, Nephi did not begin with a softened heart, but prayed for one. Thus, the story of these New World peoples begins with a hard heart that becomes softened.

---

9. McCraty & Rees, "The Heart-Brain Connection," *The Encyclopedia of Positive Psychology* (Oxford: Wiley-Blackwell, 2009). 472; for additional insights on the heart-brain connection, see Rollin McCraty, Mike Atkinson et al, *The Coherent Heart: Heart–Brain Interactions, Psychophysiological Coherence, and the Emergence of System-Wide Order* (Boulder Creek: The Institute of HeartMath, 2006).

Two verses later we meet Nephi's brothers Laman and Lemuel who, Nephi tells us, "would not hearken unto my words . . . because of the hardness of their hearts" (1 Nephi 2:18). These brothers soften their hearts periodically but always it seems reluctantly and temporarily as they continue to resist the importuning and pleading of their father, younger brother, other members of the clan, and even angels.

The nature and dimensions of a hardened heart are summarized in the following Bible dictionary entry:

> The heart, in effect, is the whole person in all of his or her distinctive human activity as a thinking, planning, willing, feeling, worshiping, and socially interacting being. And, of course, when the person is not living according to God's will, it is the heart that is described as darkened, rebellious, callous, unfeeling, or idolatrous. It is within the heart that God works; hence the human heart may be tender and soft or as hard as stone (Ezekiel 11:19). It is in this context that hardening or hardness of the heart must be understood. The heart represents the total response of a person to life around him or her and to the religious and moral demands of God. Hardness of heart thus describes a negative condition in which the person ignores, spurns, or rejects the gracious offer of God to be a part of his or her life.[10]

The drama that unfolds in the Book of Mormon can be seen as an archetypal conflict between those who strive to have softened (i.e., humble, receptive, teachable, and ultimately, loving) hearts and those who choose to retain hard (i.e., resistant, recalcitrant, callous, and ultimately, unloving) hearts. The last image we get of the heart in the Book of Mormon is in the next to last chapter of Moroni where we are told

---

10. "Hardening, Hardness of Heart," in Baker's *Evangelical Dictionary of Biblical Theology*, http://classic.studylight.org/dic/bed/view.cgi?number=T322.

the people whom Mormon is calling to repentance "harden their hearts against [the word of God]." Such hardness means that "they have no fear of death; and they have lost their love, one towards another; and they thirst after blood and revenge continually" (Moroni 9:4–5), or, as Mormon says just a few verses later, they are "without civilization" (Moroni 9:11), an amazingly damning condemnation. Thus, the Book of Mormon begins with one softened heart (Nephi's) and ends with an entire nation possessed of adamantly hardened hearts. That seems to summarize the history of these New World peoples as succinctly as one could imagine.

In the Book of Alma we have another Nephite whose heart is softened. Alma the Younger had been among those who "did not believe the traditions of their fathers . . . concerning the resurrection of the dead, neither did they believe concerning the coming of Christ," with the result that "their hearts were hardened" (Mosiah 26:1–3). When Alma came of age "he became a very wicked and an idolatrous man . . . [who] led many of the people to do after the manner of his iniquities . . . stealing away the hearts of the people" (Mosiah 27:8–9). When an angel appears to Alma and his companions and rebukes them for their wickedness, out of "the darkest abyss" of his guilt and shame, Alma beholds "the marvelous light of God" (Mosiah 27:29) and experiences a "mighty change" of heart, just as his father had earlier upon hearing the words of Abinadi. Having had his own heart softened, Alma seeks to soften the hearts of others, which leads him to renounce his role as chief judge and preach the gospel "throughout the land" of Zarahemla (Headnote to Alma 5).

After teaching the citizens of the City of Zarahemla, as discussed in the previous chapter on his "Seminal Sermon" there, Alma asks, "Have ye spiritually been born of God? Have ye received his image in your own countenances? Have ye experienced this mighty change in your hearts?" (Alma 5:14) Those questions, directly or indirectly, are the subject of the sermons of Alma and his companions throughout their missionary journeys and ultimately of all the prophets who preach and teach among the Nephites and Lamanites.

Although Alma's preaching has a positive impact on some of his hearers, not everyone in Zarahemla experiences a profound change of heart. Some continue to be "puffed up in the pride of [their] hearts," while others set their "hearts upon the vain things of the world [and] upon [their] riches" (Alma 5:53).

After leaving Zarahemla, Alma preaches in succession in Gideon, Melek, and Ammonihah where, we are told, "Satan had gotten great hold upon the hearts of the people" (Alma 8:9). Alma prays mightily that God will pour out his spirit upon the people of Ammonihah; "Nevertheless," we are told, "they hardened their hearts" (Alma 8:11), and many remained "a hard-hearted and a stiffnecked people" (9:5). Their hearts have not just been hardened but "grossly hardened" (9:30).

Hoping to persuade them to soften their hearts, Alma's missionary companion, Amulek, confesses that, like them, he once had a hardened and wicked heart (Alma 10:6), but, like his friend Alma, his heart was changed when an angel appeared to him. The narrative then turns to one Zeezrom who tries to manipulate and, ultimately, destroy Amulek by bribery and trickery, but Amulek discerns his intent: "thou hadst it in thy heart . . . that thou mightest have cause to destroy me" (11:25). Caught in his deception and realizing that he is about to be trapped in "a snare of the adversary" (12:6), Zeezrom is convinced that Alma and Amulek "knew the thoughts and intents of his heart" (12:7). This is an interesting construction—the idea of reading hearts rather than minds—but it is in accord with other Old and New Testament, as well as Book of Mormon scriptures that locate thoughts in the heart.

All of this is prelude to what transpires in Alma 12-13 where, as pointed out above, there are a dozen references within a short space to the trope of hardening one's heart. These include such expressions as "he that will harden his heart," "he that will not harden his heart" (12:10), and "if our hearts have been hardened, yea, if we have hardened our hearts against the word" (12:13). Alma quotes God himself as pleading with his children not to harden their hearts: "But God did call upon men, in the name of his Son, . . . saying: If ye will repent, and harden not your hearts, then will I have mercy upon you through mine Only

Begotten Son. Therefore, whosoever repenteth, and hardeneth not his heart, he shall have claim on mercy. . . . And whosoever will harden his heart and will do iniquity, behold, I swear in my wrath that he shall not enter into my rest'" (12:33–35). Having God speak these warning words about hardening one's heart gives more force to Alma's speaking them right after, especially when he identifies himself with his hard-hearted listeners: "And now my brethren, seeing *we* know these things, and they are true, let *us* repent, and harden not *our* hearts" (12:37, emphasis added). One could argue that it takes a softened heart to identify and empathize with a hardened heart. In essence, this is what Jesus does and what he asks us to do.

What does it mean to harden one's heart? According to Webster's 1828 dictionary, the one Joseph Smith would likely have consulted (if he consulted dictionaries), "hardness" means "to make a person or thing resistant, less sensitive; obduracy; impenitence; confirmed state of wickedness; as, hardness of heart."[11] Within the context of these chapters, it clearly means to deliberately resist the whisperings and entreaties of the Spirit, to willfully ignore and reject the messages of angels and prophets, to be proud and unteachable, to shut down the tender feelings of the heart, to spurn the gift of mercy offered through Jesus Christ, and to attempt to persuade others to likewise harden their hearts. It is to prefer darkness over light, sin over righteousness, hatred over love, and, ultimately, death over life.

It is interesting how closely having a softened heart and knowing truth are linked in these scriptures. In responding to Antionah's disin-genuous question about the Fall, Alma informs him that God "saw that it was expedient that man should know concerning the things whereof he had appointed them. Therefore he sent angels to converse with them" (Alma 12:28–29). When men "began from that time forth to call on his name . . . God conversed with men, and made known unto them the plan of redemption" (Alma 12:30). It is clear that those who have closed, calloused, or hardened hearts cannot know the things of God or, having

---

11. http://webstersdictionary1828.com/Dictionary/hardness.

once known them, reject that knowledge with ruinous consequences. Conversely, those with open and softened hearts not only seek but thirst for knowledge. As Gail Godwin states, "The intelligence of the heart is a special kind of imaginative intelligence which combines knowing and loving in a single function. It is a way of seeing with the heart."[12]

Remembering is related to both knowing and having a receptive or softened heart. According to one scientific source, "Memory is a property of diverse biological systems, including brain and heart."[13] The reality of this connection is clear from the various discourses about faith and knowledge that are recorded in the Book of Alma: those who have hardened hearts fail to remember the tender mercies of the Lord. Thus, to the people of Zarahemla who, following their conversion, had "set their hearts upon riches and upon the vain things of the world" (Alma 4:8), Alma asks, "Have you sufficiently retained *in remembrance* the captivity of your fathers? Yea, and have you sufficiently retained *in remembrance* his mercy and long-suffering toward them? And moreover, have ye sufficiently retained *in remembrance* that he has delivered their souls from hell?" (5:6, emphasis added) In other words, he is asking, "Have you sufficiently retained in your hearts the personal and cultural memory of your people's bondage? Have you sufficiently held in your hearts a memory of the mercy God showed in delivering them from their captors? Have you allowed the realization of their being free from the pains of sin, guilt, and hell to penetrate your hearts as it did in the past?" He follows these challenging questions with a simple declaration, "Behold, he [God] changed their hearts" (5:7)—with the implication that God stands ready to change *theirs* as well. Similarly, he says to the people of Ammonihah, "I would that *ye should remember* that the Lord ordained priests, after his holy order, which was after the order of his Son, to teach these things unto the people" (Alma 13:1, emphasis added). It is the heart that feels, knows,

---

12. Godwin, *Heart: A Personal Journey*. 89.
13. "Cardiac Memory and Cortical Memory," https://www.ahajournals.org/doi/10.1161/01.CIR.0000091402.34219.6C.

and ultimately remembers those feelings—or that chooses not to feel, know, or remember them.

Scientists have only recently begun to discover the wonders of the heart—or to discover what prophets, priests, and poets have always known about this mysterious organ at the center of our beings and our bodies. We now know that the heart has thousands of neurons like the neurons in our brains and, further, that the heart and brain are in constant, dynamic correspondence with one another. We know that a person's heart starts beating before his/her brain is fully formed, suggesting that it has a primary role in initiating human life. We can remain alive once the brain dies, but when the heart stops beating, mortal life ends.

Another interesting scientific finding is that "[t]he heart's electrical field is about 60 times greater in amplitude than that generated by the brain, and the magnetic field produced by the heart is more than 5,000 times greater in strength than that produced by the brain."[14] Scientists now postulate that with its own independent nervous system, the heart possesses some kind of cognitive and memory capacity, what neuro-cardiologists refer to as "the little brain in the heart."[15] Beyond this, the heart seems to have an amazing intuitive capacity that allows it to perceive "information normally outside the range of conscious aware-ness" and to "respond to an emotionally arousing stimulus seconds before it is actually experienced."[16] These heart-centered pre-cogni-tive, cognitive, and intuitional as well as memorial capabilities seem designed by God to communicate his knowledge and love via the heart to our entire systems and to enable us to communicate with him and others in like manner. In other words, God seems to be trying to reach us—to awaken our hearts, minds, bodies, and souls to the good news

14. McCraty and Rees, "The Heart-Brain connection," 472.
15. Rollin McCraty, Mike Atkinson, and Raymond Trevor Bradley, "Electro-physiological Evidence of Intuition: Part 1. The Surprising Role of the Heart," *The Journal of Alternative and Complementary Medicine*, 10 (1) (June 2004), 133–143. See also Parts 2 and 3 in the same journal.
16. McCraty & Rees, "The Heart-Brain Connection," 472.

of the gospel and to persuade us in multiple ways and through multiple channels to repent and turn to him. As he said to Zachariah, "Therefore say thou unto them, Thus saith the Lord of hosts; Turn ye unto me . . . and I will turn unto you" (Zachariah 1:3). Turning our hearts to God and turning them to others is possible only when our hearts are softened. In Chapters 12 and 13, Alma calls his people to a life of holiness by teaching them about the plan of redemption and inviting them to soften their hearts so they can experience the "mighty change" the gospel promises.

In the Chapel of the Great Commission at the Pacific School of Religion in Berkeley, California, where I teach graduate classes on Mormonism, a large, wooden cross hangs in the chancel. It is a symbol of a broken heart, but also represents a heart that is compassionate, forgiving, merciful, healing, redeeming, and, beyond all mortal comprehension, loving. Christ calls us to break our hearts upon this broken tree and to offer them to him as a sacrifice for which, as with all sacrifices he asks of us, he makes a promise: "And ye shall offer for a sacrifice unto me a broken heart and a contrite spirit. And whoso cometh unto me with a broken heart and a contrite spirit, him will I baptize with fire and with the Holy Ghost" (3 Nephi 9:20).

Alma concludes his sermon to the people of Ammonihah by speaking about his own heart. "I wish from the inmost part of my heart . . . that ye would hearken unto my words, and cast off your sins, and not procrastinate the day of your repentance; . . . and thus be led by the Holy Spirit, becoming humble, meek, submissive, patient, full of love and all long suffering"(Alma 13:27–28). In other words, Alma askes that we, as Christ's disciples, soften our hearts so that we might learn the lesson God is always hoping we will learn: to know and love ourselves, to love others as ourselves, and to love his Son and him—*by heart*. It is interesting that when Jesus commanded us to love God completely, he put the heart first: "Thou shalt love the Lord thy God with all thy heart, and with all thy soul, and with all thy mind" (Matt. 22:37) or, as God said to Abraham, "Walk in my presence! And be wholehearted" (Genesis 17:1, Everett Fox translation).

6

Imagining Peace:
The Example of the Nephites

"Imagine all the people
Living life in peace."
—John Lennon

Studying scriptures over the years, I have been struck by how often writers of sacred literature use elements of drama to teach important lessons.[1] In fact, one could argue that the extent to which God inspires and directs the writing of scripture demonstrates that he is himself a superb dramatist. The use of dramatic setting, plot, tension, and irony in scripture is similar to what one finds in great literature, from the Greeks to the present. The stories of both individuals and entire

---

1. This article is a revised version of "Children of Light: How the Nephites Sustained Two Centuries of Peace," in Andrew C. Skinner and Gaye Strathearn, eds., *Third Nephi: An Incomparable Scripture* (Provo, UT: Neal A. Maxwell Institute for Religious Scholarship, 2012), 309–328.

peoples who begin in grace and end in tragedy, or who transcend sin and evil to find redemption, make the Judeo-Christian scriptures among the great works of world literature.

By its very nature, dramatic literature has the power to engage our minds and imaginations in such ways that we are emotionally drawn into the action of the narrative. A reviewer of Paul Woodruff's *The Necessity of Theater* argues that drama is "as necessary—and as powerful—as language itself. . . . [It is] an art that—at its most powerful—can change lives and (as some peoples believe) bring a divine presence to earth."[2]

I was struck by the use of such dramatic elements in reading Third Nephi, especially when considering what happens there as illumination on what is happening in the world today. Essentially, in Third Nephi we have a dramatic presentation of the archetypal conflict between the forces of darkness/war and light/peace. This conflict was central to Nephite history from the beginning as the sons of Lehi divided into opposing tribes, with the Nephites symbolizing the quest for light (as exemplified by their industry, righteousness, and striving for peace) and the Lamanites representing the powers of darkness (as exemplified by their slothfulness, wickedness, and impulse to war). At times these two groups change sides so that the Lamanites are righteous and peace-loving and the Nephites wicked and warlike; at other times this conflict erupts within the tribes themselves, but it always seems to be ongoing except for the two hundred years of peace following Christ's visit.

Given the near continuous war during the first six hundred years of Nephite history, some have argued that the two hundred years of sustained peace following Christ's appearance in the New World is unrealistic, a clear indication of Joseph Smith's fictive invention.[3] It

---

2. "Descriptive Note," under the entry for Paul Woodruff, *The Necessity of Theater: The Art of Watching and Being Watched* (Oxford: Oxford University Press, 2008), at https://www.amazon.com/Necessity-Theater-Watching-Being-Watched/ dp/0195394801. Although Woodruff's subject is live theater, as a long-time teacher of dramatic literature, I believe that the imagintive engagement with written drama can also produce such effects.

3. See, for example, http://skepticsannotatedbible.com/BoM/abs/long.html.

might also be unrealistic considering the place of war in the history of humankind. As the historian Will Durant noted, there have been less than thirty years in recorded history in which war has not been waged somewhere on the planet.[4] Nevertheless, I believe the Book of Mormon itself provides convincing evidence that such a sustained period of peace is attainable, and it does so by using the elements of drama. In fact, the following scenes might be said to constitute a dramatic construct.

Days without Night

The penultimate conflict among the Nephites between darkness/war and light/peace is symbolized by the parallel sustained period of light that comes at Christ's birth—"But behold, they did watch steadfastly for that night and that day which should be as one day as if there were no night" (3 Nephi 1:8; see also Helaman 14:4)—and the three days of darkness that come at his crucifixion (3 Nephi 8:23). It is significant that the light precedes the darkness (a reversal of Genesis) because it intensifies the darkness. In other words, having experienced the promise of endless light (symbolized by the two days without an intervening night), the Nephites later experience what must have seemed like endless night. It appears that it is the extent and intensity of the darkness during those three days that cause them to once again embrace the light when they are given the opportunity to do so, and it is the bold and imaginative juxtaposition of these two archetypical symbols that gives the narrative much of its dramatic power.

---

4. As cited in Chris Hedges, *War Is A Force that Gives Us Meaning* (New York: Public Affairs, 2002), 10. Hereinafter *War Is A Force*. Of course, this does not mean that war has been waged continuously everywhere. Some countries have been relatively free of war and some peoples have rejected war as a strategy.

Cataclysm

Great literature always awakens and enlivens the imagination. Thus, this story compels us to imagine what it must have been like to experience those three hours in which there was "terrible tempest" and "terrible thunder" and earthquakes which changed the face of the whole earth; in which cities were covered with earth, destroyed by fire or swallowed by the sea; and in which people were drowned, carried away in whirlwinds, crushed by falling buildings, and consumed by fire (3 Nephi 8:6–19). Through the technological wonders of modern media, we have a repository of graphic images and sounds of such actual events stored in our memories which makes it easier for us to imagine a world turned inside out and upside down by powerful atmospheric, oceanic, and terrestrial upheavals. For example. the violent scenes of destruction caused by the March 2011 earthquake and tsunami in Japan may give us some idea of the kinds and degrees of destruction described in Third Nephi.

Darkness at Noon

We are told that following the cataclysmic destruction during Christ's crucifixion, "there was darkness upon the face of the land" (3 Nephi 8:19). This was not an ordinary darkness but a "thick darkness," a "vapor of darkness" so heavy that "there could be no light, because of the darkness, neither candles, neither torches; neither could there be fire kindled with their fine and exceedingly dry wood, so that *there could not be any light at all*" (3 Nephi 8:21, emphasis added). (Note the careful use of language here: not just wood, but fine and "exceedingly dry wood," dramatizing the impossibility of creating "any light at all.") Total, engulfing darkness on earth and in the heavens: "And there was *not any* light seen, *neither* fire, *nor* glimmer, *neither* the sun, *nor* the moon, *nor* the stars, for so great were the mists of darkness which were upon the face of the land" (3 Nephi 8:22, emphasis added. Note the cumulative effect of this string of six negatives.)

Now, imagine yourself, or one of your own children or grandchildren, as a child in such darkness, not for an hour or a day but for three days, seventy-two full hours, wondering if you would ever see light again. The terror you would experience is incomprehensible. No wonder "there was great mourning and howling and weeping among all the people continually; yea, great were the groanings of the people, because of the darkness and the great destruction which had come upon them" (3 Nephi 8:23; see also v. 25).

As a child completely alone in the dark hearing such lamentations, you would be aware that many children like you had perished in the holocaust, perhaps among them your own brothers and sisters and friends. Imagine crying out in this encompassing darkness, not being able to find your mother or father, or perhaps any other living soul, although you grope in the darkness toward other voices also crying out in despair. You have just witnessed the death and destruction of all that you have known, seen unimaginable terror, been thrust into the very heart of darkness. What would be your psychological state? In all wars, children, especially, suffer unspeakable terror.[5]

---

5. The lead article in the 16 April 2007 edition of *USA Today* titled, "Trauma Severe for Iraqi Children," states, "About 70% of primary school children in a Baghdad neighborhood suffer symptoms of trauma-related stress. . . . Many Iraqi children have to pass dead bodies on the street as they walk to school in the morning; . . . others have seen relatives killed or have been injured in mortar or bomb attacks." Of course, the destruction in Zarahemla lasted three hours while the conflict in the Middle East, including Iraq, continues (as of 2020). As an Iraqi psychiatrist says, "We're not certain what will become of the next generation, even if there is peace in one day." Another article titled "Children Who Survive Urban Warfare Suffer from PTSD, Too," reports, "As many as one-third of children living in our country's violent urban neighborhoods have PTSD, according to recent research and the country's top child trauma experts—nearly twice the rate reported for troops returning from war zones in Iraq," (http://articles.sfgate.com/2007-08-26/news/17256954_1_ptsd-war-zone-post-traumatic-stress-disorder). Not long after 9/11 I trained a group of counselors in the Stanton Island School District in New York City. The day I conducted the training, the New York City Board of Education published a report indicating that 92% of the school children in New York City had one or more of the symptoms of PTSD.

A Voice of Light

Now, imagine that after enduring three days of such dark terror, you hear a voice penetrating the darkness. After cataloging the vast destruction he has caused to fall upon the wicked, he addresses you and the others who have survived: "Behold, mine arm of mercy is extended towards you, and whosoever will come, him will I receive; and blessed are those who come unto me. Behold, I am Jesus Christ the Son of God. . . . I am the light and the life of the world" (3 Nephi 9:14–15, 18).

Enveloped in complete darkness, you would instinctively be drawn to the voice of a personage proclaiming to be the light of the world. Nevertheless, the darkness continues and is made more intense because "there was silence in all the land for the space of many hours" (3 Nephi 10:1–2). The darkness persists as you ponder these words from a voice of light, a male voice speaking into the darkness, lamenting the loss of those who have rejected him. Eventually you hear the voice again, addressing those like you who have been spared, speaking of himself as a mother hen who would gather you under her wings of love if you will turn to him "with full purpose of heart" (3 Nephi 10:6). This metaphor is exquisitely comforting to you since you don't know if your own mother is alive or dead and you long for her comforting love. After such terror, you cannot imagine what it would feel like to be sheltered in such love, but you long for it with all your heart.

Dawning Out of Darkness

When the morning finally comes, the darkness disperses and the earth ceases to shake, the "dreadful groanings . . . cease, and all the tumultuous noises . . . pass away, . . . and the mourning, and the weeping, and the wailing of the people . . . cease," replaced by expressions of joy, "praise and thanksgiving unto the Lord Jesus Christ, their Redeemer" (3 Nephi 10:9–10). Your voice is among those expressing such paeans of praise and gratitude.

Now imagine that it is a short time later, and once again you hear the voice, "not a harsh voice, neither . . . a loud voice, [but] a small voice" that nevertheless pierces your "very soul" and causes your "heart to burn" within you (3 Nephi 11:3). And then you see something amazing—"a Man descending out of heaven . . . clothed in a white robe" who comes down and stands near you. Once more he identifies himself as "Jesus Christ," again describing himself as "the light and the life of the world" (3 Nephi 11:8, 10–11).

Angels of Fire

As you listen to the Savior, you hear him teach the adults around you and then, turning to you, he tells them that unless they become like you, they cannot "inherit the kingdom of God" (3 Nephi 11:38). You hear him speak beautiful words about those who are blessed, and you hear him call you and others "to be the light of this people" (3 Nephi 12:14). He continues to teach, his words gentle, glowing, full of tenderness. Some of what he says even the grown-ups don't seem to understand. (3 Nephi 17:2) When he says, "Go ye unto your homes and ponder," you feel sad that you have to leave his presence. Some people around you are even crying, so he stays longer (17:2–5). People leave and return, bringing sick people and crippled people with them. Imagine that as the crowds gather forward around Jesus, you are now further back and can't see Him. You try to push forward so you will be close to him. (3 Nephi 17:6–10)

Then you hear him call for all the children to be brought to him. He asks you to sit on the ground in front of him. As you look up at this man in the white robe with a luminous face, he asks everyone to kneel. You hear him pray in language more beautiful than you have ever heard or imagined, words like the songs of unknown birds and the whisper of wind through great trees. Then he looks directly at you and calls you to come to him. When you do so, he places his hands on your head, and it seems as if his heart speaks directly to your heart. He embraces and kisses you, and as you look up, you see angels of fire descending from the sky and they too embrace and kiss you and all the other children with you, and you all become beings of light.[6] (Cf. 3 Nephi 17:11–24)

Now, imagine what your life will be like from this moment on. Among the things Jesus teaches you and the others who have survived the cataclysmic destruction is that you should cease from fighting with one another. "There shall be no disputations among you, as there hitherto have been" (3 Nephi 11:23, 28). He condemns such conflicts as originating with "the devil, who is the father of contention, and he stirreth up the hearts of men to contend with anger, one with another" (3 Nephi 11:29). (This reminds us of President Hinckley's statement "that war is the devil's own game."[7] It is interesting to note that "contention" and "war" are linked not only in the scriptures but in the addresses of modern prophets.[8])

---

6. Gordon Thomasson argues persuasively that what happens in 3 Nephi amounts to a transfiguration: "When, at the turn of the year after the crucifixion and destruction, the people gather at the temple and Christ comes down, then he prays, and first the children are transfigured (I know of no other name for what occurs with the Nephites than to compare it with what the apostles witness when Elijah and Moses are on the mount with Christ) . . . (3Ne 17:24–25), and later the adults are similarly blessed (19:14, 25, 30), and finally the testimonies . . . or keys which the children possess [—all this lays] the foundation for consecration (26:14–20). Not only are—I believe—any wounds from those three days directly healed, but both the faith and the keys are confirmed on these survivors to build a perfect society in which none of them will ever suffer such an horrendous event again" (private correspondence in my possession, 15 May 2007).

7. Gordon B. Hinckley, "We Believe in Being Honest.," *Ensign* (October 1990); www.lds.org/portal/site/LDSOrg/.

8. What the scriptures condemn as contention is not verbal disputation but physical violence or the creation of schisms in the church. In the Book of Mormon, "contention" usually means an armed skirmish or battle. We are told, for example, that Alma and "his guards, contended with the guards of the king of the Lamanites until he slew and drove them back" (Alma 2:33). Here contention means "combat," not argument. This is why it is so often coupled with "war," as in "wars and contentions" (Alma 48:20). Jesus specifically warns against the outbreak of such contention—or "conflict"—as a result of doctrinal disputes (3 Nephi 11:28–30).

A Gospel of Peace

What is significant for our understanding is that in addressing his chosen New World disciples, Jesus is teaching his followers, both anciently and contemporaneously, that it "is *not my doctrine,* to stir up the hearts of men with anger, one against another" (which leads to conflict and war); "but *this is my doctrine,* that such things be done away" (3 Nephi 11:30, emphasis added). In a powerful rhetorical manner, Christ ties the rejection of such contention, anger, and conflict to the first principles and ordinances of the gospel. He does this by repeating the phrase "my doctrine" six times within a few verses. By doing so, he subtly shifts the focus from avoiding contention and conflict (which, he says, clearly are *not* his doctrine) to the first steps in the process of salvation, confirmed by the witness of the Father and the Holy Ghost, which he identifies as "my doctrine." Further, he associates these first principles with becoming "as a little child," a phrase he had used earlier (9:22).

Blessed Are All the Peacemakers

The emphasis on becoming "as a little child" is significant because Christ identifies the contention and war-like anger that led to the Nephites' destruction with the adults, and the promised peace of salvation through him with the children. This is confirmed by his teaching his new disciples the Sermon on the Mount, including the beatitudes. Especially relevant is, "And blessed are all the peacemakers, for they shall be called the children of God" (3 Nephi 12:9). Having earlier identified these disciples (and by extension all the remaining Nephites) as "children of light," he now gives them a commission: "I give unto you to be the light of this people. . . . Therefore let your light so shine before this people, that they may see your good works and glorify your Father who is in heaven" (3 Nephi 12:14–16). Later, he connects the higher principles of the gospel (namely, "love your enemies, bless them that curse you, do good to them that hate you, and pray for them who despitefully use you and persecute you") with the purity and innocence of children, "[t]hat ye may be the children of your Father who is in heaven" (3 Nephi 12:44–45).

A Sacrament of Peace

Returning in your imagination to the scene in Bountiful: Jesus breaks bread and pours wine and gives it to you and all those present and asks all of you to partake of these emblems often in remembrance of him. You notice as he talks that he repeats the word "always" many times, and you make a promise to yourself that you will always remember him and that you will always, as he asks, "hold up your light that it may shine unto the world (3 Nephi 18:24).

When Jesus finally ascends into heaven, everyone is so excited they stay up all night talking about what has happened, telling one another what it felt like to be in his presence. Someone says Jesus has promised to return the next day, so everyone runs to tell the good news. No one can sleep they are so excited and thus they bring the light of that glorious day into night.

How Beautiful Upon the Mountains

The next day Jesus returns and quotes Isaiah. Among the words he speaks are these: "How beautiful upon the mountains are the feet of him that bringeth good tidings unto them, that publisheth peace; that bringeth good tidings unto them of good, that publisheth salvation; that saith unto Zion: Thy God reigneth!" He later adds to that idyllic picture of a time without war or contention, "And all thy children shall be taught of the Lord; and great shall be the peace of thy children. In righteousness shalt thou be established; thou shalt be far from oppression for thou shalt not fear, and from terror for it shall not come near thee" (3 Nephi 20:40; 22:13–14).

Suddenly you realize that you are fulfilling this ancient prophecy, that you are one of those whose feet are beautiful upon the mountains, one of those called to bring good tidings and publish peace, one of those promised freedom from the kind of terror that so recently enveloped you. Jesus' message to you is that you and others of your generation have been transformed from children of darkness into children of light and that your society has been transformed from the reality of a warring people to the promise of a peaceful people. Looking directly at you, you hear him say, "And now, behold, my joy is great, even unto fulness, because of you, and also this generation; yea, and even the Father rejoiceth, and also all the holy angels, because of you and this generation; for none of [you] are lost" (3 Nephi 27:30). You let these powerful words sink into your heart: you and your generation will cause Jesus, Heavenly Father, and "all the holy angels" to rejoice.

A Covenant of Peace

Because of the dramatic transformation from darkness and hatred to light and love, you and the other children of this generation hold in your hearts a remembrance of the absolute terror of that night within a night, of that darkness at noon, as it were. Because you also hold in your hearts a more vivid memory of being in the presence of divine light, of being blessed by the Lord of Light in the glory of heaven's own fire, you covenant to work for peace for the remainder of your days and to pass it on to your children and grandchildren so that it rolls forth like a mighty river.

Had you been a child during this momentous time, imagine what your life would have been like in the years following.[9] Imagine the

---

9. We can get some idea as to how light and love could have transformed these Nephite children through Ishmael Beah's *A Long Way Gone: Memoirs of a Boy Soldier* (New York: Farrar, Straus, Giroux, 2007). Beah, who was kidnapped at the age of twelve and, along with hundreds of other children his age, forced to murder others in the war between the government and the Revolutionary United Front rebels

stories you would tell to others about that devouring darkness that shrouded you in night and how, in your moment of deepest despair, the light came, first as a voice and then as a ray that blossomed into a person as bright as the sun, and how his light flowed into your eyes and into your heart, making your whole body as luminous as sunlight.

Now imagine that you are older, and your life is drawing to a close. As you gather your extended family around you, your children and grandchildren and great-grandchildren, they say, "Grandma, tell us that story again." You pause for a long moment, remembering your promise to always remember these remarkable events, and then you say, "That was a long time ago, but I remember it as if it were this morning. There are no words in all of the languages, even the beautiful language spoken by our first parents when they came from Jerusalem to this promised land, to tell you what happened or how it felt. But when he embraced me and kissed me, I felt as if my heart was in his heart and his was in mine, as if somehow all the light in the universe was flowing from him into me, like sunlight in my veins. The peace in my heart was as full as the great seas over which our people sailed and as vast as the night skies spangled with stars which God showed to our father Abraham. I pray for all of you to feel what I felt then as you embrace the Savior in your hearts and as you feel his peace in your souls." You then take them one by one, as the Lord had taken you and the other children, and you bless them to carry his peace forward.

As their history unfolds for the next hundred plus years, especially for a society that depended on storytelling as the Nephites must have, these great events, these powerful personal narratives of light over-powering darkness, would have been told and retold, sung and danced, expressed in powerful poetry, in graphic images, in dramas, in weaving and other expressive arts, down the generations.

---

in Sierra Leone, speaks of his descent into the dark world of the African killing fields as a time when his "heart was frozen" (126). Through the love and light of caring people, Beah ultimately escaped the horror of his living nightmare and was transformed into a person of light.

Of the great transformation among the Nephites, we read that, abiding by the doctrine of Christ, "the people were *all* converted unto the Lord, . . . and there were *no* contentions and disputations among them, and *every man* did deal justly one with another. And they had *all* things in common among them; therefore, there were not rich and poor, bond and free, but they were *all* made free, and partakers of the heavenly gift." Further, "There was *no* contention in the land, because of the love of God which did dwell in the hearts of the people. And there were *no* evyings, *nor* strifes, *nor* tumults, *nor* whoredoms, *nor* lyings, *nor* murders, *nor* any manner of lasciviousness; and surely there could not be a happier people among *all* the people who had been created by the hand of God (4 Nephi 1:2–3, 15–17; emphasis added). Again, note the rhetorical effect of the string of indefinite pronouns (*all, every*) and negatives (*no, nor*) dramatizing the totality of conversion, similar, one imagines, to that of the City of Enoch. Of this epoch of sustained peace, Apostle Orson F. Whitney, perhaps echoing the image of the mother hen or introducing the image of the dove of peace, wrote, "For two hundred years peace spread her white wings over . . . the entire people. Nephites and Lamanites, were converted unto Christ, were brethren and sisters, and all socially equal."[10]

Peace Gives Way to War

Although the Nephite peace lasted for two centuries, ultimately it came to an end when the Nephites, again being lifted up in pride, seeking for riches and engaging in secret combinations, "began to build up churches unto themselves to get gain, and began to deny the true church of Christ, . . . insomuch that they did receive all manner of wickedness" (4 Nephi 1:26–27). (The use of "receive" is a telling verb, suggesting that they not only sought wickedness but passively accepted

---

10. Orson F. Whitney, "Zion and Her Redemption." In *Collected Discourses*, ed. Brian H. Stuy. (Burbank, CA: BHS, 1987), 1:364, 2008).

it when it came to them in its various forms.) As a result, "the wicked part of the people began again to build up the secret oaths and combinations of Gadianton." Note the irony of "build up," suggesting a carefully designed and deliberate wickedness. "And it came to pass that the robbers of Gadianton did spread over all the face of the land; and there were none that were righteous save it were the disciples of Jesus" (4 Nephi 1:42, 47). Note also the irony of the change from "*all* converted to the Lord" to "*none* that were righteous," the latter an echo of Jesus' condemnation of the wickedness that led to the destruction described earlier in this chapter—"there were none righteous among them" (3 Nephi 9:11).

All this leads the people to turn once more to war and its destructive darkness. Even though they know the endgame of broken bodies and spilled blood that destroyed the Jaredites and has plagued their own history, they once more surrender to pride and class divisions, to inequality and injustice, to hatred and war. And so, they descend deeper and deeper into darkness for the next two hundred years until the Nephites become more degenerate and warlike than the Lamanites. As Mormon states, they become so brutal and depraved that they "are without civilization" (Moroni 9:11), as noted in the previous chapter, a shocking condemnation.

A Message for our Times

The dramatic narrative in Third Nephi seems particularly compelling for modern readers. By its own account and by the confirmation of modern prophets, we know the Book of Mormon was written for future generations, perhaps especially our own. As Hugh Nibley says, "Suddenly the Book of Mormon has become as modern as today's newspaper,"[11] or as Stephen Walker says, "History repeats itself with a

---

11. Hugh Nibley, *Since Cumorah: The Book of Mormon in the Modern World* (Salt Lake City: Deseret Book Company, 1970), 375. Hereinafter *Since Cumorah.*

vengeance in 4th Nephi, which reads like a twenty-first century news report."[12]

Since the purpose of drama is to engage us intellectually, imaginatively, and spiritually so that we may see ourselves in the distant mirrors of others' experiences, the dramatic narrative presented in Third Nephi places a special burden on us to be among those who work to end war and establish peace. How are we to do this? To begin with, we can accomplish what the Lord and his Latter-day prophets have urged us to do: "[R]enounce war and proclaim peace, and seek diligently to turn the hearts of the children to their fathers, and the hearts of the fathers to the children" (D&C 98:16). Note the strength of these imperatives: *renounce, proclaim, diligently seek.* Renouncing war does not mean silently sitting by while war does its destructive work. It means using our voices to counter those who argue for and endorse war in all its destructive measures and instruments. It means supporting those individuals, groups, and organizations committed to ending war. Proclaiming peace is more than hoping or praying for it; it is actively using the energy of our hearts and souls as well as our time and economic means to work for it. As Nibley elaborates, "'Renounce' is a strong word: we are not to try to win peace by war, or merely call a truce, but to renounce war itself, to disdain it as a policy while proclaiming . . . peace without reservation."[13]

During the First World War, President Joseph F. Smith stated, "For years it has been held that peace comes by preparation for war; the present conflict should prove that peace comes only by preparing for peace, through training the people in righteousness and justice, and selecting rulers who respect the righteous will of the people."[14] In times of war "the righteous will of the people" is often ignored and even silenced. As Chris Hedges says in *War is a Force that Gives Us Meaning,*

---

12. Steven Walker, "Last Words." In *The Reader's Book of Mormon*, ed. Robert A. Rees and Eugene England (Salt Lake City: Signature Books, 2008), 7: xiv.
13. *Since Cumorah*, 375.
14. Joseph F. Smith, "Editor's Table," *Improvement Era 17* (1914), 1074–75.

"States at war silence their own authentic and humane culture. When this destruction is well advanced, they find the lack of critical and moral restraint useful in the campaign to exterminate the culture of their opponents. By destroying authentic culture—that which allows us to question and examine ourselves and our society, the state erodes the moral fabric. It is replaced with a warped version of reality. The enemy is dehumanized; the universe starkly divided between the forces of light and the forces of darkness."[15]

Another lesson we can learn from the drama presented in Fourth Nephi is that pride leads to social inequality and injustice, discrimination against the poor, violence, and, ultimately, war. Note that it is the reemergence of class distinction that begins the Nephites' rapid descent toward their fatal end: "And now, in this two hundred and first year there began to be among them those that were lifted up in pride, such as the wearing of costly apparel, and all manner of fine pearls, and of the fine things of the world," leading to a "great division among the people"(4 Nephi 1:24, 35).

Thus, an additional step we can take toward ending war and establishing peace is to work for greater economic and social equality, both at home and abroad. In an 1873 general conference address, President Lorenzo Snow stated that what led to the sustained peace among the Nephites was their willingness to have all things in common: "When the Church was established among the Nephites, as recorded in the Book of Mormon, this doctrine was preached by them, and practiced nearly two hundred years, resulting in peace, union, great prosperity, and miraculous blessings, greater than were ever experienced by any people of whom we have record. The most remarkable miracles were constantly wrought among them; . . . These extraordinary manifestations of the approbation of God continued so long as they remained one in their temporal interest, or were control[l]ed in their financial matters according to the Order of Enoch."[16]

---

15. *War Is A Force*, 63.
16. General Conference address, 7 October 1873; reported by David W. Evans in *Journal of Discourses*, 26 vols. (Liverpool: Joseph F. Smith, 1874), 16:274.

While the Nephite peace is an ideal likely beyond our power given the present condition of the world, including in our own Latter-day Saint and American society, we could at least strive for greater balance so that instead of a large portion of national wealth being concentrated in the hands of an increasingly smaller percentage of the population, there could be a more just and equitable distribution of wealth, resources, and opportunities. According to Forbes, the three richest Americans own more wealth than the bottom fifty percent, the richest 400 Americans own more than thirty-three million median income earners and more than all black American families–an amount equivalent of the GDP of Great Britain.[17] According to the U.S. Census Bureau, in 2017 fifteen percent or forty million Americans lived below the poverty line.[18] And a 2018 report from the Annie E. Casey Foundation found that 42 million Americans (13% of the populace), including 13 million children, live in poverty.[19] Such statistics represent an astonishing disparity. We could strive for the kind of society the Nephites enjoyed following Christ's visit by, first, sharing our abundance with the poor, the destitute, and the disadvantaged and, second, by supporting the efforts of government and non-governmental organizations committed to eliminating poverty and injustice.

Love as the Path to Peace

Finally, I would like to suggest that we consider following an even more radical lesson from the Book of Mormon—that we love our enemies. I have been struck in my recent reading of the Book of Mormon by how often the Nephites and Lamanites, striving to be Christ-like, respond to their enemies, not with contempt but with compassion, not with

---

17. https://www.forbes.com/sites/noahkirsch/2017/11/09/the-3-richest-americans-hold-more-wealth-than-bottom-50-of-country-study-finds/#128f36b53cf8.

18. Center for Poverty Research, https://poverty.ucdavis.edu/faq/what-current-poverty-rate-united-states.

19. https://www.aecf.org/blog/poverty-talk-basic-terms-you-need-to-know-now/.

loathing but with love. Although some Lamanites and some Nephite dissenters plunder, enslave, and wage all-too-frequent war against the Nephites, the more noble Nephites refuse to respond in kind. In spite of the damage and destruction they experience at the hands of the Lamanites, and in spite of the fact that at times the Lamanites seek their utter destruction, the Nephites continue to strive to heal their fraternal bonds, speaking of the Lamanites as their "beloved brethren," forgiving them easily and often, and continually trying to persuade them to make peace.

This principle is reflected in a 1981 Christmas message from the First Presidency: "To all who seek a resolution to conflict, be it a misunderstanding between individuals or an international difficulty among nations, we commend the counsel of the Prince of Peace, 'Love your enemies, bless them that curse you, do good to them that hate you, and pray for them which despitefully use you, and persecute you; That you may be the children of your Father which is in heaven.' . . . This principle of loving one another as Jesus Christ loves us will bring peace to the individual, to the home and beyond, even to the nations and the world."[20]

Frances Menlove reminds us that Christ did not say blessed are the peace lovers or peacekeepers, but rather "blessed are the peacemakers."[21] James says, "Righteousness is sown in peace of them that make peace" (James 3:18). Making peace is not a passive activity. It is interesting to note that the scriptures use verbs like "proclaim," "execute," and especially "establish" peace. King Benjamin suggests that making peace should be integral to our lives when he says we should "live peaceably" (Mosiah 4:13), and, near the end of the Nephite record, Moroni quotes his father Mormon, in addressing the members of the church in his day, but likely intending ours as well, calling them "the peaceable followers of Christ" (Moroni 7:3).

---

20. *Church News* (19 December 1981), 2.
21. Panel presentation, "How Mormons Have Helped Perpetuate the War in Iraq: What We Could Do to Help End It," 2007 Sunstone Symposium, Salt Lake City, Utah.

One might argue that the prolonged peace among the Nephites was possible only because Jesus came and dwelled among them and that we cannot hope for such peace until he comes again, but such peace was achieved by the people of Enoch and the generations who were born after Christ's visit to the New World. The promise is that we too can have it if we choose to do so.

Imagining Peace

If what turned the hearts of the Nephites from war was the light of Christ, which the prophets tell us is the birthright of all humanity, then that light can shine in and through us as well. As Paul says, "For ye were sometimes darkness, but now are ye light in the Lord: walk as children of light" (Ephesians 5:8). Walking in his light, I believe we can work for peace and forge that peaceful messianic future which the scriptures promise. As Stephen Mitchell in *The Gospel According to Jesus* points out, "The messianic dream of the future may be mankind's sweetest dream. But it is a dream nevertheless, as long as there is a separation between inside and outside, as long as we don't transform ourselves."[22] As Abinadi says of Christ, "He is the light and the life of the world; yea, a light that is endless, that can never be darkened; yea, and also a life which is endless, that there can be no more death" (Mosiah 16:9). May we strive for that light and the peace it promises. And may we use our understanding of this great dramatic conflict between darkness and light in Third Nephi to once more transform our war-like world into Christ's peaceable kingdom.

Imagine such a world.

---

22. *The Gospel According to Jesus* (New York: HarperCollins, 1991), 11.

7

Irony in the
Book of Mormon

*"We cannot use language maturely until we
are spontaneously at home in irony."*
—*Kenneth Burke*

*"Every good reader must be . . . sensitive
in detecting and reconstructing ironic
meanings."*
—*Wayne Booth[1]*

Irony has been an indelible part of Western literature and culture from
ancient times to the present. Irony abounds in the Bible and was one
of the main characteristics of Greek drama, from which it derives its
name. It is an indelible part not only of our literature but also of our

---

1. Both Burke's and Booth's quotations come from Booth's *A Rhetoric of Irony*
(Chicago: University of Chicago Press, 1975), 1. Hereinafter *A Rhetoric of Irony*.

culture. In many ways we live in an ironical age, something that the critic, Jedediah Purdy, laments in his book, *For Common Things: Irony, Trust, and Commitment in America Today* (1999).

Irony largely has defied simple definition or easy categorization. As D. J. Enright says, "It is unfortunate, it is even ironical, that for so ubiquitous and multifarious and, some say, alluring a phenomenon there should be but one word."[2] D. C. Muecke writes, "Getting to grips with irony seems to have something in common with gathering the mist."[3] However, since "gathering the mist" has never deterred literary critics, a number have attempted to capture this elusive creature.

At the outset, it is important to distinguish between three kinds of literary irony—verbal, dramatic, and situational. All three have to do with levels of communication, meaning, and understanding between what is said or expected to be understood on one level and what is implied or understood on another.

Verbal Irony Karl A. Plank, professor of religion at Davidson College, North Carolina, provides a useful summary of "several recurring features" of verbal irony:

> First, irony occurs through an *indirect use of language* and expresses a covert meaning. The meaning of ironic language lacks self-evidence and must be reconstructed by the reader. Second, the indirect use of language reflects a *contrast between appearance and reality*. In the ironic text things are not simply as they appear to be. Third, irony works through the *introduction or implication of a second perspective* from which the text's 'obvious meaning' can be reinterpreted.

To summarize, the three features of verbal irony to look for in scripture are: 1) "covert meaning"; 2) "a contrast between appearance and

---

2. *The Alluring Problem: An Essay on Irony* (Oxford: Oxford University Press, 1986), 7.
3. *The Compass of Irony* (London: Methuen & Co., 1969), 3.

reality"; and 3) "a second perspective" on a text's ostensible meaning. Of interest to students of scripture, Plank adds, "Irony functions not to undermine a text's meaningfulness, but to give access to it by indicating the vantage point from which the text's full meaning can be perceived."[4] Being aware of irony in scripture can, then, enhance our understanding of sacred texts.

In his "Irony in Scripture," Mark Wenger identifies four subcategories of verbal irony: overstatement or hyperbole, understatement, oxymoron (words that contradict one another), and paradox (a statement that on its face is or appears to be absurd or self-contradictory).[5]

Dramatic Irony   As elusive as "getting to grips" with verbal irony may be, dramatic irony also defies simple definition or explanation. For purposes of this discussion, however, I cite Muecke's explanation of the "three essential elements" in dramatic irony:

> "In the first place irony is a double-layered or two-story phenomenon . . ."
>
> "In the second place there is always some kind of opposition between the two levels, an opposition that may take the form of contradiction, incongruity, or incompatibility."
>
> "In the third place there is in irony an element of 'innocence'; either a victim is confidently unaware of the very possibility of there being an upper level or point of view that invalidates his own, or an ironist pretends not to be aware of it."[6]

Situational irony   Situational irony "occurs when incongruity appears between expectations of something to happen, and what actually

---

4. *Paul and the Irony of Affliction* (Atlanta, GA: Scholars Press, 1987), 37.
5. Mark Wenger, "Irony in Scripture," https://www.academia.edu/7114303/Irony_in_the_Bible
6. *Compass of Irony*, 19–20.

happens instead."[7] A good example of this is seen in the episode in which Nephi announces to his older brothers that he has been commanded to build a ship and begins making tools to do so. They respond, "Our brother is a fool, for he thinketh that he can build a ship, and he also thinketh that he can cross these great waters." They add, "We knew ye could not construct a ship, for we knew that ye were lacking in judgment" (1 Nephi 17:17–19). The irony is heightened by the likely incredulousness of readers of the text who know Lehi's family to be desert-dwelling people who may never have been on a ship in their lives, let alone seen one built by someone—and a younger brother at that—who has no experience in shipbuilding. Laman and Lemuel's consternation is likely heightened by looking at the endless, intimidating expanse of sea upon which they feel their younger brother seems foolhardy enough to plan to launch a ship. Nevertheless, Nephi surprises his brothers by building an actual ship: "And it came to pass that after I had finished the ship, . . . my brethren beheld that it was good, and that the workmanship thereof was very fine; wherefore, they did humble themselves again before the Lord" (1 Nephi 18:4). An example of both dramatic and verbal irony is seen in the fact that Nephi not only builds a ship but tells his brothers (and us as his readers) that it isn't just any ship but one in which the workmanship is "exceeding fine." Further, even though Nephi reports that his brothers helped him build the ship ("we did work timbers of curious workmanship" [18:1]), he takes the credit for having done so ("I did build the ship . . . after I had finished the ship" [18:2,3]).

Book of Mormon irony mirrors biblical irony.[8] A familiar kind of dramatic irony in the Bible is the presentation of a person who is first shown as weak or foolish and then, after being touched by the hand of

---

7. https://literarydevices.net/situational-irony/

8. For more on biblical irony, see Edwin M. Good, *Irony in the Old Testament* (Sheffield, England: Almond Press, 1965); Lillian R. Klein, *The Triumph of Irony in the Book of Judges* (Sheffield England: Almond Press, 1988); and Karl A. Plank, *Paul and the Irony of Affliction* (Atlanta, GA: Scholars Press, 1987).

God, is transformed into an extraordinary person. An example of this from the Old Testament is Abraham who finds God's declaration that he and Sarah will have a child not only incredulous but amusing, causing him to fall "upon his face" and laugh (Genesis 17:17). Much later when the son of this miraculous birth has grown into a young man, God tests Abraham's faith by asking him to sacrifice that very son on an altar.

Ironies abound in this story. Earlier, God had commanded Abraham to leave his father's people precisely because they were sacrificing children and were even threatening to sacrifice Abraham himself. This is doubly ironic because God had promised Abraham innumerable posterity through this very son (see Genesis 17:15–16 and Abraham 1:5–16). Thus, he who lacked faith that God could bless Sarah to bear a son becomes known as "the father of the faithful"; he who laughed at God becomes God's trusted friend and chosen prophet; he who could not conceive of God's blessing him with offspring is promised that through his seed "shall all the nations of the earth be blessed"; and he who was willing to sacrifice his only son becomes known as the father of nations and is promised that through his lineage God's only son would be born and that his (Abraham's) seed would become as numerous "as the stars of the heaven, and the sand which is upon the sea shore" (Genesis 22:17–18).

An Example of Biblical Irony in The Book of Mormon

There are vivid examples of verbal, dramatic, and situational irony throughout the Book of Mormon. In fact, an entire book could be written on the subject. An example of how all three kinds of irony can be seen in a single narrative is found in the story of Abinadi and King Noah in the Book of Mosiah.[9] When we first meet Abinadi we are told, "There was a man among them whose name was Abinadi; and he went forth

---

9. I am indebted to my Book of Mormon teacher, Robert K. Thomas, for some of the insights detailed herein.

among them, and began to prophesy" (Mosiah 11:20). Abinadi is a reluctant prophet—at least he makes clear to his hearers that being a prophet is not his idea but God's: "Behold, thus saith the Lord, and thus hath he commanded me, saying, Go forth, and say unto this people, thus saith the Lord. . . . and thus saith the Lord, and thus hath he commanded me" (11:20, 25). Abinadi's repetition of "thus" in such a short space (he uses it five times!) has the effect of his pointing to heaven and saying to his antagonists, "This is all *his* idea, not mine!"

King Noah, responding with the kind of extreme hubris that is characteristic of both Hebrew scripture and Greek and modern drama, asks, "Who is Abinadi, that I and my people should be judged of him, or who is the Lord, that shall bring upon my people such great affliction?" (11:27) Such pride is almost always an ironic foreshadowing of a dramatic downfall, and its presentation early in the story prepares us for the reversal of fortune that King Noah and his also prideful priests will undergo later in the narrative. The irony of King Noah's descent is heightened by our being told that he has built "elegant and spacious buildings" (11:8) similar to that which Lehi saw the wicked inhabiting in his dream (1 Nephi 8). It also recalls the Tower of Babel and foreshadows the Rameumptom tower of the Zoramites that we will see later in the Book of Alma to which it bears a close resemblance: Noah has built "a very high tower, even so high that he could stand upon the top thereof and overlook . . . all the land round about" (11:12). When Noah boasts, "Behold, we are strong, we shall not come into bondage, or be taken captive by our enemies"(12:15), readers of the text know how wrong he is, which heightens the irony,

Offended by Abinadi's words, King Noah summarily calls for his death: "I command you to bring Abinadi hither, that I may slay him" (11:28). Learning of Noah's intention, Abinadi flees for his life. Again suggesting his reluctance to take on his prophetic calling, he stays away for two years, enough time for him to disguise himself so he will not be recognized: "And it came to pass that after the space of two years that Abinadi came among them in disguise, that they knew him not" (12:1). But then, again in a manner typical of Hebrew irony, we are shown

Abinadi being a bit dim-witted, for no sooner does he open his mouth than he gives away his disguise: "Thus has the Lord commanded me, saying—Abinadi, go and prophesy" (12:1). Oops!

Having blown his cover, Abinadi proceeds to preach the same doom and destruction as he had two years previously, only this time he augments his offense by prophesying Noah's death: "And it shall come to pass that the life of king Noah shall be valued even as a garment in a hot furnace; for he shall know that *I* am the Lord" (12:3, emphasis added). This prophesy is ironic because it answers the King's galling, if not blasphemous, question, "Who is the Lord?" and because it foreshadows the death by fire of the king and his priests. To no one's surprise, surely not even Abinadi's, his preaching produces the same result it had two years earlier: "And it came to pass that they were angry with him; and they took him and carried him bound before the King" (12:9).

Because those who bring Abinadi to the king seem a bit shaken by his prophesies not just of the king and his priests' demise but of "great pestilence" and "bondage" to come upon the whole nation (12:2, 4–7), King Noah asks his priests to advise him as to what he should do with Abinadi. Seeking legalistic grounds for an accusation, they begin "to question [Abinadi], that they might cross him, that thereby they might have wherewith to accuse him" (12:19). In an attempt to catch Abinadi in a trap, the priests confront him with a difficult scripture from Isaiah, asking him to tell them what it means. Instead of answering them, however (which he likely was incapable of doing to their satisfaction), he cleverly turns the tables and asks, "Are you priests, and pretend to teach this people, and to understand the spirit of prophesying, and yet desire to know of me what these things are?" (12:25) The irony is heightened by the fact that the scripture the priests give to Abinadi is one of the most meaningful and powerful scriptures in the entire Old Testament (12:21–24; cf. Isaiah 52: 7–10; Grant Hardy's formatting):

> How beautiful upon the mountains
> are the feet of him that bringeth good tidings;
>   that publisheth peace;

that bringeth good tidings of good;
    that publisheth salvation;
that saith unto Zion, "Thy God reigneth!"
Thy watchmen shall lift up the voice;
    with the voice together shall they sing;
for they shall see eye to eye
    when the Lord shall bring again Zion;
Break forth into joy,
    sing together ye waste places of Jerusalem;
for the Lord hath comforted his people,
    he hath redeemed Jerusalem.
The Lord hath made bare his holy arm in the eyes of
    all the nations,
        and all the ends of the earth shall see the salvation
        of our God.

It is ironic that neither King Noah nor his priests recognize the significance of this scripture nor its centrality in Hebrew history and theology. Among other things, It is a powerful poetic response to Noah's question, "Who is Abinadi?" and "Who is the Lord?" And it is a rebuke to the priests who should be—but clearly are not—fulfilling their role as watchmen. This is a scripture they should know by heart but clearly do not because their hearts are hardened. As Abinadi says to them, "Ye have not applied your hearts to understanding" (12:27).

When the priests declare that they teach the law of Moses, Abinadi challenges their obedience to the Ten Commandments—but, apparently, he can remember only two of the ten, for after recounting the first two, he asks, "Have ye done *all* this?" (12:37, emphasis added). It is difficult not to see that "all" as ironic, not only because Abinadi apparently can't remember the other eight commandments but because the priests likely have not kept *any* of the ten! Later, Abinadi somehow gets a copy of the Ten Commandments and says, "Now I *read* unto you the remainder of the commandments of God" (13:11, emphasis added).[10]

Some scholars argue that Abinadi reads the Ten Commandments to the priests during a Passover celebration, arguing that "No other day on the ancient Israelite calendar fits the message, words, and experience of the prophet Abinadi more precisely than does the ancient Israelite festival of Pentecost."[11] That makes the story even more ironic because Pentecost also marks the anniversary of God's giving the Torah to Israel and thus once more dramatically and ironically answers King Noah's question, "Who is the Lord?"

Having seen Abinadi as a prophet reluctant to accept his calling, as a returning fugitive who inadvertently gives away his disguise, and as someone who apparently does not know all of the Ten Commandments, we see him rise to the stature of his prophetic calling, demonstrating great courage, integrity, and devotion by willing to give his life in God's service. When the wicked priests attempt to take him away to be slain, he addresses them with dignity and majesty: "Touch me not, for God shall smite you if ye lay your hands upon me" (13:3). (Joseph Smith may

---

10. Richard Rust does not agree with my interpretation here. He observes, Abinadi's "subsequent purpose in reading the ten commandments is not that he needs to read them in order to get them right. Quite the contrary: He takes (I'm presuming this) the written commandments that are available to these corrupt priests and reads them (to the condemnation of the priests) because, he says, 'I perceive that they are not written in your hearts.' By contrast, Abinadi is one who has the ten commandments written in his heart. He also has Isaiah (lots of Isaiah) written in his heart" (personal correspondence, 3 August 2001).

11. John W. Welch, Gordon C. Thomasson, and Robert F. Smith in "Abinadi and Pentecost" argue that Abinadi read the Ten Commandments to King Noah's priests during what would have been Passover in the New World: "At precisely the time when Noah's priests would have been hypocritically pledging allegiance to the Ten Commandments (and indeed they professed to teach the law of Moses; see Mosiah 12:27), Abinadi rehearsed to them those very commandments (see Mosiah 12:33). On any other day this might have seemed a strange defense for a man on trial for his life, but not on Pentecost—the day on which the Ten Commandments were on center stage!" *Reexploring the Book of Mormon*, ed. John W. Welch (Salt Lake City, UT: Deseret Book, 1992), 135–38.

have remembered this scene when he himself stood in chains in Liberty Jail many years later.)[12]

From this point on, Abinadi assumes the mantle of a divinely appointed prophet, "for the Spirit of the Lord was upon him "13:5), as he preaches a powerful Jeremiad against Noah and his corrupt priests. Emboldened, he confronts them with their lack of adherence to the Law of Moses, quotes Isaiah to them, tells them the meaning of the scripture with which they had tried to confound him earlier (perhaps having taken time to prepare a response), prophesies of Christ, teaches them the plan of salvation, and foretells their destruction—declaring that they will suffer the same death they will cause him to suffer. "And now when the flames began to scorch him, he cried unto them saying: Behold, even as ye have done unto me, . . . ye shall suffer, as I suffer, the pains of death by fire" (17:14–18). Ironically, as pointed out earlier, this is exactly what happens to Noah and his priests (see Alma 25:7–11).

An additional irony in the story of Abinadi, and one that seems clearly intentional, is that this at first reluctant spokesman for God— seemingly limited in judgment at times and even in knowledge of the scriptures—converts only one person to the gospel, but that one person, Alma, turns out to be a great leader who is instrumental in turning the tide of Nephite history. Thus, in the hands of God, Abinadi is transformed into a luminous prophet whose "face shown with exceeding luster, even as Moses' did while in the mount of Sinai" (13:5), and who preaches the gospel with power and clarity, thus revealing that in chains he is more powerful than the King and all of his priests. This is exactly the kind of dramatic irony one finds in the Bible; and, I contend, the arrangement of dramatic structure, exposition of character, and rhetorical skill require a mind capable of narrative artistry and compositional sophistication.

---

12. Parley P. Pratt, *The Autobiography of Parley Parker. Pratt: One of the Twelve Apostles of the Church of Jesus Christ of Latter-Day Saints, Embracing His Life, Ministry, and Travels* Chapter 26; http://mldb.byu.edu/ppprat26.htm.

Stylistic Irony

Wayne Booth identifies a fourth kind of irony, not yet mentioned: an abrupt shift in style so that our usual expectations are turned upside down. As Booth says, "When you're reading anything that seems to have been written carefully, and you run into something odd in the style, watch out: it may be ironic."[13] While Booth speaks of such a change in the work of a single author, I think it can be argued that dramatic stylistic shifts in any text may be evidence of intended (or possibly unintended) irony.

An example of something "odd in style" can be seen in the dramatic shifts in style among the seven record keepers whose brief accounts come between Jacob and Mosiah. It isn't just the differences in style of these narrators that is striking, but also what their narratives reveal about their respective personalities.

Keeping a record of their history is among the most significant tasks entrusted to the keepers of the Nephite record. In Nephi we have one of the Book of Mormon's great writers and historians. Though less expansive than his older brother, Jacob is no less righteous and serious a steward of their people's history. In both authors' records we find important historical facts, revelations, and doctrinal teachings; both show evidence of having studied the Brass Plates; and both demonstrate literary eloquence (e.g., Nephi's Psalm and Jacob's allegory of the olive tree).

Those who next inherit the responsibility of keeping the record are, by comparison, a rather motley group. Taken together, the styles of these writers constitute an abrupt and even stark contrast with the writers who come before and after, and thus reveal irony of the kind Booth identifies.

Enos is the first of the seven narrators between Jacob and the Words of Mormon who together account for about four hundred years of Nephite history. Enos's style reveals his egocentricity: "And I will tell

---

13. *A Rhetoric of Irony*, 38.

you of the wrestle which I had before God, before I received a remission of my sins" (1:2). In his brief narrative, he uses personal pronouns (I, me, my, and mine) on a per-page basis more than any other Book of Mormon writer. In fact, he uses the personal pronoun twenty times in just the first seven verses and sixty-six times in the twenty-seven verses of his narrative.

This is a marked contrast with the next narrator, Jarom, Enos's son, who is more businesslike than his father, and less focused on himself: "I shall not write the things of my prophesying, nor my revelations" (1:2). In a few short verses, Jarom summarizes the history of his times, but, recognizing his limitations as a writer, refers his readers to the more official record: "Ye can go to the other plates of Nephi; for behold, upon them the records of our wars are engraven, according to the writings of the kings, or those which they caused to be written" (1:14). It is almost as if Jarom is saying, "Yes, I know I have been appointed to keep the record, but if you really want to know what is happening, read Nephi. He's much better at this than I am."

The next writer, Omni, is self-focused like his grandfather, but, unlike Enos, he is wicked, a fact which he readily admits: "Wherefore, in my days, I would that ye should know that I fought much with the sword to preserve my people, the Nephites, from falling into the hands of their enemies, the Lamanites. But behold, I of myself am a wicked man, and I have not kept the statutes and commandments of the Lord as I ought to have done" (1: 2). Omni is a warrior, not a writer, and his three short verses constitute his full literary output.

Omni's son, Amaron, is similarly brief before passing the record on to his brother, Chemish, whose one verse is almost comical for its brevity and vacuity: "Now I, Chemish, write what few things I write, in the same book with my brother; for behold, I saw the last which he wrote, that he wrote it with his own hand; and he wrote it in the day he delivered them unto me. And after this manner we keep the records, for it is according to the commandments of our fathers. And I make an end" (Omni 1:9). "All I have to say is that we are supposed to write something by hand here. I know this because I watched my brother do it when he gave the plates to me. That's all I have to say."

Chemish's son, Abinadom, is nearly as taciturn as his father, contributing only two verses to the record. Like Omni before him, Abinadom is a warrior, not a writer or prophet. He boasts, "I, with my own sword, have taken the lives of many of the Lamanites," and admits to no interest in chronicling his people: "I know of no revelation save that which has been written, neither prophecy; wherefore, that which is sufficient is written. And I make an end" (Omni 1:10–11). In other words, he takes up precious space on the plates to tell us that he has nothing to say!

The last of the seven keepers of the record between Jacob and King Benjamin is Amaleki, the son of Abinadom. Amaleki is the most loquacious of the group, contributing a hefty thirty verses to the record. Despite its brevity, Amaleki has important historical facts and cultural insights to add to the narrative, including the first account of the Mulekites and the Jaredites.

The irony presented by these seven brief narratives is primarily one of contrast—between the magnificent and the mundane, between those who have important things to say and those whose poverty of language and imagination leave them nearly speechless, and also between true stewardship and mere perfunctory obligation. One function of including these writers in the history (for Mormon could simply have summarized the history himself) is to cause the reader to have a greater appreciation for and pay greater attention to those more substantial portions of the text. The inclusion of such writers in the narrative seems a highly unlikely invention of someone inventing and orally delivering a text, as Joseph Smith is reported to have done. One has to question why someone who ostensibly is in the process of perpetuating a fraud (as some claim was true of Joseph Smith) would include a group of writers with nothing (or at least not much) to say, instead of creating more impressive, rhetorically rich narrators/scribes.

Conclusion

As mentioned earlier, the Book of Mormon is replete with examples of verbal, dramatic, and situational irony (as well as stylistic irony), including those discussed in earlier chapters as well as many others not discussed due to limitations of space. What is the source of all this irony? There is little evidence that Joseph Smith was an ironist; certainly, there is no evidence that he had the rhetorical or expressive skills necessary to produce the rich variety of irony one finds in the book he claims to have translated. D.C. Muecke says, "An ironist, therefore, is not just *like* an artist, but *is* an artist, governed by the artist's need for perfection of form and expression and all 'the nameless graces which no methods teach.'"[14] I contend that the presence of irony in the Book of Mormon cannot be explained as the result of unconscious genius, absorption of biblical texts, or automatic writing (See chapter 8). The most logical explanation is that the ancient writers of the Book of Mormon were consciously writing in an ironic tradition that was part of their Hebraic literary heritage.

As someone who has studied, written about, and taught ironic texts for the past nearly sixty years, I am aware that to some extent when we discuss irony we are dealing with matters of observation, perception, and interpretation. And yet the examples of irony discussed here are imbedded in the text. It is always possible to read too much or too little into a text, and certainly critics may disagree about what a particular text says or means. Nevertheless, for me the evidence is compelling that writers of these narratives made deliberate choices in arranging the detail and structure of narratives to reveal examples of irony that seem reflective of the literary tradition of which they claim to be a part.

---

14. *Compass of Irony*, 15.

8

The Book of Mormon and Automatic Writing

"The Lord has a hand in bringing to pass his strange act, and proving the Book of Mormon true in the eyes of all the people. . . . Surely 'facts are stubborn things.' It will be and ever has been, the world will prove Joseph Smith a true prophet by circumstantial evidence, in experiments, as they did Moses and Elijah."
—*Joseph Smith, September 1842[1]*

Having exhausted the more bizarre and byzantine explanations of the coming forth of the Book of Mormon (that it was written by Joseph Smith, plagiarized from Solomon Spaulding or Ethan Smith, written by

---

1. *Times and Seasons*, 15 September 1842, as cited in Terryl L. Givens, *By the Hand of Mormon: The American Scripture That Launched a New World Religion* (Oxford: Oxford University Press, 2002), 118. Hereinafter, *By the Hand of Mormon*.

Oliver Cowdery or Sidney Rigdon, dictated under the spell of epileptic seizures, etc.), some naturalist critics have postulated what appears
to be a more rational explanation,[2] namely, that it was the product of
"automatic writing." Automatic writing, also called "spirit writing," "psychography," "abnormal writing," "direct writing," "trance writing," and
"independent writing," is a term used to explain a self-induced flow of
language from the unconscious, or a form of writing the source of which
supposedly comes from outside the conscious or subconscious mind of
the person receiving the communication. In other words, the "author"
is merely a conduit for some other intelligence, an amanuensis for ideas
and expressions from another source. This latter definition is the one I
focus on in this paper wherein I explore the proposition that the Book
of Mormon can be explained as a product of automatic writing.

Claims about the existence of automatic writing have existed since at
least the nineteenth century, although some contend that "records of its
occurrence are found in the most ancient works on the subject [of psychic
phenomena], and it was perfectly familiar to those early and mediaeval
students of occult phenomena whose researches throw so much light on
that which we now find so perplexing."[3] Automatic writing of this kind is
normally classified as paranormal. That is, by some mysterious process,

---

2. By "more rational" I mean that to the extent one can make a case for the existence of automatic writing (a reasonable possibility to entertain since there are so
many examples of the phenomenon and such a wide variety of styles), this theory
becomes a more plausible explanation for how the Book of Mormon was produced
than many other explanations that, when seriously considered, prove to be either
ridiculous or without credible evidence. For a more recent discussion of automatic
writing and the Book of Mormon, see Brian C. Hales' excellent article, "Automatic
Writing and the Book of Mormon: An Update," *Dialogue: A Journal of Mormon
Thought* 52:2 (Summer 2019), 1–36.

3. W. Stainton Moses, *Direct Spirit Writing (Psychography): A Treatise on One of the
Objective Forms of Psychic or Spiritual Phenomena* (London: Psychic Book Club,
n.d.), 19. Stainton Moses was himself a famous medium and recorder of automatic
writing during the height of the Spiritualist movement in England and the United
States. See "The Mediumship of Stainton Moses," members.tripod.com/cryskernan/
mediumship_of_stainton_moses.htm.

"psychic forces," "angelic voices," "discarnate personalities," "goddesses of wisdom," or other sources, dictate a rapid and voluminous flow of words that somehow turns out to be coherent, inspiring, and often amazing in its brilliance and inclusion of esoteric facts, some of which may be beyond the author's experience or knowledge.

Challenges of Evaluating Automatic Writing

One problem with exploring this phenomenon is that it covers such a wide array of experiences. Some human "conduits" of communications from another realm use Ouija boards on which the communication is spelled out letter by letter; others use crystals or stones in which words and sentences are reported to appear (as with Joseph Smith's seer stone); and still others merely listen to, see, or understand the messages being sent (sometimes in visions, dreams, or trance states). Scribes for these communications may use pens (sometimes writing in shorthand), typewriters, or computers to quickly record what is being dictated or revealed; or they may dictate messages to a recording device. Some communications take place during a single period with a flurry of "communication"; others, like *A Course in Miracles*[4] or *The*

---

4. According to the official Course in Miracles website, through a process called "inner dictation," *A Course in Miracles* was "dictated" by Jesus to Dr. Helen Schucman, a clinical and research psychologist and tenured associate professor of medical psychology at Columbia University's College of Physicians and Surgeons in New York City. The course of study is defined as follows: "This is a course in miracles. It . . . does not aim at teaching the meaning of love, for that is beyond what can be taught. It does aim, however, at removing the blocks to the awareness of love's presence, which is your natural inheritance. The opposite of love is fear, but what is all-encompassing can have no opposite. This course can therefore be summed up very simply in this way: 'Nothing real can be threatened. Nothing unreal exists. Herein lies the peace of God'" (www.acim.org). *A Course in Miracles* has been translated into many languages and is used as a course of spiritual study throughout the world.

Urantia Book,[5] which are well known to adherents of automatic writing, take place over a period of years.

Complicating the matter is the fact that the communications claim to come from a wide and unusual (and in some instances even strange) array of personalities. These include: historic figures like William James and Oscar Wilde; unknown personalities like Patience Worth, a 17th-century English Quaker; creatures from other planets like "an Orvonton Divine Counselor, chief of the corps of superuniverse personalities," who revealed the Urantia (earth) chronicles; previously unknown prophets from the past like Tahkamenon, Seth, and Levi; and even Jesus Christ.

The task of evaluating these various communications is even more complicated and challenging because some contradict others. The portrayal in Patience Worth's *The Sorry Tale* (hailed by some contemporary critics as a "fifth gospel"), which is a supposed account of the last days of Christ along the lines presented in the New Testament, is contradicted by *A Course in Miracles.* The latter claims to have been dictated by Christ himself, yet it rejects the central Christian doctrines of the atonement, crucifixion, and resurrection, a position that, in turn, is at variance with *The Aquarian Gospel of Jesus the Christ*, an account of the "lost" 18 years of Christ's life that the "author" (Levi Dowling) also claimed was dictated to him by Jesus Christ. While the account of Christ's life in *The Urantia Book* (as "supplied by a secondary midwayer

---

5. "*The Urantia Book*, first published by the Urantia Foundation in 1955, was authored by celestial beings as a special revelation to our planet, Urantia. The book's message is that all human beings are one family, the sons and daughters of one God, the Universal Father. It instructs on the genesis, history, and destiny of mankind and on our relationship with God. It also presents a unique and compelling portrayal of the life and teachings of Jesus, opening new vistas of time and eternity, and revealing new concepts of Man's ever-ascending adventure of finding the Universal Father in our friendly and carefully administered universe" (Urantia Foundation, www.urantia.org). The Urantia text was a "revelation" dictated to and "transcribed" by an anonymous group living in Chicago. Like *A Course in Miracles*, *The Urantia Book* has been translated into many languages and is studied in many countries.

who was onetime assigned to the superhuman watchcare of the Apostle Andrew") is essentially the portrayal of Christ that one finds in the Gospels, it contradicts that original account in some important particulars, including its claim that Christ's physical body was not resurrected. Rather, it claims that he came forth out of the sealed tomb "in the very likeness of the morontia personalities of those who, as resurrected morontia ascendant beings, emerge from the resurrection halls of the first mansion world of this local system of Satania."[6] The problem becomes even more challenging if one includes in the category of automatic writing the account of Jesus Christ found in the Book of Mormon.

Skeptics of psychic experiences, including automatic writing, tend to explain such phenomena as clever frauds, unconscious processes, or "dissociation," which the dictionary defines as "the separation of whole segments of the personality (as in multiple personality disorder) or of discrete mental processes (as in the schizophrenias) from the mainstream of consciousness or of behavior."[7] In other words, these communications are produced as conscious deceptions, unconscious delusions, or subconscious dissociations, all of which at one time or another have been proposed as explanations of Joseph Smith's production of the Book of Mormon.

As one examines the wide range of texts claimed to have been received through the process of automatic recording of communication from another realm, it is difficult, if not impossible, to conclude that all such communications are authentic and legitimate. This is an arena in which some writers of automatic texts seem to record information from their subconscious memories and in which magicians and others have used trickery or manipulated data to produce the illusion of automatic writing.

While some such phenomena can be explained as the skeptics suggest, other phenomena apparently cannot. What, for example, does

---

6. *The Urantia Book* (Chicago: The Urantia Foundation, 1955), 2021–22.
7. *Merriam-Webster's Collegiate Dictionary*, 11th ed., s.v. "dissociation."

one make of the reported cases in which the communicant begins conversing in a language that, although unknown to the medium or scribe, is recorded with linguistic precision? Examples include communications in a variety of languages, including Greek, Welsh, Hungarian, and, in one of the most interesting cases, a Chinese dialect not spoken in China for centuries. As an observer of this last case, Dr. Neville Whymant, lecturer in Chinese at Oxford University, reported, "The Chinese to which we were now listening was as dead colloquially as Sanskrit or Latin." To test the authenticity of the speaker, who identified himself as Confucius, Dr. Whymant recited the first and only line he knew of an obscure and difficult ancient Chinese poem and asked its meaning. He reports, "The voice took up the poem and recited to the end" using intonation characteristic of archaic Chinese.[8]

There are other instances in which the medium who was the conduit of the automatic writing performed tasks that seem impossible to explain as the result of conscious, unconscious, or subconscious processes. That is, these individuals received historical facts and used linguistic styles that were not available in their information environment,[9] and they expressed them in language and forms that were far

---

8. Robert Almeder, *Beyond Death: Evidence for Life After Death* (Springfield, IL: Charles C Thomas, 1987), 60–62. Obviously, such anecdotal reports are not the same as controlled scientific studies, and yet the number of such reported incidences offers at least the possibility that some may be reliable.

9. A term used by Gordon Thomasson in "Daddy, What's a 'Frontier?'": Thoughts on the 'Information Environment' That Supposedly Produced the Book of Mormon," unpublished manuscript in my possession, 18. Thomasson provides the most detailed account yet as to what information might have been available to someone living in eastern New York in the late 1820s.

According to Thomasson, "There are two types of critical tests which can be made on Book of Mormon data: [1] The first type involves subjects about which an information vacuum can be shown to have existed in 1830—and about which the Book of Mormon takes a position which can be compared to new data revealed by contemporary scholarship (textual comparison of the Book of Mormon with otherwise unparalleled Qumran and/or Nag Hammadi documents might fall in this category). [2] The second class of tests includes those cases in which the information environment of 1830 can be shown to have documented a particular

beyond their expressive talents. One of the intriguing and most widely studied automatic writers was Pearl Curran, a St. Louis, Missouri, housewife who claimed to have received an enormous volume of material from a spirit personage over a ten-year period. According to Curran, the personage identified herself as Patience Worth and said she had lived in the 17th century.

It is interesting to speculate about the possibility of a variety of communications coming from beyond the veil—some inspired and some not, some truthful and some not, some rational and some not. That is, since mortals, having free will, can communicate with one another in ways that are manipulative and deceitful as well as in ways that are open and truthful, since communications range from the brilliant to the dull and from the clear to the incoherent, and since they express conscious as well as unconscious material, might it not be possible that those in the spirit world can communicate with the living in the same ways? This runs counter to our general assumption about the spirit world, but since "whatever principle of intelligence we attain unto in this life . . . will rise with us in the resurrection" (Doctrine and Covenants 130:18), it may also be that other aspects of our personality and character follow us into the next world and influence our communication with the living, if indeed such communications are possible, as some contend.

Asserting a Connection

What, if anything, does all of this have to do with the Book of Mormon? In an article entitled "Automaticity and the Dictation of the Book of Mormon," Scott C. Dunn argues that the Book of Mormon is an example of automatic writing. He contends that "a number of parallels exist

---

position which the Book of Mormon took exception to—and these two conflicting ideas can be compared to current scholarly opinion. These are tests which the Book of Mormon can pass or fail—taking into consideration the open-ended dialogue which is true scholarship. These are tests to which it generally has not been subjected."

between Joseph Smith's production of scripture and instances of automatic writing."[10] He uses the case of Pearl Curran to make his point. Curran claimed to receive communications from Patience Worth through use of a Ouija board, communications that she in turn dictated to various scribes. One of the most curious aspects of these communications is that they were given, Dunn writes, in "an antique and archaic figurativeness," in an amalgam of dialects from earlier English periods, and in a diction that was 90 percent Anglo-Saxon (as compared to 42 percent for the Declaration of Independence). According to linguistic experts, the dictated text contained no modernisms. Over the decade of these communications, Curran recorded history, fiction, poetry, proverbs, and prayers. Those who knew her intimately and those who studied her carefully, including some of the leading psychologists and literary and linguistic scholars of the time, were convinced that there was nothing in Curran's background, study, or experience that could account for this material.[11]

Dunn compares Curran's experience to that of Joseph Smith and the Book of Mormon: "Like believers in the Book of Mormon, followers of Patience Worth adduced linguistic evidence to show that the writing dictated through Pearl Curran did indeed belong to antiquity. Although some of the language was more ungrammatical than archaic [which, by the way, one might expect of a person of Patience Worth's purported education and background], there appear to be occasional uses of genuinely obsolete English words which Curran would probably not have known." Dunn continues, "Another startling thing about the works attributed to Patience Worth is their accuracy on factual

---

10. Scott C. Dunn, "Automaticity and the Dictation of the Book of Mormon," in *American Apocrypha: Essays on the Book of Mormon*, ed. Dan Vogel and Brent Lee Metcalfe (Salt Lake City: Signature Books, 2002), 26. Hereinafter "Automaticity."
11. See Stephen E. Braude, "Dissociation and Latent Abilities: The Strange Case of Patience Worth," *The Journal of Trauma and Dissociation* 1/2 (2000): 13–48. See commentaries on Braude by Jean Goodwin and Jennifer Radden in the same issue.

details that Curran apparently could not have known, a defense often applied to writings given through Joseph Smith."[12]

Extending his argument, Dunn writes, "Like Joseph Smith, Pearl Curran appears to have lacked the education necessary to produce such works. . . . Just as Joseph Smith eventually began to dictate revelations without the aid of a seer stone, so Curran began to dictate the words of Patience Worth without any physical object. Curran 'simply saw the pictures and the words in her head and called them out, as coming from the hand of Patience Worth.'" According to Dunn, "Pearl Curran is like Joseph Smith in still another way: for both, available evidence militates against the likelihood of conscious fraud."[13]

Dunn then asks, "But beyond these general parallels to the experience of automatic writers, what is the evidence that Joseph Smith's translation is an example of this phenomenon?" His answer: "To begin with, the content of automatic texts is often similar to that of the Book of Mormon: Examples include multiple authorship, use of archaic language, accounts of bygone historical figures, accurate descriptions of times and places apparently unfamiliar to the writer, narratives with well-developed characters and plot, accounts of various ministries of Jesus Christ, poetics, occasionally impressive literary quality, doctrinal, theological, and cosmological discussions, and even discourses by deity."[14]

Dunn also argues that the manner in which the Book of Mormon was produced "bears strong resemblance to the process of automatic writing," including "the speed and ease with which Smith worked" on his translation. After countering the arguments of some critics who feel the Book of Mormon is not a good example of automatic writing, Dunn concludes, "It is clear that Smith's translation experience fits comfortably within the larger world of scrying, channeling, and

---

12. "Automaticity," 27.
13. Ibid., 29.
14. Ibid., 30.

automatic writing. Indeed, the automatic processes . . . provide the best model for understanding the translation of the Book of Mormon."[15]

The Extent of Common Ground

To what extent are Dunn's observations accurate? To begin with, if one takes all the texts that might fit into the category of automatic writing, a great number of books, many of which make no claim to have been written or dictated by anyone other than the author, might also be said to have content similar to automatic texts. Indeed, the works identified as automatic texts have very little in common with one another. They range from the absurd to the inspired, from the mundane to the eso-teric, from short story to voluminous chronicle, from realistic narrative to what could best be described as speculative fiction. And their styles are as varied as their subject matter. So, while it may be true, as Dunn argues, that the Book of Mormon "fits comfortably within the larger world of . . . automatic writing," it also fits comfortably within the larger world of narrative fiction and the narrower world of sacred literature.

It is surprising that Dunn seems to take at face value the claims of other automatic scribes about the source of their manuscripts but doesn't seem to accept Joseph Smith's own account of his sources as valid. That is, if Dunn uncritically accepts the witness of writers of automatic texts regarding the processes by which they received their material, why question the source or sources Joseph Smith claimed for the Book of Mormon?[16] Joseph was clear and specific about the manner in which he received the ancient record he claims to have translated. As Terryl L. Givens summarizes: "His self-described excavation of the plates, repeated secreting of them in bean barrels, under hearthstones, and in smocks, his displaying of them to eight corroborating witnesses,

---

15. Ibid., 33.

16. I believe Dunn may be disingenuous when he states, "It may be argued that automatic writing is God's true means of giving revelations and translations [in the case of Joseph Smith]," "Automaticity," 36.

and his transcription of them into hieroglyphics and translation of them into English—this continual, extensive, and prolonged engagement with a tangible, visible, grounding artifact is not compatible with a theory that makes him an inspired writer reworking the stuff of his own dreams into a product worthy of the name scripture."[17] Nor, one could argue, is it compatible with the theory that he was an automatic writer in the sense in which that term is generally understood.

What is true of Dunn's argument is that there are many similarities between the processes described by automatic writers and that described by Joseph Smith and his various scribes. Joseph receiving information from some source outside himself; seeing words by means of the Urim and Thummim, in the seer stone, or in his mind's eye; dictating a sort of stream-of-consciousness narrative; being able to pick up dictation/translation after interruptions and delays, sometimes for days, with no break in the narrative flow; producing a large body of material over a short period of time; and leaving the final text essentially unrevised—all of these have similarities to the producers of some credible or claimed automatically written texts.

But if one postulates that some automatic texts or some sacred literature really is the product of communication beyond the veil, then one would expect some correspondence between such texts and a text that the translator claimed was given to him by an angel, assisted in its translation by use of various means or instrumentalities and inspired by the Holy Ghost.[18] That is, if some communications do come from the spirit world, it seems likely that they may come in different ways, under different circumstances and for different purposes, and one that purports to be the scriptural record of ancient Israelites and a second testament of Jesus Christ should make a compelling claim for our

---

17. *By the Hand of Mormon*, 177–78.
18. See Richard Van Wagoner and Steve Walker, "Joseph Smith: 'The Gift of Seeing,'" *Dialogue* (15/2, Summer 1982); revised and reprinted in Bryan Waterman, ed., *The Prophet Puzzle: Interpretive Essays on Joseph Smith* (Salt Lake City: Signature Books, 1999), 87–112.

consideration, especially considering the arguments made in earlier chapters about the difficulty of seeing Joseph Smith as the author of the Nephite record.

For those who believe that the veil between the mortal and immortal worlds is penetrable by those who have special gifts or sensitivities, it is not difficult to believe in the possibility of automatic conveyance or inspired/revealed translation (although as I argue below, from what we know of the Book of Mormon translation, it does not qualify as an automatic text). If one accepts the possibility that Jehovah could reveal his law to Moses on Mt. Sinai and that Jesus could reveal to John the strange and wonderful things contained in the book of Revelation, surely one must accept that the Lord could reveal the record of his New World peoples to Joseph Smith. How he would do so seems much less important than that he could do so. And if personages such as Moroni, Elijah, Moses, John the Baptist, and Peter, James, and John could appear to Joseph Smith, as he claimed and as Mormons believe, then it is easy to accept the possibility that revelations from Nephi, Mormon, Alma, and others could have come to him as well. In fact, it is interesting to speculate, as some early scholars of the Book of Mormon did, that these figures actually appeared to Joseph and told their stories in the same way that the authors of some automatic texts claim past prophets and historical figures appeared to or communicated through them.[19]

Considering Scientific Evidence

What evidence exists that such communications from the spirit world might actually take place? While there is good reason to doubt the authenticity of some, if not most, texts claimed to be the result of automatic writing, not all examples of such writing can be explained as the result of naturalistic influences or causes. Obviously, this is a landscape on which believers and skeptics have contended for centuries—and

---

19. "Automaticity," 38n.

likely will continue to contend, since at present we seem to lack the scientific tools and technology to incontrovertibly establish the existence
of communication from another sphere, including what is sometimes
referred to as "the spirit world." Nevertheless, respected researchers
are probing this possibility, some with support from the National
Institutes of Health. One such researcher is Dr. Gary E. Schwartz, professor of psychology, medicine, neurology, psychiatry, and surgery at
the University of Arizona and director of the university's Laboratory
for Advances in Consciousness and Health.

Dr. Schwartz and his associates at the University of Arizona have
conducted scientific research on communication between the living and the dead. In his book *The Afterlife Experiments: Breakthrough
Scientific Evidence of Life After Death*, Schwartz reports on studies using
established mediums (people who seem to have a gift for spirit communication) whose integrity he and his colleagues had come to trust. They
set up controlled, double- and triple-blind laboratory experiments in
which the mediums were asked to communicate with personalities
purportedly in the spirit world on behalf of people unknown to them
(i.e., the mediums). In one experiment the mediums averaged an 83
percent accuracy rate in describing specific elements relating to the
person with whom they allegedly were communicating (e.g., names
of deceased relatives and their relationships, unique details of their
history together, causes of death, etc.), as compared to a 36 percent
average for the control group. Dr. Schwartz concludes, "The statistical
probability of this difference occurring by chance alone was less than
one in ten million."[20] Of later more scientifically rigorous experiments,
Dr. Schwartz reports, "We performed statistical analyses indicating

---

20. Gary E. Schwartz, *The Afterlife Experiments: Breakthrough Scientific Evidence of
Life after Death* (New York: Pocket Books, 2002), 121. Hereafter, *Afterlife Experiments*.
See also Gary E. R. Schwartz and Linda G. S. Russek, *The Living Energy Universe*
(Charlottesville, VA: Hampton Roads, 1999).

that the results could have occurred by chance fewer than one in a 100 trillion times."[21]

In reviewing these experiments and evaluating them in light of the high standards for scientific integrity he and his colleagues had established, their own skeptical safeguards, and the challenges of nonbelieving critics, Dr. Schwartz concludes, "I went through all the experiments—each and every [psychic] reading, both within and beyond the formal data collection periods—and examined it all on the basis of the eleven key summary points that form the core [of the experiments]. I can no longer ignore the data and dismiss the words. They are as real as the sun, the trees, and our television sets, which seem to pull pictures out of the air." His conclusion: "In the experiments, information was consistently retrieved that can best be explained as coming from living souls. . . . The data appear to be as valid, convincing and living as the mediums, sitters, skeptics, and scientists themselves. That's what the experimental data unmistakably show." [22]

Another body of research that seems to have some bearing on the subject of "spirit communication" is that conducted by the Institute of HeartMath on intuition and epigenetics. Epigenetics is defined as the "science that studies how the development, functioning, and evolution of biological systems are influenced by forces operating outside the primary DNA sequence of the genome (i.e., intracellular, environmental, and energetic influences)."[23] Based on research studies conducted under rigorous, conservative conditions on "how the body receives and processes prestimulus information about a future event,"[24] HeartMath scientists conclude that "*both the heart and brain* appear to receive and respond to

---

21. *Afterlife Experiments*, 222.
22. *Afterlife Experiments*, 257, 266.
23. "Emotional Energetics, Intuition, and Epigenetics Research," The Institute of HeartMath, http://www.heartmath.org/research/research-intuition/overview.html.
24. Rollin McCraty, Mike Atkinson, and Raymond Trevor Bradley, "Electrophysiological Evidence of Intuition: Part 1. The Surprising Role of the Heart," *The Journal of Alternative and Complementary Medicine* 10:1 (2004): 141.

information about a future emotional stimulus prior to actually experiencing the stimulus."[25] Although differing in some aspects of their methodology, these studies confirm or are related to others conducted by Dean Radin, senior scientist at the Institute of Noetic Sciences;[26] William A. Tiller, professor emeritus of Materials Science and Engineering at Stanford and current head of The Institute for Psychoenergetic Science; and others. Tiller's *Psychoenergetic Science: A Second Copernican-Scale Revolution* (2007), summarizes these and other psychoenergetic scientific studies, including those relating to remote viewing, psychokinesis, precognition, telephony, and clairvoyance.[27] While such studies remain controversial, some of their findings are compelling.

Studies by the Institute of HeartMath on the heart provide "strong evidence for the idea that intuitive processes involve accessing a field of information that is not limited by the constraints of space and time. More specifically, they provide a compelling basis for the proposition that the body accesses a field of potential energy—that exists as a

---

25. Rollin McCraty, Mike Atkinson, and Raymond Trevor Bradley, "Electrophysiological Evidence of Intuition: Part 2. A System-Wide Process?" *The Journal of Alternative and Complementary Medicine* 10/2 (2004): 334. In another study, HeartMath researchers conclude, "Even more surprising was our finding that the heart appears to receive this 'intuitive' information before the brain. This suggests that the heart's field may be linked to a more subtle energetic field that contains information on objects and events remote in space or ahead in time. Called by Karl Pribram and others the 'spectral domain,' this is a fundamental order of potential energy that enfolds space and time, and is thought to be the basis for our consciousness of 'the whole'" (Rollin McCraty, Raymond Trevor Bradley, and Dana Tomasino, "The Resonant Heart," *Shift: At the Frontiers of Consciousness* 5 [Dec. 2004–Feb. 2005], 15–19).
26. See Dean I. Radin, "Unconscious Perception of Future Emotions: An Experiment in Presentiment," *Journal of Scientific Exploration* 11:2 (1997): 163–80. See also Radin's *The Conscious Universe: The Scientific Truth of Psychic Phenomena* (San Francisco: HarperEdge, 1997); *Entangled Minds: Extrasensory Experiences in a Quantum Reality* (Harper Collins, 1997); and *Supernormal: Science, Yoga, and the Evidence for Extraordinary Psychic Abilities* (Deepak Chopra Books, 2013).
27. *Psychoenergetic Science: A Second Copernican-Scale Revolution* (Pavior Publishing: Walnut Creek, CA, 2010).

domain apart from space-time reality—into which information about 'future' events is spectrally enfolded."[28]

Whatever scientific evidence or lack thereof for communication beyond the veil, one has to consider the possibility that at least some of the cases of automatic writing might indeed be authentic communication across the liminal threshold that divides the mortal and immortal worlds. In view of this decidedly speculative conclusion, Joseph Smith's claims as to the source of the Book of Mormon and the process by which he translated it must be accorded at least some validity given the elaborate explanations that must be marshaled as evidence that, alternatively, the book came out of his or some other nineteenth-century author's (or authors') mind, experience, and imagination. In other words, if communication from the spirit world can produce even fragments of information, and if texts can be written that cannot be explained as the result of naturalistic causes, then it may be possible for someone to be the conduit of a book as complex and original as the Book of Mormon. Having said that, I would like to illustrate ways in which I think the Book of Mormon does not fit the usual model of automatic writing.

Countering the Connection

To begin with, some writers of automatic texts, such as those discussed earlier in this chapter, aver that their information comes from specific personages who often have names, come from specific epochs, and have definite personalities. Unlike these mediums of extra-mortal communication, Joseph Smith never claimed that anyone was dictating to or communicating through him. While he saw specific words and phrases by means of a seer stone or the Urim and Thummim, he did

---

28. McCraty, Atkinson, and Bradley, "Electrophysiological Evidence," 334. For additional information on HeartMath research see www.heartmath.org.

not identify them as coming from a source beyond what was recorded on the gold plates.

Another way in which Joseph Smith's claim differs from the producers of automatic texts is that he is the only one of whom I am aware who claimed to have an actual tangible text from which his dictation was derived. The gold plates revealed by Moroni and placed into Joseph's hands constitute the source of the record he claims to have translated. At least 11 other witnesses attested to the existence of the plates.[29]

The Book of Mormon Uniquely on Target

Joseph Smith, as far as I can tell, is also unique in including in his text information that was not available anywhere in his or anyone else's information environment during the period in which he produced his text. While Patience Worth spoke highly specialized English dialects and used archaic vocabulary that seem impossible for her medium, Pearl Curran, to have known, the fact remains that such dialects and vocabulary were available in the English-speaking environment of certain districts of England contemporaneous with Curran. The same could be said of Patience Worth's use of topical information about the Holy Land in *A Sorry Tale*, her fictional narrative about Jesus. As one critic noted, "While the scenes are mainly in Palestine, it touches Rome occasionally, and it deals not only with Jews but with Romans, Greeks, and Arabians, revealing an intimate and accurate knowledge of the political, social, and religious conditions of the times, the relations of each of these peoples to Rome, and their essential differences

---

29. Dan Vogel attempts to discredit these witnesses and to undermine their testimonies of the existence of the plates by seeing their experiences as the result of hallucination, hypnotism, or "induced visionary experiences" ("The Validity of the Witnesses," in *American Apocrypha*, 79–121). Vogel's piece is so shot through with subjunctive qualifiers (*if, probably, perhaps, seems, might, assuming that, likely, probable, possibility*, etc.) that it is difficult to take his argument seriously.

of character, custom and tradition."[30] Nevertheless, this information could have been found in sources extant at the time of the dictation. Information not available to Joseph Smith at the time of the publication of the Book of Mormon includes the following:

Ancient travel   The Book of Mormon contains information that, as far as can be determined, was not known to anyone in the world at the time it was published. For example, as revealed in an earlier chapter, Eugene England points out that the route that Lehi and his people took across the Arabian Desert was counter to what all the travel guides of the nineteenth century described or advised. England summarizes, "For Joseph Smith to have so well succeeded in producing over twenty unique details in the description of an ancient travel route through one of the least-known areas of the world, all of which have been subsequently verified, requires extraordinary, unreasonable faith in his natural genius or his ability to guess right in direct opposition to the prevailing knowledge of his time."[31] S. Kent Brown adds a number of items to England's list of details about Lehi's route that were not known anywhere in the nineteenth century.[32]

Mesoamerica   Another example of material in the Book of Mormon that was unknown and unknowable in 1830 is the vast amount of detail about Mesoamerica. As John L. Sorenson, one of the leading authorities in this field, states, "At point after point the scripture accurately reflects the culture and history of ancient Mesoamerica. . . . Where did such information come from if not through Joseph in the manner

---

30. Casper S. Yost, "The Problem of Knowledge," in Walter Franklin Prince, *The Case of Patience Worth* (Hyde Park, NY: University Books, 1964), 380.

31. Eugene England, "Through the Arabian Desert to a Bountiful Land: Could Joseph Smith Have Known the Way?" *Book of Mormon Authorship: New Light on Ancient Origins*, ed. Noel B. Reynolds (Provo, UT: Religious Studies Center, 1982), 153.

32. S. Kent Brown, "New Light from Arabia on Lehi's Trail," in *Echoes and Evidences of the Book of Mormon*, ed. Donald W. Parry, Daniel C. Peterson, and John W. Welch (Provo, UT: FARMS, 2002), 55–125.

he claimed? Literally no person in Joseph Smith's day knew or could have known enough facts about exotic Central America to depict the subtle and accurate picture of ancient life that we find as background for the Book of Mormon."[33] Sorenson cites such things as geographical consistency, the pattern of cultural history (which was "totally unknown in 1830," for "not even the best-informed scholars in the world at that time, let alone Joseph Smith, had any notion of a pattern behind ancient American history that would come to light over a century later"), language ("How remarkable that the record keepers of the Book of Mormon allude again and again to their writing systems and, even more remarkable, that the Book of Mormon statements fit so well with what we know about the primary type of script in use in early Mesoamerica"), Nephite political economy ("Nothing Joseph Smith could have known in his day about 'the Indians' or the biblical Israelites would have prepared him to dictate such a consistent picture of Nephite and Lamanite government and society as he actually did. Only in recent decades have scholars learned enough to describe these ancient Mesoamerican power mechanisms that prove to have been so much like what the Book of Mormon portrays"), elements of material culture ("No one in the nineteenth century could have known that cement, in fact, was extensively used in Mesoamerica beginning at about . . . the middle of the first century b.c."), and warfare (only during the "the last quarter century [has] a tide of new studies" validated the Book of Mormon's portrayal of war).[34] In relation to the last item on Sorenson's list, contrary to what some have proposed and what one might normally expect, warfare in the Book of Mormon does not reflect warfare in the United States prior to and including the time of the publication of the Book of Mormon.[35]

---

33. John L. Sorenson, "How Could Joseph Write So Accurately about Ancient American Civilization?" in *Echoes and Evidences*, 261–62.
34. Sorenson, "Ancient American Civilization," *Echoes and Evidences*, 269, 281, 286, 287, 292.
35. See Richard Bushman, "The Book of Mormon and the American Revolution," in *Book of Mormon Authorship: New Light on Ancient Origins*, ed. Noel B. Reynolds

Ancient languages Similarly significant is the Book of Mormon's inclusion of words, rhetorical practices, rituals, and cultural practices whose meanings have been discovered since 1830. A striking example is the word *Hermounts* (identified in Alma 2:37 as "that part of the wilderness which was infested by wild and ravenous beasts"). As Hugh Nibley pointed out, this word is almost identical with "Hermonthis," a land named after the Egyptian god of wild things and wild places.[36] And Gordon Thomasson argues persuasively that the word *Mormon* itself, which is first presented in the Book of Mormon as a place infested by wild beasts, has the same Arabic root, *RMN*, as *Hermounts*.[37] Other Egyptian elements appear in the names Korihor, Pahoran, and Paanchi, the last of which is a seventh-century BC name (i.e., contemporary with Lehi) not known in the West until the end of the nineteenth century.[38] Nibley also suggested that the Book of Mormon's use of Hebrew names, many of which are nonbiblical, "preserve the authentic forms of the Hebrew names of the period as attested in newly discovered documents."[39]

A further example of Book of Mormon language unknowable to Joseph Smith is the place-name Nahom (1 Nephi 16:34), where Nephi's people buried Ishmael and mourned his passing. As various scholars have pointed out, this word seems related not only to the Arabic root *NHM*, which means "to sigh or moan" (suggesting grief) and the Hebrew "nahum"(meaning "comfort"),[40] but also to a recently discovered ancient burial site, Nehhm (alternately, Nihm, Nahom, Nehem), which lies very close to the area where Ishmael was buried. As Terryl

---

and Charles D. Tate (Provo, UT: Brigham Young University, 1982),189–212.

36. See Hugh Nibley, *Since Cumorah: The Book of Mormon in the Modern World* (Salt Lake City: Deseret Book, 1970), 192). Hereinafter, *Cumorah.*

37. See Gordon Thomasson, "Book of Mormon Language, Names, and [Metonymic] Naming," *Journal of Book of Mormon Studies* 3/1 (1994): 1–27.

38. *Since Cumorah*, 192–93.

39. *Since Cumorah*, 194.

40. Hugh Nibley, *Lehi in the Desert: The World of the Jaredites; There Were Jaredites* (Salt Lake City, UT: Deseret Book and FARMS, 1988), 79.

Givens argues, "Found in the very area where Nephi's record locates Nahom, these altars may thus be said to constitute the first actual archaeological evidence for the historicity of the Book of Mormon."[41] While the name "Nehhm" appears on Carsten Niebuhr's map of Arabia published in 1774 and 1778, S. Kent Brown argues that Joseph Smith could not have had access to such a map "because the English translation of Niebuhr's book and accompanying map were unavailable to him either at the Dartmouth library, which did not acquire a copy of the English translation until December 1937, or from John Pratt's library, which did not own it."[42]

While some automatic texts claim to have been dictated by biblical figures, and therefore have in common with the Book of Mormon the literary, religious, and cultural background of the Hebrew scriptures, none has come close to matching the Book of Mormon's reflection of the complex rhetorical style and stylistic patterns of Hebrew literature or its ritual patterns. The Book of Mormon is replete with stylistic elements characteristic of Hebrew speech and thought patterns, including adverbials, cognate accusatives, compound prepositions, pronoun repetition, simile curses, climactic forms, and various kinds of biblical parallelisms, among them complex and intricate examples of chiasmus.[43] If, as some critics contend, Joseph Smith somehow absorbed all of this or intuited it from his familiarity with the Hebrew scriptures, he accomplished something that no other author in the history of the world that includes those scriptures has, especially given his lack of deep knowledge of and acquaintance with the Hebrew scriptures.

Literary complexity   The sheer complexity of the Book of Mormon narrative is far beyond that of any automatic text of which I am aware. As Givens notes, there are some 2,000 authorial shifts in the narrative.[44]

---

41. *By the Hand of Mormon*, 120.
42. "New Light from Arabia on Lehi's Trail" in *Echoes and Evidences*, 55–125.
43. See Dennis Largey, ed., *Book of Mormon Reference Companion* (Salt Lake City: Deseret Book, 2003), 182–86, 321–26.
44. *By the Hand of Mormon*, 156.

And while it is true that some automatic texts contain more than one authorial style and some spirit communicants apparently speak in more than one voice (one thinks particularly of Patience Worth), none that I know of contains the number of distinctive authorial styles (two dozen or so) found in the Book of Mormon.

Doctrinal richness   Even more significant, I believe, is the substantive richness of the Book of Mormon's message. While many automatic texts contain inspirational literature and some contain specific doctrine (Christian and otherwise), none in my estimation matches the Book of Mormon's doctrinal richness and density nor its theological consistency with the Bible.

Concluding Thoughts

One might cite many more examples of things in the Book of Mormon that were unavailable in Joseph Smith's information environment or completely foreign to his experience. The chances that he could have guessed at even one of these, let alone hundreds, are astronomical. No naturalist critic of whom I am aware has come close to explaining their presence in the Book of Mormon. I believe all of this constitutes a significant refutation of Dunn's dismissive statement, "There does not appear to be anything of a historical, theological, philosophical, or literary quality in the scriptural writings of Joseph Smith that has not been matched by those well outside the Mormon tradition."[45]

As someone who considers the validity of both spiritual and empirical processes in the search for truth, I have tried honestly and fairly to evaluate the data and arguments presented by both apologist and naturalist critics of the Book of Mormon, including those relating to automatic writing. Naturalist critics, to my mind, raise important issues about the origin and nature of the text. I honor their efforts

---

45. "Automaticity," 36.

when they derive from a sincere attempt to come to terms with the book using the best tools for intellectual inquiry and rational exploration. Some of the challenges they present are legitimate and deserve serious consideration.

On the other hand, apologist critics also make invaluable contributions to the dialogue, and their work, when based on rigorous scholarship and on responsible spiritual witness, should also be taken seriously. For the most part, I have found such scholars to be people of integrity who use their best intellectual and spiritual abilities to understand and explain the Book of Mormon. When they defend the book on a purely spiritual basis, they must understand that they enter a realm where few naturalist critics are willing to follow. However, when they combine their empirical inquiry with rigorous spiritual standards (including the integrity to honestly test their spiritual convictions against the best considered knowledge), they should be given respect for their conclusions.

I believe that the evidence suggested by some automatic writing, as well as the intuition studies of the Institute of HeartMath and the afterlife experiments of Gary Schwartz, as well as other reputable scientific explorations of unexplainable communications such as those involved in automatic writing present a compelling argument for the *possibility* of communication from the immortal to the mortal world. As Schwartz says of his findings in testing "the living soul hypothesis": "Scientists and nonscientists alike are experiencing a test of faith—In this case, whether we can put our belief in the scientific method itself. Because if we are to put our faith in the scientific method, and trust what the data [we have produced] reveal, we are led to the hypothesis that the universe is more wondrous than imagined in our wildest dreams."[46]

It is important to acknowledge that the material in the Book of Mormon had its origin in specific physical and cultural loci. In order for it to have come from Joseph Smith's conscious or subconscious mind, it had to have somehow gotten there. As Casper S. Yost observed

---

46. *Afterlife Experiments Experiments*, xxiii.

about Pearl Curran, "The subconscious has a larger store of information than the conscious part of the mind, but it has no objective knowledge not acquired by individual experience, it has no objective impressions that are not made through the senses. It knows nothing externally, that is to say, that it has not learned by seeing, hearing, touch, tasting or smelling. . . . No objective knowledge is in any part of Mrs. Curran's mind that has not been acquired through her own sensory experience."[47]

Perhaps Yost's observation should be revised to say that the mind contains no objective *terrestrial* knowledge that has not been received through the senses. This leaves open the possibility that memory and knowledge may have some other locus of origin, such as premortal experiences or revealed dreams and visions. The point is that if one contends, as do some naturalist critics, that the rich tapestry of narrative we know as the Book of Mormon came from the mind and imagination of Joseph Smith, one has to account for the means or process(es) by which it got there and from there to the pages of the Book of Mormon. No one in my opinion has offered a more satisfactory or more convincing explanation than the one Joseph Smith himself gave.

Some naturalist critics speculate that all of the information contained in the Book of Mormon came from Joseph Smith's nineteenth-century environs. In citing the example of an automatic writer who apparently "picked up and stored material that was in her field of vision as she worked [a] crossword puzzle," Scott Dunn says, "It should not be surprising, therefore, to find Smith's scriptural productions repeating things he may have heard or overheard in conversation, camp meetings, or other settings without any concerted study of the issues."[48]

Dunn would be hard-pressed to show that anyone could have overheard the kinds of information and knowledge presented above at camp meetings or anywhere else in the Palmyra area (or elsewhere in the world) during the time the Book of Mormon was translated. The

---

47. Yost, "The Problem of Knowledge," in Prince, *Patience Worth*, 369.
48. "Automaticity," 35.

remarkable thing about the Book of Mormon is that there is not a single fact, character, or allusion contained in it that can be tied exclusively to nineteenth-century America. Most parallels that environmentalist critics find between the book and Joseph Smith's cultural environment are of such a general and superficial nature that they could be found at many times and in many cultures.[49] As Richard L. Bushman contends, the milieu of the Book of Mormon has much more in common with ancient Hebrew culture than nineteenth-century America. He summarizes his analysis by saying that the Book of Mormon is "strangely distant from the time and place of its publication."[50] Along the same line, Givens concludes, "In sum, there is simply little basis for arguing that the worldview of Joseph's era had any influence on the make-up of the Book of Mormon itself."[51] As a specialist in the literary history of the period in which the Book of Mormon emerged, I can state categorically that it is unlike any book written in the entire scope of American literature.

---

49. As Gordon Thomasson states, "Upon finding a possible parallel between the Book of Mormon and some bit of early American history, it is all too often assumed that the source for the idea has been found and further study is neglected or even ridiculed. Such an at-best naïve, reductionist approach ignores the fact that where parallels occur they almost invariably relate to what are perennial questions—themes which recur in countless religious histories—and which are by no means unique to the Burned-over District in space or time, and/or may correlate even more significantly with ancient evidence than it does with the more recent" ("Frontier," 9).

50. Richard L. Bushman, "The Book of Mormon and the American Revolution," in *Believing History: Latter-day Saint Essays,* ed. Reid L. Neilson and Jed Woodworth (New York: Columbia University Press, 2004), 47–64, esp. 57. Bushman states: "The Book of Mormon was an anomaly on the political scene of 1830. Instead of heroically resisting despots, the people of God fled their oppressors and credited God alone with deliverance. Instead of enlightened people overthrowing their kings in defense of their natural rights, the common people repeatedly raised up kings, and the prophets and the kings themselves had to persuade the people of the inexpediency of monarchy. Despite Mosiah's reforms, Nephite government persisted in monarchical practices, with life tenure for the chief judges, hereditary succession, and the combination of all functions in one official" (57).

51. *By the Hand of Mormon,* 169.

In conclusion, while I do not find the Book of Mormon a credible candidate as an automatic text, I believe it is more closely related to automatic writing than, say, normative narrative fiction, the former (in some instances) coming from some place outside the author's mind and imagination and the latter coming entirely from within them. That is, on the basis of what I rationally accept as evidence, there seem to be supernatural forces at work in some written communications, automatic or otherwise. Just as I accept the conclusion that Pearl Curran could not have been the author of the Patience Worth manuscripts and that some of the communications recorded by Dr. Schwartz could not be the products of the mediums they engaged in their experiments, so I don't believe that Joseph Smith was or could have been the author of the Book of Mormon.

9

Joseph Smith and the Writers of the American Renaissance

". . . a book I have made,
The words of my book nothing, the drift of it everything,
A book separate, not link'd with the rest nor felt by the
intellect,
But you ye untold latencies will thrill to every page."
—*Walt Whitman,* Leaves of Grass

In considering the provenance of the Book of Mormon, the central question is whether it is reasonable to argue that Joseph Smith could have written the book out of his native gifts, life experience, and formal and informal learning rather than translating it by some process from ancient records as he claimed. Could he reasonably be considered the book's author, given his literary imagination and talent; his maturity as a writer when the book was published; the amount of time he had to produce such a book; his education; his information/knowledge base; and the sophistication necessary to conceive, design, and execute such a complicated narrative with such a rich array of characters and so many varied literary forms and styles? In considering such questions, I believe it is helpful to compare Joseph Smith with authors who were his contemporaries, including those who constitute the pantheon of American Literature from early to mid-nineteenth century.

The Book of Mormon came out of the richest creative period of American culture, what the critic F.O. Matthiessen termed the "American Renaissance." In his book of the same title, subtitled *Art and Expression in the Age of Emerson and Whitman*,[1] Matthiessen chronicles what literary critic Van Wyck Brooks called "the Flowering of New England," which he identified as taking place between 1815 and 1865.[2] That flowering included such masterpieces as Poe's stories and poems (1827–1848), Emerson's *Essays* (1836–1850) Hawthorne's *Twice-Told Tales* (1837, 1842) and *The Scarlet Letter* (1850), Melville's *Moby Dick* (1851), Thoreau's *Walden* (1854), and Whitman's *Leaves of Grass* (1855), not to mention the astonishing poetry of Emily Dickinson and a host of minor masterpieces by other authors that were composed and published during the same period in which the Book of Mormon was published. Was the Book of Mormon a product of what David S. Reynolds has called "the subversive imagination in the age of Emerson and Melville" (the subtitle of his *Beneath the American Renaissance*),[3] or was it what Joseph Smith claimed it to be—an ancient sacred text whispering out of the ground to modern readers?

This chapter compares Joseph Smith with some of the major writers of the first half of the nineteenth century listed above in terms of their literary imagination and talent, education, cultural milieu,

---

1. *American Renaissance: Art and Expression in the Age of Emerson and Whitman* (New York: Oxford University Press, 1941). Hereinafter *American Renaissance*.
2. *The Flowering of New England* (New York: Dutton, 1952).
3. *Beneath the American Renaissance: The Subversive Imagination in the Age of Emerson and Melville* (Cambridge, Mass: Harvard University Press, 1988).

information/knowledge base, and sophistication. The following chapter will compare Joseph Smith and the composition of the Book of Mormon with the five major American writers discussed below in relation to their respective major literary compositions.

Literary Imagination and Talent

> *"The highest species of reasoning upon divine subjects is . . . the fruit of a sort of moral imagination."*
> —Emerson, Journal, 18 April 1824

> *"Blessed are those who have no talent."*
> —Emerson, Journal, February 1850

While many critics disagree on a number of aspects of Joseph Smith's character, there is almost universal agreement that he had an unusually creative and energetic imagination. Fawn Brodie, one of his early biographers, observed that "The rare quality of his genius was due not to his reason but to his imagination. He was a mythmaker of prodigious talent."[4] The late Harold Bloom, one of the preeminent humanistic scholars of our generation, praised Smith as being an authentic religious genius.[5] Yet, what we know of Joseph Smith at the time he produced the Book of Mormon reveals no proclivity for literary expression. That he was imaginative there is no doubt; that he had the ability to channel that imagination into what some critics regard as a five-hundred-page fictional narrative, there is substantial doubt. That is, there is an enormous difference between being able to conceive of something imaginatively and being able to shape it into a concrete, complex, and coherent artifact. Many of us may think of wonderful

---

4. *No Man Knows My History: The Life of Joseph Smith the Mormon Prophet*, 2nd ed. revised and enlarged (New York: Vintage Books, 1995), ix.
5. *The American Religion: The Emergence of the Post-Christian Nation* (New York: Chu Hartley, 1992), 73. Hereinafter *American Religion*.

novels we would like to write, or symphonies we would like to compose, or films we would like to direct, but only those with true gifts and the discipline and attention to both coherence and style are able to produce significant novels, symphonies, and films.

Was Joseph Smith a gifted creative writer? Did he possess narrative or fictional capabilities similar to those of such contemporaries as Cooper, Melville, or Hawthorne? Did he have any poetic ability similar to Dickinson, Emerson, Lowell, or Whitman? Was he a lesser light like John Neal, Louisa May Alcott, or William Gilmore Simms? Or could he even conceivably be placed in this latter category?

Although Harold Bloom praises Joseph Smith's charisma and imagination, he sees him as "an indifferent writer."[6] While in his own writings Smith achieves moments of eloquence, and while there is evidence he was beginning to develop a mature style by the time he was murdered, in none of his writings is there evidence of either the narrative or expressive complexity one finds in the Book of Mormon. In fact, as the literary critic Richard Rust claims, "I have spent a good deal of time reading the journals and letters of Joseph Smith, and I consider his style to differ markedly from the style (really, the styles) I find in the Book of Mormon."[7] In his *Understanding the Book of Mormon: A Reader's Guide,* Grant Hardy argues persuasively that the Book of Mormon has "three major narrators: Nephi, Mormon, and Moroni," each of whom "has a distinctive story, perspective, set of concerns, style, and sensibility. Furthermore, they have a sense of who their audience will be and they deliberately shape their message accordingly."[8]

The case Hardy makes demonstrates that those who consider Joseph Smith or one or several of his contemporaries as the author or authors of the Book of Mormon simply haven't read it carefully. Consider what it would have taken for Smith to have composed the

----

6. *American Religion,* 71.
7. Letter to Robert A. Rees, 20 July 2000.
8. *Understanding the Book of Mormon: A Reader's Guide* (Oxford: Oxford University Press, 2010), xiv, xv.

history of the Nephites while orally dictating the various sub-narratives and rhetorical styles found in the Book of Mormon. It would have required him to keep in mind not only the general sweep of the narratives with their respective complicated plots and subplots, but also the distinctive rhetorical styles and vocabulary of each major narrator and minor character. This would mean mentally cataloguing and somehow keeping track of the way each speaker expressed himself while dictating the narrative. For example, since Alma the Younger has by far the largest vocabulary of any figure in the Book of Mormon, were he composing the narrative, Smith would have had to be conscious of using vocabulary and patterns of speech peculiar to Alma that he would not use with any other speaker. Even if he had been a brilliant novelist and had had a photographic memory, it seems inconceivable that he would have been capable not only of imagining and constructing the narrative of the Book of Mormon, but that he would have had the ability (and the time!) to memorize what he had composed or written in order to dictate it in an essentially seamless manner. Why would he have chosen such a seemingly impossible means of producing his text when other, simpler choices were available to him?

I contend that not only was the composition of the Book of Mormon far beyond Joseph Smith's capabilities, but it is likely that he had no idea as to the subtleties and complexities of the text he was dictating. There is no evidence that he knew anything about writing intricate parallel literary structures, that he was able to invent the wide range of characters found in the Book of Mormon, that he had the inventiveness to create complicated fictional plots, that he had the ability to write in a variety of styles, or that he was able to invent the wide range of characters found in the Book of Mormon. In regard to the latter, Heather Hardy observes, "One source for my endless fascination with the Book of Mormon is that I think several of its characters—Nephi, Alma, and Moroni immediately come to mind—were careful, thoughtful, reflective intellectuals, which is not how I would characterize Joseph Smith, even in the Nauvoo period. I truly cannot imagine how anyone can create the words of characters that are demonstrably 'smarter'/more intellectually competent than you are."[9] Again, quoting from Harold Bloom, Joseph Smith's "life, personality, and visions far transcended his talents at the composition of divine texts."[10]

Education and Cultural Milieu

> "Books are for the scholars' idle times. When he can read God directly, the hour is too precious to be wasted in other men's transcripts of their readings."
> —Emerson, "The American Scholar"

All the authors of the American Renaissance had educations vastly superior to Joseph Smith's. Hawthorne graduated from Bowdoin and Emerson and Thoreau from Harvard. Melville attended Albany Academy, and Whitman, although having only about six years of formal education, was a schoolteacher, and for many years he engaged in various aspects of journalism, including reporting, writing, and editing. In addition, all these authors were intimately involved in the cultural life of their communities, attending lyceums and concerts, lecturing, publishing, and with the exception of Thoreau (who said, ironically, that he had "travelled a good deal in Concord"!), traveling far beyond their local environs, including to foreign lands and to large metropolises with their rich social, political, and cultural diversity. This is a stark contrast to the education and culture of Joseph Smith. His formal education was limited to only a few years of schooling, and that, most likely, involved sporadic attendance.[11] In his earliest history (1832), composed two years after the publication of the Book of Mormon,

---

9. Private correspondence in my possession.

10. *American Religion*, 72.

11. Dan Vogel postulates that in addition to attending school in Royalton, Vermont, between 1808 and 1813, Joseph may have attended school during other periods of his youth but that he "was probably not a regular attender" (*Early Mormon Documents*, Vol. 1 [Salt Lake City: Signature Books, 1996], Note 3, p. 27).

Smith summarized his education as follows: "We [the nine Smith children] were deprived of the bennifit of an education suffice it to say I was mearly instructid in reading and writing and the ground [rules] of arithmatic which constuted my whole literary acquirements"[12] (spelling and punctuation in the original).

For the writers of the American Renaissance, not only is there evidence of early compositions that influenced their masterpieces, but there is ample evidence that they all benefited from being part of a literary culture, one that was full of cross-fertilization. Emerson's influence on Thoreau and Whitman is well documented, as is Hawthorne's on Melville, and vice versa. Although Emerson's shadow on the age is the longest, Emerson himself reveals and acknowledges indebtedness to a number of writers, including Swedenborg, Carlyle, Coleridge, and Goethe.

While there is no question that Joseph Smith was significantly indebted to the King James Bible in terms of style and language, where, one wants to ask, are the European or American writers who served as models or inspiration for him? There are no allusions in his writings or in the Book of Mormon to such important writers and thinkers of American culture as Cotton Mather, Edward Taylor, John Neal, James Fenimore Cooper, Charles Brockden Brown, Washington Irving, or even the more popular writers of the time who were, as David S. Reynolds says, "part of a heterogeneous culture which had strong elements of the criminal, the erotic, and the demonic."[13]

The popular hunger for such sensational, sentimental literature seems not to have infiltrated Joseph Smith's creative imagination. Reynolds describes the "seamy fiction" written in "a succinctly American irrational style whose linguistic wildness and dislocations were also visible in the grotesque American humor that arose during this period."[14]

---

12. The Personal Writings of Joseph Smith, ed., Dean C. Jessee (Salt Lake City: Deseret Book, 1984), 4.

13. *Beneath the American Renaissance: The Subversive Imagination in the Age of Emerson and Melville* (Cambridge, Harvard University Press, 1988), 169. Hereinafter *Beneath the American Renaissance*).

14. *Beneath the American Renaissance,* 170.

It is curious that Reynolds makes no mention of the Book of Mormon, possibly the most subversive text written in nineteenth-century America (in the sense that it had the potential to overturn so many established ideas about religion and culture). Literary historian Daniel Walker Howe observes that "the Book of Mormon should rank among the great achievements of American literature, but it has never been accorded the literary stature it deserves."[15] One might add, even among the majority of Latter-day Saint readers.

Harold Bloom in *The American Religion* has praised Joseph Smith in relation to his contemporary writers, although more as charismatic creator of a new religion than as a writer: "I myself can think of not another American, except for Emerson and Whitman, who so moves and alters my own imagination. . . . So self-educated was he that he transcends Emerson and Whitman in my imaginative response, and takes his place with the great figures of our fiction, since at moments he appears larger than life, in the mode of a Shakespearean character. So rich and varied a personality, so vital a spark of divinity, is almost beyond the limits of the human, as we normally construe those limits."[16] Like other critics, Bloom offers no proof of Joseph's self-education but simply takes it for granted.

And yet Bloom, a master at deciphering and delineating texts, seems to have missed much of the intricate complexity of the Book of Mormon. He saw it, along with other scriptures in the Latter-day Saint canon, as "stunted step-children of the Bible."[17] One could argue that the standard chapter and verse organization and formatting of the Book of Mormon as scripture likely kept many readers, including Bloom, from seeing its literary richness. Grant Hardy freed the book from such limitations when he produced his reformatted text, *The*

---

15. *What Hath God Wrought? The Transformation of America, 1815–1848* (Oxford: Oxford University Press, 2009), 314; hereinafter, *What Hath God Wrought?*
16. *American Religion*, 129.
17. *Ibid.*, 72.

Book of Mormon: A Reader's Edition,[18] thus making much more available and transparent for readers.

Frankly, I don't believe Bloom gave the book his best critical effort. This seems evident from his comment, "I cannot recommend that the book [of Mormon] be read either fully or closely, because it scarcely sustains such reading."[19] That a scholar of Bloom's reputation could conclude that the Book of Mormon was the result of "magical trance-states" only demonstrates, once again, that scholars like Bloom (who says he sees "all religion [as] a kind of spilled poetry"[20]) have difficulty seriously considering any non-naturalist explanation of the book's origin. In private conversation, one of Bloom's former students told me that Bloom confessed to him that he had not read the Book of Mormon! Bloom would not be the first critic to have an opinion of the book without having read it. As we know, it is even possible to compose a successful Broadway musical about the book with practically no knowledge of its contents.

Information/Knowledge Base:
What Did Joseph Smith Know?

And I know that the hand of God is the promise of my own,
And I know that the spirit of God is the brother of my own.
—Walt Whitman, Song of Myself, *Stanza 5*

In an interview with her son, Joseph Smith III, Emma Smith, who knew Joseph more intimately than anyone, said her husband had limited knowledge of spelling and "could neither write nor dictate a coherent and well worded letter; let alone dictate a book like the book of Mormon." She added, "I am satisfied that no man could have dictated

---

18. (Urbana, ILL: University of Illinois Press, 2005). Hardy has also edited a study edition of The Book of Mormon published by The Maxwell Institute.
19. *American Religion,* 78.
20. *Ibid.*

the writing of the manuscripts unless he was inspired; for, when acting as his scribe, your father would dictate to me hour after hour; and when returning after meals, or after interruptions, he would at once begin where he had left off, without either seeing the manuscript or having any portion of it read to him. This was a usual thing for him to do. It would have been improbable that a learned man could do this, and for one as unlearned as he was it was simply impossible."[21]

Hiram Page spoke of Joseph's inability to produce such a book on his own: "[It would be unreasonable] to say that a man of Joseph's ability, who at that time did not know how to pronounce the word Nephi, could write a book of six hundred pages, as correct as the book of Mormon, without supernatural power . . ."[22] David Whitmer said, "Sometimes Joseph could not pronounce the words correctly, having had but little education."[23]

Early theories that Smith copied the book from another author or that it was written by Oliver Cowdery or someone else were based on the assumption by those who knew him that Joseph Smith simply did not have the education, intelligence, or talent to write such a book. According to Louis Midgley, "The gossip about the presumed activities of the young Joseph Smith published in [E. D.] Howe's book yield a portrait of someone incapable of the intellectual effort necessary to produce a long, complicated history like the Book of Mormon."[24] Richard Bushman says, "We must remember that he was only twenty-two, truly unlearned,

21. "Last Testimony of Sister Emma," *Saints' Herald* 26 (1879), 290, in Dan Vogel, ed. *Early Mormon Documents*, 5 vols. (Salt Lake City: Signature Books, 1996–2003), 1:538–39.

22. Letter to William E. McLellin, 30 May 1847, *Ensign of Liberty*, 1 (January 1848): 63, as quoted in Richard L. Anderson, "Personal Writings of the Book of Mormon Witnesses," in Noel B. Reynolds, ed., *Book of Mormon Authorship Revisited: The Evidence for Ancient Origins* (Provo, UT: Foundation for Ancient Research and Mormon Studies), 25. Hereinafter *BMAR*.

23. James H. Hart interview, 1884, as quoted in Royal Skousen, "Translating the Book of Mormon: Evidence from the Original Manuscript," *BMAR*, 66.

24. "Who Really Wrote the Book of Mormon? The Critics and Their Theories," *BMAR*, 110.

with no worldly standing, living in an obscure rural backwater, and with only a few visionary glimpses of what lay ahead."[25]

How much of the information contained in the Book of Mormon would have been available to someone living in Joseph Smith's environs prior to the publication of the book? Latter-day Saint scholar Gordon C. Thomasson contends, "Critics of, and apologists for, the Book of Mormon have at various times both under- and over-estimated the extent of the information environment of early America, and especially the Burned-over district."[26] Of the information that could have been found in Joseph Smith's information environment, one has to ask the extent to which he was likely to have had access to it. Beyond that is the more serious question—the extent to which he was capable of integrating such information into a composition of his own devising.

What would a relatively uneducated person living on the edge of the American frontier have needed to know in order to write a history of ancient Hebrew peoples who emigrated to the New World? Here are a few of the many things, selected almost at random:

1. He would have had to have a deep and thorough knowledge of the Bible. Like nearly every American living in America during the early part of the nineteenth century, Joseph Smith was heavily influenced by the King James Bible, the most ubiquitous text in America thanks to the American Bible Society which distributed 21 million copies between 1816 and 1866 (to a population of 31 million).[27] Everyone read the Bible and many considered it the only essential text (*sola scriptora*), because it was

25. "The Recovery of the Book of Mormon," *BMAR*, 29.

26. "'Daddy, What's a 'Frontier?': Thoughts on the 'Information Environment' That Supposedly Produced the Book of Mormon," unpublished MS in my possession, 18. Hereinafter "Frontier." Thomasson provides a detailed account as to what information might have been available to someone living in Eastern New York in the late 1820s.

27. *What Hath God Wrought?*, 47.

believed to contain all the truth necessary for salvation. Joseph's contemporary Alexander Campbell was of the opinion that "[t]he Bible contains more real learning than all the volumes of men."[28]

How well did Joseph know the Bible? In her memoirs, Lucy Mack Smith recalled that as a boy of eighteen (i.e., in 1823 or 1824, six years before the publication of the Book of Mormon) Joseph "had never read the Bible through in his life." Moreover, she said, "he seemed much less inclined to the perusal of books than any of the rest of our children."[29] Bloom's contention that "Smith had drowned in the Bible, and came up from it in a state of near identification with the ancient Hebrews"[30] is speculative, at best, and is really quite incredible when one considers that "absorbing" the Bible is a far cry from being able to replicate its forms, styles, and patterns in highly specific, sophisticated ways. And this must be seen in light not only of Lucy Mack Smith's statement about her son's acquaintance with the Bible but David Whitmer's observation about Joseph during the time he was translating the record of Lehi: "In translating the characters Smith, who was illiterate and but little versed in biblical lore, was oftentimes compelled to spell the words out, not knowing the correct pronunciation."[31]

Joseph acknowledged his indebtedness to the Bible. In his earliest account of his first vision, he reports, "At about the age of twelve years, my mind [had] become seriously impressed with regard to the all-important concerns for the welfare of my immortal soul, which led me to searching the scriptures—believing, as I was taught, that they

---

28. *What Hath God Wrought?*, 446.

29. Lavina Fielding Andersen, ed., *Lucy's Book: A Critical Edition of Lucy Mack Smith's Memoir* (Salt Lake City: Signature Books, 2001), 344.

30. *American Religion*, 78.

31. Lyndon W. Cook, ed., *David Whitmer Interviews: A Restoration Witness* (Orem, Utah: Grandin, 1991), 174, as quoted in Royal Skousen, "Translating the Book of Mormon: Evidence from the Original Manuscript," *BAMR*, 76.

contained the word of God and thus applying myself to them."[32] It is, however, one thing to have studied the Bible and quite another to have known it so intimately and thoroughly as to have created an entire new scripture based on its language, narrative variety, rhetorical styles, and compositional complexity. That is, Joseph could have been influenced by the Bible, but he couldn't have relied on the Bible for some of the more esoteric and previously unknown material found in the Book of Mormon, nor would extensive knowledge of the Bible have been sufficient for him to construct a narrative like the Book of Mormon.

Is it reasonable to conclude, given the hardscrabble nature of his life prior to the publication of the Book of Mormon, that Joseph Smith would have had time to immerse himself so completely in the Hebrew scripture as to have mastered its literary styles and cultural complexities? When he states that Smith imaginatively recovered "elements of the archaic Jewish theurgy" (which had evaded both "normative Judaism" and Christianity, Bloom was speaking more of the Pearl of Great Price than the Bible.[33]

What else would he have needed to know?

2. As pointed out in Chapter 8, he would have had to know how to take his characters from Jerusalem through the Arabian Desert. Again quoting Eugene England, "For Joseph Smith to have so well succeeded in producing over twenty unique details in the description of an ancient travel route through one of the least-known areas of the world, all of which have been subsequently verified, requires extraordinary, unreasonable faith in his natural genius or his ability to guess right in direct opposition to the prevailing knowledge of his time."[34]

---

32. "First Vision Accounts," https://www.churchofjesuschrist.org/study/manual/gospel-topics-essays/first-vision-accounts

33. *American Religion*, 99.

34. "Through the Arabian Desert to a Bountiful Land: Could Joseph Smith Have Known the Way?" *BAMR*, 153.

3. He would have had to know that the use of Baal and El names were out of favor during Lehi's time but not during the time of the Jaredites.[35] I would guess that even if Joseph Smith understood the significance of such names, he would have had no idea when it was and wasn't appropriate to use them in his text.

4. He would have had to have a thorough knowledge of olive horticulture. How likely is it that someone raised on an American farm would have known the detailed information contained in Zenos's parable of the olive tree? Joseph Smith would have known wheat and beans, but he wouldn't have known beans about olives![36] Those who speculate that he could have found this information in books or other sources have failed to identify those sources or demonstrate that Smith had or could have had access to them.

5. He would have had to know the rich variety of Hebraic literary forms and devices, including chiasmus—not only to know that chiasmus was an ancient poetic form and mnemonic device, but also to be able to compose numerous examples, some of them extremely complex, and to dictate them spontaneously. As John W. Welch has stated, the Book of Mormon, "especially in its most literary portions, is replete with precise and extensive

---

35. *Collected Works of Hugh Nibley* (Salt Lake City: Deseret Book, 1989), Vol.8, 387–388.

36. See Wilford M. Hess, "Botanical Comparisons in the Allegory of the Olive Tree," *The Book of Mormon: Jacob through Words of Mormon*, ed. Monte S. Nyman and Charles D. Tate, Jr. (Provo, UT: Brigham Young University Press, 1990), 87–102. Gordon C. Thomasson cites Johannes Jahn's *Biblical Archeology* (1823) as reporting that in Arabian culture "a subtle olive culture was practiced in which the branches of wild olives were grafted into barren orchard trees to cause them to become fertile" ("Frontier," p. 36). This shard of information, however, could hardly account for the many specific particulars of olive horticulture found in the book of Jacob.

chiastic compositions." After citing an example of chiasmus in Mosiah 5:10–12, Welch, states, "Again, the
repetition here is precise, extensive and meaningful. It
simply strains reason to imagine that such structure in
this oration occurred accidentally." Welch concludes,
"The use of chiasmus is . . . a conscious creation of an
imaginative and mature artist. . . . No one seriously
contends that Joseph Smith or anyone associated with
him knew or could have known of chiasmus or had the
training to discover this principle for himself. The evidence is overwhelming against such a claim."[37] This is
not external, but internal evidence. That is, the chiasms
(at least some of those so identified) are clearly there;
they are not the invention of modern readers. No naturalist critic of whom I am aware has seriously answered
the question as to their origin.[38] As Mark Thomas says
in "A Rhetorical Approach to the Book of Mormon,"

---

37. "What Does Chiasmus in the Book of Mormon Prove?" *BMAR*, 205, 207, 208.
See also Welch, "Chiasmus in the Book of Mormon," in Welch, ed., *Chiasmus in
Antiquity: Structures, Analyses, Exegesis* (Hildesheim: Gerstenberg, 1981).

38. In a paper presented at the August 2001 Sunstone Symposium in Salt Lake City
entitled, "The Use and Abuse of Chiasmus in Book of Mormon Studies," Dan Vogel
argues "that there are fundamental problems with the whole theory of chiasmus"
(p. 1, typescript in my possession). While Vogel is correct in postulating that some
scholars have played fast and loose in finding chiasmus in the Book of Mormon,
and while his challenging of some purported examples of chiasmus is persuasive,
the facts remains that there are examples of genuine chiasmus in the Book of
Mormon and that even non-chiastic parallel passages required either conscious
composition or absorption of parallel structures so completely as to produce them
unconsciously, which strains credibility. There is a difference between the simple
parallel structures which Vogel finds in the writings of Joseph Smith and others and
the sometimes lengthy, intricate, and complex parallel forms one finds in the Book
of Mormon as, for example, in Mosiah 5 and Alma 36. It is the presence of such
examples that has yet to be explained as coming out of Joseph Smith's information
environment or from his inventive mind.

"Letting the text speak requires attention, sincerity, and integrity."[39]

Those who assisted Joseph in the translation of the Book of Mormon testified that he dictated the narrative of the people of Lehi at times for hours on end, day after day, without notes or reference materials, and that, repeating Emma's report quoted earlier, he would pick up the dictation the following day at the very place where he left off, with no prompting to tell him where the narrative had ended or was to continue. Had he been "free-composing" his narrative, rather than translating as he claimed, he would have had to keep in his consciousness not only the various threads of his narration, but the structure and intricate pattern of the history he was inventing, the array of characters who peopled that history, the cultural and religious traditions that informed their lives, and the various forms of their literary style.

Consider the magnitude of such a feat. To my knowledge, in all of literary history there is not a single example to match such an accomplishment. The only thing to approach it is the theorized ancient oral spinning of epic tales, but that was done only by poets who had spent years memorizing vast "word hoards" of narrative formulae, tropes and images which they would then weave into constantly changing epic poems. If Joseph Smith composed the Book of Mormon out of his imagination and in the manner in which his scribes said he did (and we have no reason to disbelieve them), I can't think of any writer who has accomplished such a feat. As shown in Chapter 11, John Milton dictated his epic poem *Paradise Lost* only after a lifetime of study and writing and only with the help of scribes who could read his text back to him for approval or correction.

---

39. *New Approaches*, 55.

Sophistication

> *"I always feel like drinking that heroic drink [brandy] when we talk ontological heroics together."*
> —*Melville to Hawthorne, 29 June 1851*

Joseph Smith was, according to contemporary accounts, a rather typical frontier figure with little education, culture, or polish. Jan Shipps, a leading non-Mormon scholar, calls him "an unsophisticated farm boy."[40] From all we can tell, by his early twenties he had little knowledge of history, languages, politics, or the arts and humanities. Except for a few passages in the Doctrine and Covenants and some of his sermons, all of which were written after he had expanded his education (much of it by self-education), there is nothing in Joseph Smith's other writing that reveals what we might call a sophisticated literary style. In fact, like many of his American contemporaries, he wrote in a plain style. This is very different from the style or styles one finds in the Book of Mormon.

As reported in an earlier chapter, I first learned of the literary complexity of the Book of Mormon from my BYU teacher and mentor, Robert Thomas. Thomas, who had written his undergraduate thesis at Reed College on the Book of Mormon as Hebrew literature, was the first scholar to see the book's intricate biblical parallelism.[41] Richard Dilworth Rust in his valuable study, *Feasting on the Word: The Literary Testimony of the Book of Mormon*,[42] gives a much more detailed and comprehensive analysis of the book's many literary forms and styles, thus opening the text in many new ways. A number of other scholars, including especially Grant Hardy, have identified elements in the Book of Mormon that give evidence of an elevated level of intelligence, sophistication, and compositional artistry.

---

40. "The Mormons: Looking Forward and Outward," in *Where the Spirit Leads: American Denominations Today*, ed., Martin E. Marty (Richmond, Va.: John Knox, 1980), 29–30, as quoted in Midgley, *BMAR*, 103.
41. "A Literary Analysis of the Book of Mormon," A.B. thesis, Reed College, 1947.
42. (Salt Lake City: Deseret Book, 1997).

Another distinguishing mark of a sophisticated mind is the conscious use of irony. As discussed in Chapter 7, "Irony and the Book of Mormon," the Book of Mormon contains examples of verbal and dramatic irony similar to that distinguished by classical rhetoricians and used by classical authors, including the writers of Hebrew scripture. The book is also devoid of the style of irony popular in Joseph Smith's frontier environs, including the tall tale, earthy language, regional dialect, deliberate overstatement, and exaggeration characteristic of what is known as Southwestern humor—of which, judging from his sometimes colorful language and use of humor, he most certainly was aware. It is important to note that Joseph Smith's own early writing is devoid of the conscious use of irony, which is what one would expect in a naïve writer.

Conclusion

> "In this world of lies, Truth is forced to fly like a scared white doe in the woodlands; and only by cunning glimpses will she reveal herself, as in Shakespeare and other masters of the great Art of Telling the Truth—even though it be covertly, and by snatches."
>
> —Melville's review of Hawthorne's Mosses

I have tried to demonstrate that Joseph Smith did not possess the literary imagination or talent, the authorial maturity, the education, the knowledge base, or the sophistication necessary to write the Book of Mormon; nor, had he possessed all of these, was the time and circumstance under which the book was produced sufficient for him to have composed such a lengthy and elaborate narrative.

As a scholar, I believe that the best and most inclusive, as well as most persuasive, objective evidence leads to the conclusion that no one living in the world in the 1820s, let alone an untutored, inglorious farmer, could have produced the Book of Mormon. And yet it bears the unmistakable imprint of Joseph Smith's own nineteenth-century mind and heart. By that I mean that the words on the pages of the book came through his mind and native tongue as he saw and dictated the text.

Coda

Not "Revelation" 'tis that waits,
But our unfurnished eyes.
—Emily Dickinson, Letter to
Thomas Wentworth Higginson, 1862–63

When he gave his Address to the Divinity School at Harvard in 1838, Emerson made a dramatic break from both traditional Christianity and from the long line of clergymen in his own family. He scandalized the faculty with his call for "perpetual revelation" ("It is my duty to say to you that the need was never greater of new revelation than now"; "God is, not was; . . . He speaketh, not spake") and for personal revelation ("Intuition . . . cannot be received at second hand").[43] Emerson, who had been trained to be a minister, but who early broke with the Congregational Church over what he saw as a distortion of the teachings of Jesus, had come to the conclusion, to use the words spoken several decades before in the Sacred Grove to the boy Joseph Smith, that the creeds of the churches "were an abomination" and that their ministers "were all corrupt." He spoke words that Joseph himself might have said: "Men have come to speak of . . . revelation as somewhat long ago given and done, as if God were dead."[44]

Had Ralph Waldo Emerson met Joseph Smith, I believe he would have felt an immediate affinity to and kinship with him and would have recognized the prophetic mantle of his visionary countryman. He might have recognized him as the prophet he himself imagined coming to the New World: "I look for the hour when that supreme

---

43. "Address [to the Divinity School]," *Ralph Waldo Emerson: Essays and Lectures* (New York: Literary Classics of the United States, 1983), 79, 83. Hereinafter "Address."
44. "Address," 83.

Beauty, which ravished the souls of those Eastern men, and chiefly of those Hebrews, and through their lips spoke oracles to all time, shall speak in the West also. . . . I look for the new Teacher that shall follow so far those shining laws that he shall see them come full circle; shall see their rounding complete grace; shall see the world to be the mirror of the soul; shall see the identity of the law of gravitation with purity of heart; and shall show that the Ought, that Duty, is one thing with Science, with Beauty, and with Joy."[45]

As noted earlier, Harold Bloom placed Joseph Smith in the same pantheon as Emerson and Whitman. He adds, "Ralph Waldo Emerson and Walt Whitman were great writers. . . . Joseph Smith did not excel as a writer or as a theologian, . . . but he was an authentic religious genius, and surpassed all Americans, before or since, in the possession and expression of what could be called the religion-making imagination."[46] That imagination may have allowed for revolutionary "religion making," as Bloom believes, but it did not lead to the kind of literary expression and composition that characterize the Book of Mormon. That is, there is simply too much evidence of its being an ancient text to consider the Book of Mormon as a novel, speculative fiction, or other product of the imagination.

As mentioned earlier, the period of spiritual and imaginative expression that flowered in early to mid-nineteenth-century America is called the Age of Emerson, but given the growing reputation of the Vermont farm boy and the book he miraculously brought forth to the world (which is more widely read than any book written in the nineteenth century), one could speculate that at some time in the future this same period might be renamed the Age of Joseph Smith.

---

45. "Address," 91–92.
46. *American Religion*, 96–97.

The Conception and Creation of a Major Work of Literature

"A good Book is the precious life-blood of a master spirit, embalmed and treasured up on purpose to a life beyond life."
—*John Milton,* Areopagitica

What I attempted to show in the previous chapter is that in comparison with the major writers of the American Renaissance, at the time he produced the Book of Mormon, Joseph Smith lacked the compositional skills, literary gifts, and cultural background necessary to write a book as structurally complex, rhetorically varied, and culturally "strange" as the Book of Mormon (by strange, I mean the Egyptian, Hebrew, and New World elements one finds in the history of these Promised Land peoples). That is, Emerson, Thoreau, Hawthorne, Melville, and Whitman all had educations superior to Joseph Smith's, all lived under more substantial and stable socio-economic conditions, and all had much greater family, community, and cultural environments to support their writing than he did.

Recently in working on a dramatic script about Emerson and his contemporaries while at the same time teaching the Book of Mormon at Graduate Theological Union and the University of California, Berkeley, I realized there was an important dimension of the comparison between the American prophet and his contemporaries to which I had not given sufficient consideration: the biographical and bibliographical context in which each writer produced his magnum opus. This chapter is an attempt to address that dimension because it completes the picture of these writers and their respective places in this incredibly fertile chapter of American literary and cultural history in relation to the Mormon prophet and the book with which he is most closely and famously identified.

In his great novel *Moby-Dick*, Melville has a chapter titled "Try-Works," about the two large kettles or "try pots" situated on the decks of nineteenth-century whaling ships that were used to "try out" or reduce whale oil by boiling the blubber. As with many of the elements and episodes in the novel, try-works can symbolize various things. One of the ways in which *try-works* functions is as a symbol of the process of writing, the fire of discipline and imagination necessary to boil away the rhetorical blubber that plagues most authors, especially in their early years. In this sense, it stands for the process a successful writer must go through in order to refine and perfect his or her craft. Thus, for Melville, the five novels he wrote prior to *Moby-Dick* (*Typee, Omoo, Mardi, Redburn,* and *White-Jacket*) constitute the try-works that prepared him for the more complex rhetorical style, universal themes, and timeless scope of *Moby-Dick* as well as the subtleties and other stylistic felicities that constitute the novel's amazing ontological density.

Melville was aware he had written a much deeper, more profound novel than his previous works of fiction, which is evident in his response to Hawthorne's praise of *Moby-Dick*: "I have written a wicked book, and feel spotless as the lamb. Ineffable socialities are in me. I would sit down and dine with you and all the gods in old Rome's Pantheon. It is a strange feeling—no hopefulness is in it, no despair. . . . I speak now of my profoundest sense of being, not of an incidental feeling. . . . I feel that the Godhead is broken up like the bread at the Supper, and that we are the pieces."[1]

Compositional Maturity

In order to produce a mature work of literature, a writer has to be seasoned in the craft of literary invention, construction, and revision. Few if any masterpieces spring fully formed from the writer's mind and imagination without prior experience in working out style, scope, and subject matter. Without exception, Joseph Smith's contemporary authors produced their major works when they were mature writers. Each writer's magnum opus took years in preparation and a substantial period of time in composition and revision. The works of each author show progressive development from early literary expressions to later master works. In most cases their early works reveal writers attempting to find their voice as well as their subject matter. For example, although, as the critic F. O. Matthiessen observes, Emerson's *Nature* "contains in embryo nearly all his cardinal assumptions,"[2] the essay is philosophically opaque and stylistically dense. Even though Hawthorne's early style "shows remarkable finish,"[3] the contrast between his first novel, *Fanshaw* (1828), and *The Scarlet Letter* (1850) is dramatic. This is also true of Melville, who stated in a letter to Hawthorne in June 1851 when he was thirty-two, "My development has been all within a few years past. . . . From my twenty-fifth year [when his first novel was published] I date my life. Three weeks have scarcely passed, at any time between

---

1. Melville to Hawthorne, 17 November 1851, www.melville.org/letter7.htm.
2. *American Renaissance*, 12.
3. *American Renaissance*, 203.

then and now, that I have not unfolded within myself."[4] But, as his first novel (*Typee*) written at this time reveals, his development had scarcely begun. Whitman's early journalistic writing reveals only the vaguest promise of the powerful poetry that he would later produce. In fact, it wasn't until he read Emerson's comments on the first edition of *Leaves of Grass* (1855) that he seemed to fully realize his vocation as a poet. As he later wrote, "I was simmering, simmering, simmering; Emerson brought me to a boil."[5]

By way of comparison, we have only two minor extant examples of Joseph Smith's writings before 1830, the year the Book of Mormon was published—a letter to Oliver Cowdery and a one-paragraph introduction to the "Anthon Transcript."[6] Neither shows any promise of literary expression. In fact, there is no evidence before 1830 that Smith was developing as a writer or that he had any ambitions as an author. The material written in the years immediately following the publication of the Book of Mormon shows Smith as a writer with little literary style or polish. His handwritten account of the First Vision written in 1832 is ungrammatical, is written with little sense of punctuation or compositional structure, and, though sincere and authentic, shows little evidence of stylistic or compositional confidence. Certainly, there is evidence of the beginnings of an eloquent voice, but that voice is tentative and immature. Nowhere in Joseph Smith's early writing does one find evidence of the kind of literary skill necessary to write a book which has been translated into more languages and sold more copies than any book written by his illustrious contemporaries.

---

4. http://www.melville.org/letter3.htm.

5. *American Renaissance*, 523.

6. In his *Early Mormon Documents* (Salt Lake City: Signature, 1996), Dan Vogel lists Smith's letter to Oliver Cowdery of 22 October 1829 as the only extant pre-Book of Mormon document written by Joseph Smith (Vol. 1, 223–24). Dean C. Jessee includes the introduction to the Anthon Transcript as possibly having been written in 1828 (*The Personal Writings of Joseph Smith* [Salt Lake City: Deseret Books, 1984]), 224. Hereinafter *Personal Writings*.

By way of comparison, Nathaniel Hawthorne had in a sense been composing *The Scarlet Letter* for twenty-five years before it was actually published. That is, most of the themes, character types, and situations in his novel were developed to one extent or another in the notes, sketches, and stories he wrote from 1825 to 1850. As to the actual time of the writing of the novel, Arlin Turner notes that by the end of August 1849, Hawthorne "was writing immensely, so his wife phrased it."[7] Typically, Hawthorne would put in nine hours a day at his desk. He wrote his friend Horatio Bridge that the book had been finished on February 3, 1850,[8] making a total of more than five months' time for the novel's composition.

Melville's previous novels of the sea were all novels in which he was working out both his subject matter and his style. *Moby Dick*, which took him more than eighteen months to complete, reveals indebtedness to all of his earlier works. At the same age at which Joseph Smith produced a book as large as *Moby Dick*, Melville was just beginning to feel confident as a writer, and *Moby Dick* was still far in the future.

Henry David Thoreau spent nearly nine years writing *Walden, or Life in the Woods.* His early compositions both prepared him for and contained many of the ideas and themes of his major opus. Ralph Waldo Emerson wrote nothing as sustained as *The Book of Mormon*, but his essays, which represent his major contribution to the literary age that bears his name, were produced over a lifetime. Walt Whitman wrote and rewrote his great collection of poems, *Leaves of Grass*, over his entire adult life, seeing it through many permutations and numerous editions.

Thus, each of these authors was significantly older and more mature as a writer when he published his literary masterpiece. Emerson was thirty-eight when his first volume of essays was published, Thoreau was thirty-seven when he published *Walden*, Hawthorne was forty-six when

---

7. *Nathaniel Hawthorne, a Biography* (New York: Oxford University Press, 1980), 187, 193.
8. *Personal Recollections of Nathaniel Hawthorne* (New York: Harper and Brothers, 1893), 100.

The Scarlet Letter was published, and Melville thirty-two when *Moby Dick* was published. Whitman was thirty-six when he sent an autographed first edition of *Leaves of Grass* to Emerson. Based on what he had written before the publication of the Book of Mormon when he was twenty-four, Joseph Smith could hardly have been considered a writer at all.

Time

> *"Time is but the stream I go a-fishing in."*
> —*Thoreau,* Walden

All writers know that writing takes time and generally lots of it to get the writing right. As the venerated American poet Donald Hall said, "It's typical for me to spend three to five years on a poem, but not working on it every day but maybe every day for six months, then nothing for six months, then starting it again. At the beginning, every draft changes a lot, but toward the end I may spend a lot of time changing a word from the end of one line to the beginning of the next. . . . There are several poems I've worked on over twenty years."[9]

In an article entitled "For Authors, Fragile Ideas Need Loving Every Day," the novelist Walter Mosley speaks of the importance of a routinized, disciplined approach to writing. Arguing that writing is a quotidian endeavor, Mosley says that interruptions and distractions (which Joseph Smith experienced in abundance during the translation of the Book of Mormon) cause the life to drain out of one's writing: "The words have no art to them; you no longer remember the smell. The idea seems weak, it has dissipated like smoke." He adds, "Nothing we create is art at first. It's simply a collection of notions that may never be understood. Returning every day thickens the atmosphere. Images appear. Connections are made. But even these clearer notions will fade if you stay away more than a day. . . . The act of writing is a kind of

---

9. *The Language of Life: A Festival of Poets*, ed., James Haba (New York: Doubleday, 1995), 144. Hereinafter, *Language of Life*.

guerrilla warfare; there is no vacation, no leave, no relief. In actuality there is very little chance of victory. You are . . . likely to be defeated by your fondest dreams."[10]

Most writers recognize that good writing is seldom easy and rarely flows seamlessly from the writer's pen or keyboard, and certainly, as the chapter on Milton and the Book of Mormon in this collection reveals, not in unprepared or unrehearsed dictation. The more complicated, complex, and sophisticated the text, the more time it takes to compose. While some writers speak of writing mellifluously flowing lines as if under a spell, in reality this seldom happens, and if it does, it doesn't last. When asked about the place of impulse or inspiration in writing poetry, Hall states, "It's twenty seconds of impulse and two years of attention."[11]

How much time did Joseph Smith have to write the Book of Mormon? This much seems to be part of the historical record: After losing the first 116 pages of the book through Martin Harris's negligence, Joseph did not resume his work of translation until 22 September 1828 when he was twenty-two years old, although even then he seems to have written little until Oliver Cowdrey became his scribe on 5 April 1829. Between that date and 30 June 1829, a period of approximately eighty-five days, Joseph and Oliver completed the bulk of the translation. By any measure, that is an astonishing accomplishment. As a straight work of translation or dictation alone, this would be a formidable task.

Scholars have noted that during the time he was translating the book, Smith was plagued with numerous mundane concerns—moving his family from Harmony to the Whitmer farm, finding work, feeding his family, protecting the plates, and other pressing concerns. In other words, there were so many stresses and strains that, for the most part, sustained, daily writing would have been impossible.

The Book of Mormon is a complicated narrative with many twists, turns, returns, foreshadowings, and allusions; numerous kinds of

---

10. *New York Times*, 3 July 2000, B2.
11. *Language of Life*, 146, 143.

parallelism reflective of Hebrew scripture, including extensive and complicated chiasms; and many different expressive styles. This is not the kind of book one dashes off in a few months as one might a romance novel. As a conscious composition, this kind of writing takes time, deep and deliberate thinking, and rigorous revision. As theologian Marcus Bach observed many years ago, the Book of Mormon "was solemn and ponderous and heavy as the plates on which it was inscribed. No Vermont schoolboy wrote this, and no Presbyterian preacher [Solomon Spaulding] tinkered with these pages."[12]

My intention here, as in the previous chapter, is to consider in comparison with Joseph Smith the respective intellectual, emotional, and cultural states of his contemporary writers and the circumstances and conditions under which they created their most important work—those for which history most remembers them. Let's consider each in his turn.

Ralph Waldo Emerson (1805–1882)[13]

Emerson was likely the most influential writer and thinker of his generation. Today he is remembered as a poet and quasi-philosopher, but during the period in which he flourished, he was recognized as somewhat of a prophet and sage, which is why this period is sometimes referred to as the Age of Emerson. Emerson was fortunate to

---

12. *Faith and My Friends* (New York: Bobbs-Merrill, 1951), 255.

13. While any standard critical biography presents the facts of the compositional evolution for each of the respective authors of the American Renaissance discussed here, the reader is referred to F. O. Matthiessen's groundbreaking *American Renaissance*, mentioned above. For more specific information, the following are excellent sources: Robert D. Richardson, Jr., *Emerson: The Mind on Fire* (Berkeley: University of California Press, 1995); Robert D. Richardson, Jr., *Thoreau: A Life of the Mind* (Berkeley: University of California Press, 1988); David S. Reynolds, *Walt Whitman's America: A Cultural Biography* (New York: Alfred A. Knopf, 1995); Hyatt Waggoner, *Hawthorne: A Critical Study* (Cambridge, MA: Harvard University Press, 1955); Hershel Parker, *Melville: A Biography: Vol 1, 1819–1851; Vol 2, 1851,–1891.* (Baltimore: Johns Hopkins University Press, 1996, 2005).

be blessed with conditions conducive to producing an accomplished writer. He had an excellent education at the Boston Latin School and Harvard College (from which he graduated at age eighteen) and Harvard Divinity School (age twenty-two), published his first article at age nineteen, travelled to Europe when he was twenty-nine, and gave his first public lecture when he was thirty. He published his first major piece, *Nature*, when he was thirty-three. In addition, he was a prolific correspondent and an indefatigable keeper of journals (running to some ten published volumes) in which he worked out many of the ideas and stylistic expressions for his writing and public speaking. For the next nearly four decades, he was the most popular lecturer in America, delivering some fifteen hundred lectures throughout the Northern, New England, and Midwestern states as well as in Europe over the course of his lifetime.

Further, Emerson lived in one of the most creative and intellectually stimulating environments in American history. He was at the center of an amazing array of poets, artists, philosophers, educators, innovators, explorers, adventurers, and other luminaries. He was heralded not only in America but in Europe, where he met other writers who influenced him—people like Wordsworth, Coleridge, Eliot, and Carlyle. Although Emerson never produced a singular major work, his collections of essays (1841, 1844, and 1846) and poems (1846) mark him as a major American writer. Thus, Emerson had a long apprenticeship before he produced his most mature work in his late thirties and early forties. In addition, having been the recipient of two inheritances, he lived a life of relative comfort and leisure, giving him abundant time to develop his expressive talents. Since he was at the hub of a cultural revolution, he was also fortunate in associating with luminaries in the political, social, and cultural world of Boston, New York, and elsewhere.

Henry David Thoreau (1817–1862)

Like his fellow townsman Emerson, Henry David Thoreau was well educated, having attended Concord Academy (where he later taught) and
Harvard College. Like Emerson, he was an avid journal writer. However,
in contrast to Emerson's extensive travel and lecturing, Thoreau was an
immersive student of nature. His wry, self-deprecating remark, "I have
travelled a good deal in Concord,"[14] belies a serious intent: he deliberately set out to know the microcosm of his own environs. A wide
reader and deep thinker, Thoreau published poetry and essays as well
as a memoir, *A Week on the Concord and Merrimack Rivers* (1849), at age
thirty-one before producing one of the most important and influential
works of American literature, *Walden Pond*, six years later (1854).

Thoreau lived for a time in Emerson's house and tutored Emerson's
children and (at Stanton Island) Emerson's brother William's children.
He enjoyed the association of a number of other writers and thinkers,
including Hawthorne and Whitman. He lectured in Concord and published several essays, including the influential "Civil Disobedience."
Although in many ways different from Emerson, Thoreau benefited
from Emerson's friendship, as Emerson did from his. What one sees
with Thoreau, as with Emerson, is a significant apprenticeship as a
writer from the time he was a teenager until he published *Walden Pond*
at age thirty-seven.

Nathaniel Hawthorne (1804–1864)

Nathaniel Hawthorne showed an early proclivity for writing when at
age sixteen he wrote and published *The Spectator*, a short-lived news-
magazine. The next year, he entered Bowdoin College where he was
classmates with Henry Wadsworth Longfellow and the future U.S.
President, Franklin Pierce. After graduation, Hawthorne withdrew

---

14. *Walden, or Life in the Woods,* Chapter 1, para. 1.

from the world to devote full time to writing. He published his first novel, *Fanshaw*, at age twenty-four and began publishing short stories under a pseudonym. His most famous and influential collection of stories, *Twice-Told Tales*, was published in 1837 when he was thirty-three.

In 1842 Hawthorne moved into Emerson's ancestral home in Concord with his new bride, Sophia Peabody, of the prominent Peabody sisters, an excellent critic and editor of her husband's works. For the next several years, Hawthorne had one of his most creative and productive writing periods, producing additional short fiction, children's stories, and a second story collection, *Mosses from an Old Manse* (1846). In 1849, Hawthorne began work on his major novel, *The Scarlet Letter*, which he published the following year (1850) at age forty-six. What followed were additional novels: *The House of the Seven Gables* (1851); *The Blithedale Romance* (1852); and *The Marble Faun* (1860). In addition to writing, Hawthorne served as U.S. Ambassador to Liverpool for four years (1853–57) during which time he interacted with distinguished British writers. Thus, the time between his first novel at age twenty-four and *The Scarlet Letter at* age forty-six was twenty-two years.

Herman Melville (1819–1891)

Herman Melville's formal education, which began when he was five, included attendance at the New York Male School, Lansingburgh Academy, the Columbia Grammar and Preparatory School, and Albany Academy. As pointed out earlier, like his contemporary writers discussed in this chapter, Melville had a long literary apprenticeship before he undertook to write *Moby Dick*. His life as a sailor and his extensive travel, often to exotic places, also prepared him to write about universal themes. In addition, his formal and informal education provided both breadth and depth to his writing, which began in his adolescent years. According to Merton Sealts, Melville's "study of ancient history, biography, and literature during his school days left a lasting impression on both his thought and his art, as did his almost encyclopedic knowledge of both the Old and the New Testaments."[15]

One sees the influence of Melville's education in his fascination with Shakespeare. In a collection of the Bard's plays he purchased in 1849, there are nearly five hundred markings, and Shakespeare's influence can be seen in many places, including some passages in *Moby Dick* that scan iambic pentameter, the primary metric rhythm employed by Shakespeare. As David Cope observes, "Melville's *Moby-Dick* contains nearly measureless references to the reading of Shakespeare . . . featuring the whaling epic's persistent Shakespearean verbal echoes, the composition and sequencing of scenes, and the construction of Ahab as a tragic hero-villain. . . . The verbal echoes pop up so often that Shakespeareans may look forward to enjoying the variety of uses to which Melville put the bard."[16]

Perhaps equally influential in his writing was Melville's intimate, sustained relationship with Hawthorne, the writer with whom he had the greatest affinity and whose imprint on Melville's imagination was indelible. In the long space between the completion of his formal education (1837) and the publication of his first novel, *Typee* (1846), Melville had ample time to develop his skills as a writer of fiction. Additionally, in the five-year span between *Typee* (1846) and *Moby Dick* (1851), he published four additional novels. What is also relevant, after *Moby Dick*, he continued to publish stories, sketches, novels, and poems (including a long poem, *Clarel*, on the Holy Land). Two of his masterpieces, *Benito Cereno* and *Billy Budd,* were written in his later years (although the latter was unfinished at his death). Thus, from the beginning to the end of his career as a writer, one can see the progressive unfolding of Melville's literary gifts and talents.

---

15. Merton M. Sealts, Jr., *Melville's Reading.* Revised and Enlarged Edition (University of South Carolina Press, 1988), 18

16. David Cope, "Melville/Shakespeare." http://cms.grcc.edu/sites/default/files/docs/shakespeare/contemporary/melville_shakespeare.

Walt Whitman (1819–1892)

Unlike Melville and the other writers discussed in this article, Walt Whitman did not have a substantial formal education, a rich family culture, or a close intellectual community in which he could develop his literary talent. His father took him out of school when Walt was eleven, at which time he began working in printing, journalism, and the various trades he pursued during his lifetime. In 1848–49 (age nineteen/twenty) he established and edited the Brooklyn *Weekly Freeman*, which, in addition to other liberal causes, opposed slavery.

Although he was a journalist and dabbled in fiction, Whitman's real love was poetry. In 1855, at age 36, he anonymously published the first edition of his revolutionary collection, *Leaves of Grass*, a work he would continue to revise and expand throughout his life. During the Civil War, Whitman worked as a nurse in a military hospital in Washington, D.C., was employed at several federal agencies, and continued to expand and polish his great poem. After the last edition (1892), Whitman exclaimed, "L. of G. *at last complete*—after 33 y'rs of hackling at it, all times & moods of my life, fair weather & foul, all parts of the land, and peace & war, young & old."[17] *Leaves of Grass,* which Whitman expanded and revised almost literally to the end of his life, from the dozen poems in the first edition to the nearly four hundred in the last, chronicles the evolution not only of America's greatest poem but its most accomplished and most influential poet. In a sense, Whitman spent most of his adult life working on his masterpiece.

In comparison with Joseph Smith, each of the writers discussed here had the ample time that the writing of significant literature takes. Emerson, who was relatively wealthy, had long periods for contemplation, reading, and writing. For the most part he could choose to spend his time writing. Thoreau was an independent spirit who came and

---

17. David S. Reynolds, *Walt Whitman's America: A Cultural Biography* (New York: Alfred A. Knopf, 1995), 5.

went as he wished. For a time, he lived at Walden Pond with entire seasons devoted to observation, reading, and writing. Hawthorne secreted himself in his mother's house while he worked out his literary style and was reclusive for long stretches of time during other periods of his life, which he devoted to composition, including writing *The Scarlet Letter.* Melville lived his life essentially as a writer, although at times he struggled to find the time and money to support his profession. As a single, independent man, Whitman was able to devote substantial time to the writing and revision of his major work throughout his life.

What is true of these authors under discussion here could also be said of many other literary figures of the period, including Margaret Fuller, Edgar Allan Poe, James Russell Lowell, Henry Wadsworth Longfellow, and Emily Dickinson. Although none produced a single major work on which his or her reputation rests, all produced a substantial body of literary expression, whether poetry or prose.

Joseph Smith (1805–1844)

Just as with Joseph Smith's contemporary writers, it is important to consider his life in the years preceding the publication of the Book of Mormon in 1830 when he was twenty-four years old. In other words, what was he doing when Emerson, Thoreau, and their fellow writers during comparable periods of their lives were keeping journals, going to school, seeking higher education, starting their professions, travelling, and mingling with the leading lights of their respective intellectual and cultural communities?

According to Richard Bushman's award-winning biography, *Joseph Smith: Rough Stone Rolling,* two years after the publication of the Book of Mormon, Joseph, speaking of his family, wrote, "We were deprived of the bennifit of an education. Suffice it to say I was mearly instructed in reading writing and the ground rules of Arithmatic which constuted my whole literary acquirements."[18] If Joseph's spelling is any indication,

---

18. (New York: Vintage, 2005), 41–42. Hereinafter *Rough Stone.*

the word "mearly" accurately describes his level of education. Bushman adds, "Joseph may have attended school briefly in Palmyra, and a neighbor remembered the Smiths holding school in their house and studying the Bible."[19] While some have challenged the extent and degree of Joseph's education or suggested that his "home schooling" might have entailed more than has been claimed,[20] the contrast between his education and those of the writers discussed above, with the possible exception of Whitman, is striking. Harvard and Bowdoin, though not colleges or universities in the sense we think of them today, offered the best classical education available in the United States and exposure to gifted teachers, rich libraries, and other resources.

What we find in the historical record is that the hardscrabble life of the Smith family in general and of Joseph in particular seems to have left little space or leisure for the kind of thinking and writing necessary to produce a manuscript of the length and complexity of the Book of Mormon. Before Moroni's first visit in 1823 and Joseph's acquisition of the plates in 1827, Joseph was preoccupied with the family's declining fortunes, working the family farm, hiring himself out as a laborer, and hunting for treasure as, in his own words, "it required the exertions of all that were able to render any assistance for the support of the Family."[21] Thus, the idea that Joseph had time to read broadly, undertake research, construct various drafts, and work out the plot, characters, settings, various points of view, and multiple rhetorical styles that constitute the five-hundred plus page narrative of the Book

---

19. *Rough Stone*, 41–42.

20. The anonymous author of "Could Joseph Smith Have Written the Book of Mormon," *Mormon Think*, http://mormonthink.com/josephweb.htm#introduction, avers that Joseph, "was home schooled quite extensively," without any supporting evidence to either describe what such "schooling" might have entailed or to back up such a claim. While it may have been true that the Smith family had the rudiments of basic educational lessons in the home, what the Smith children got was nothing close to what Emerson and Thoreau got at Harvard, Hawthorne at Bowdoin, Melville at the various academies he attended, or even what Whitman got during his curtailed formal education.

21. *Rough Stone*, 41.

of Mormon is simply incredible (in its original Latin sense of "not worthy of belief").[22]

Further, according to his wife Emma, who was well acquainted with her husband's compositional, expressive, and literary talents at the time he was translating the Book of Mormon, Joseph was still somewhat of a rustic when it came to writing. Let me again quote her exact words: "Joseph Smith could neither write nor dictate a coherent and well-worded letter; let alone dictating a book like the *Book of Mormon.*" Although some critics have suggested that Joseph was somehow composing and memorizing the text he was dictating to his wife and other scribes, Emma testified, "He had neither manuscript nor book to read from. If he had anything of the Kind he could not have concealed it from me."[23]

Joseph's life just before and during the time he was translating was hardly conducive to writing. As Bushman states, Joseph "was entangled with the money-diggers and struggling to scrape together rent money for his family." Also, during this period, as Bushman documents, "Joseph had to provide for Emma while attempting to translate

---

22. An example of the facile, uninformed arguments about the composition of the Book of Mormon all too common these days is: "Could Joseph Smith Have Written the Book of Mormon?" referred to in footnote 20. The anonymous author argues, "First, translation of the BOM did not take place in less than three months; it spanned a time period of over a year and Joseph may have been working on the text for years. Second, the 'most correct of any book on earth' has undergone more than 3,000 textual and grammatical corrections. Some of these corrections included significant changes in doctrine. Third, a large portion of the BOM simply quotes the Bible, including translation errors unique to the King James Version. Fourth, stories in the BOM directly parallel stories from Joseph's life, such as his father's dream of the tree of life when Joseph was five years old. Fifth, the BOM is no more complicated than other works of fiction, such as Tolkien's *Lord of the Rings* and related works. Finally, the ideas in the BOM bear strong parallels to ideas popular in New England at the time and several other books. Sixth, Joseph may have had help." *Mormon Think,* http://mormonthink.com/josephweb.htm#introduction.

23. Interview of Emma Smith by her son, Joseph Smith III, February 4–10, 1879, published in *The Saints' Herald,* 26:19 (October 1, 1879), 289–90. See Bushman, *Rough Stone,* 70.

in a house that her parents reluctantly provided as a place to work." It was also during this period that "Emma gave birth to a son after an exhausting labor." Bushman reports, "Whatever happiness the child brought was short-lived. The baby, named Alvin after Joseph's older brother, died that very day, . . . Emma came close to death herself, and Joseph attended her night and day."[24] It was shortly after this great sadness that Joseph was thrown into despair over Martin Harris's loss of the first translated pages of the Book of Mormon. It is hard to imagine circumstances less conducive to an attempt to compose a lengthy manuscript!

In an article entitled "For Authors, Fragile Ideas Need Loving Every Day," the novelist Walter Mosley says that interruptions and distractions (such as those Joseph Smith had in abundance) cause the life to drain out of one's writing: "The words have no art to them; you no longer remember the smell. The idea seems weak, it has dissipated like smoke." He adds, "Nothing we create is art at first. It's simply a collection of notions that may never be understood. . . . But even these clearer notions will fade if you stay away more than a day. . . . The act of writing is a kind of guerrilla warfare."[25]

Aside from the issue of interruptions and distractions, where are the "try-works" of the Book of Mormon? There are none that we know of or even evidence that there might have been. In other words—and this is important—whereas we see copious journal entries, essays, letters, lectures, and other writings revealing Emerson working out his mature expressions in poetry and prose; whereas we see Hawthorne's significant volume of early fiction (short and long forms), journals, and other writings leading up to and illuminating the writing of *The Scarlet Letter*; whereas we see Thoreau's copious journals, notebooks, essays, lectures, fields notes, and other writings as preludes to *Walden*; whereas we see Melville's many novels, stories, and other writings preparing

---

24. *Rough Stone*, 63–69.
25. "For Authors, Fragile Ideas Need Loving Every Day" (*New York Times*, 3 July 2000, B2).

him to write *Moby Dick*; and whereas as we see Whitman's journalistic writings, poetry, and numerous drafts of his major poem *Leaves of Grass*, we have practically nothing of Joseph Smith's mind or writing to suggest that he was capable of authoring a book like the Book of Mormon, a book that is much more substantial, complex, and varied than his critics have either been able to see or been willing to admit. We need to remember that the Book of Mormon is considered one of the most influential books in American history and one that has been scrutinized by scholars for over a century.

Although we have ample examples of early writings of Emerson, Thoreau, and other writers of the time and a history of their evolving from immature to mature writers, as noted above, we actually have very little of Joseph's writing before the publication of the Book of Mormon. In other words, there are no writings that demonstrate that Joseph was creating the major characters of the Nephite and Jaredite histories and working out the major themes and ideas found in the Book of Mormon, nor is there any evidence that he exhibited any proclivity to compose narrative forms or differential styles or much of anything at all like the complex, interwoven, episodic components of the Book of Mormon.

What do we have from Joseph's pen before the publication of the Book of Mormon in 1830? To reiterate, according to Dean C. Jessee's *The Personal Writings of Joseph Smith*, very little: a short note summarizing Martin Harris's experience with Charles Anthon, possibly written in 1828, and a letter to Oliver Cowdery dated 22 October 1829.[26] Because the Lord directed him to begin keeping a record of his experiences, Joseph commenced keeping a journal in 1832 *following* the completion of the Book of Mormon, although he was anything but a regular or systematic record keeper. Joseph was more likely to dictate his words to scribes. The reason, according to Jessee, was Joseph's insecurity in expressing himself in his own words. As Jessee explains, reporting some of Joseph's own words on the subject, "A complicated life and feelings of literary inadequacy explain his dependence. He lamented his 'lack of fluency in

---

26. (Salt Lake City: Deseret Books, 1984), Vol. 1, xv.

address,' his 'writing imperfections,' and his 'inability' to convey his ideas in writing. Communication seemed to him to present an insurmountable barrier. He wrote of the almost 'total darkness of paper pen and ink' and the 'crooked broken scattered and imperfect language.'"²⁷ This stands in stark contrast to the articulate, fluent, and confident style of Emerson and other writers of the period.

Although Joseph eventually gained more confidence as a writer, he continued to rely on the words and rhetorical styles of others more than on his own. To demonstrate the fact, Jesse provides an example of the obvious contrast in rhetorical styles between Joseph's own writing and that of his clerk Willard Richards, the one (1835) ungrammatical and unpolished and the other (1843) quite the opposite.²⁸

Over the past five decades, a number of scholars have documented the complicated and at times even complex structure of the Book of Mormon. In his excellent study, *Understanding the Book of Mormon* (2010), Grant Hardy has identified the reason the Book of Mormon cannot be read as critics have been reading it for nearly two hundred years: rather than the book revealing the style and point of view of a single author, it is instead told primarily from the respective points of view and through the respective styles of three primary narrators/editors—Nephi, Mormon, and Moroni—each of whom has a unique and distinctive expressive voice and style.

As I summarized in a review of Hardy's book, "By focusing on the three major narrators of the Book of Mormon, Hardy is able to demonstrate that each has 'a particular point of view, a theological vision, an agenda, and a characteristic style of writing, all of which can be found within the confines of the text itself.' Such a 'narrator-centered approach . . . opens up the Book of Mormon to literary appreciation.' Although traditionally it has been accused by outside critics as having extreme incoherence, what emerges from this approach is a clear demonstration of rhetorical and spiritual coherence both within the

---

27. *Ibid.*, xv.
28. *Ibid.*, xv.

sub-narratives as well as in the book as a whole."[29] As noted earlier, Hardy's *The Book of Mormon: A Reader's Edition* (2003) transformed the text by freeing it from its format restrictions and limitations (double columns, narrow margins, textual references, etc.). In other words, Hardy has made it possible for readers to see the unencumbered text for the first time.

In the chapter on Automatic Writing (Chapter 8), I attempted to demonstrate the proposition that Joseph Smith wrote the Book of Mormon under some kind of a spell or through the process known as automatic writing simply does not stand up when one compares the book with other texts claimed to have been written in this way. The chapter on Irony in the Book of Mormon (Chapter 7) demonstrates that the Book of Mormon contains abundant evidence of sophisticated rhetorical and dramatic irony, evidence of which is absent in Joseph Smith's known writing both before and after the publication of the Book of Mormon.

While one could argue that it is impossible to compare Joseph Smith and the Book of Mormon with the prophet's contemporary writers and their major works, nonetheless both their master compositions and the Book of Mormon constitute major literary achievements; whether autobiography, fiction, history, scripture, philosophical treatise, poetry, or some other genre, each has a significant cultural and compositional history and context. This is why Emerson, holding a copy of Whitman's *Leaves of Grass* for the first time, could say, "I greet you at the beginning of a great career, which yet must have had a long foreground somewhere, for such a start. I rubbed my eyes a little, to see if this sunbeam were no illusion; but the solid sense of the book is a sober certainty."[30] Had Joseph Smith sent Emerson a copy of The Book

---

29. Robert A. Rees, "The Figure in the Carpet: Grant Hardy's Reading of the Book of Mormon," *The John Whitmer Historical Association Journal* 31:2 (Fall/Winter 2011), 137.

30. R.W. Emerson to Walt Whitman, July 21, 1855, http://www.whitmanarchive.org/criticism/reviews/ leaves1860/anc.00038.html

of Mormon when it came off the press in 1830, though perplexed by its content and style, Emerson might have said something similar. If he knew of the Prophet's background—and of the absence of any "foreground" of literary apprenticeship—he likely would not have believed it came from Joseph's pen.

Each of the writers of the masterpieces under consideration here, with the exception of Joseph Smith, had a long gestation period during which he "tried out" his ideas, metaphors, allusions, coloring (tone), points of view, personae, and rhetorical styles before tackling a larger, more complex, and more sophisticated form, whether as a collection of poems and essays (Emerson), an extended personal narrative (Thoreau), a novel (Hawthorne and Melville) or a major poem (Whitman). There are no parallel try-works for Joseph Smith, nor any evidence of his apprenticeship as a writer. In fact, all evidence points in the opposite direction.

Unless and until some hitherto undiscovered record demonstrating that Joseph Smith did in fact leave evidence of the reading, thinking, writing, and imaginative expression—the try-works—that would have been necessary for him to have written the Book of Mormon, we are left with the choice of accepting his explanation of the book's origin or making the case for some alternative explanation, which to my mind no one has satisfactorily done to date.

The Matter of Dictation: Joseph Smith and John Milton

"For books . . . do contain a potency of life in them to be as active as that soul was whose progeny they are."
—*John Milton,* Areopagitica

In my Introduction to Mormonism class at Graduate Theological Union (GTU) in 2013, among other topics we discussed the Book of Mormon and its possible provenances. The assignments for the class included my article "Joseph Smith, the Book of Mormon, and the American Renaissance" (Chapter 9) in which I compare Joseph Smith with his illustrious contemporaries—Ralph Waldo Emerson, Henry David Thoreau, Nathaniel Hawthorne, Herman Melville, and Walt Whitman—in terms of their literary imagination, talent, authorial maturity, education, cultural milieu, knowledge base, and intellectual sophistication. In Chapter 10, "The Conception and Creation of Major Works of Literaturee," I take the comparison one step further by examining the evolution of each writer's literary masterpiece from inception to completion.

In that GTU class, one of my students, Ryan Eikenbary, who had significant experience studying and analyzing John Milton's *Paradise Lost*, argued that a more plausible comparison with Joseph Smith in terms of authorial composition was not writers of the American Renaissance but rather John Milton, whose dictation of his great epic poem was in some ways similar to Joseph Smith's dictation of the Book of Mormon. Eikenbary's thesis was that just as Milton had absorbed an enormous amount of material through his education and his informational and cultural environment that allowed him, even after going blind, to dictate his masterful epic, so Joseph Smith did the same in mentally and imaginatively preparing for and then composing and dictating the Nephite-Jaredite narrative. This chapter examines the validity of that comparison.

It would be difficult to find two authors whose educations, backgrounds, and cultural milieus differ more dramatically than those of Joseph Smith and John Milton. Milton had a classical education that was vastly superior to Smith's in every particular. He had a superior formal education; he enjoyed the stability and support of his family as well as the wealth and leisure to sustain long periods of study and reflection; he held prominent positions in government and was involved in affairs of state at the highest level for two decades; he was a voracious and voluminous reader; he traveled widely and was exposed to the best of European culture; he published many works of literature, politics, and theology before undertaking his major work; he had a large and essentially appreciative audience; and he had an assembly of readers, amanuenses, and reviewers during the long period he was composing and dictating *Paradise Lost*.

Milton "from a very early age . . . [was] cherished by his family as something of an educational phenomenon, given to reading, translating, and writing."[1] According to Milton scholar Harris Fletcher, Milton's

---

1. . Ray Flannigan, *John Milton: A Short Introduction* (Oxford: Blackwell, 2002), 5.

education, like that of other English boys of the time, was in three stages: "'the Institution,' or grounding in the fundamentals"; the grammar school; and the university.[2] Milton's father, a scrivener (clerk or scribe), "carefully planned and directed the education of his son," so that from an early age, even before he attended school, Milton had tutors in "the elements of classical learning." As Milton later wrote, "My father destined me from a child to the pursuits of literature."[3]

After this period of "home schooling," Milton went to the prestigious St. Paul's School, where he studied the scriptures, Latin grammar and literature, writing in imitation of Latin as well as Greek and Hebrew models. In addition, he learned the mathematical arts of the quadrivium (arithmetic, geometry, music, and astronomy) as well as the trivium (grammar, rhetoric, and logic). As was the custom, the students at St. Paul's memorized classical and scriptural texts and were required to translate Latin texts to English, and vice versa. In addition to the classical languages Milton learned at school, his father had him tutored in Spanish, French, Italian, and possibly Aramaic and Syriac. Even as a boy, Milton was a serious student, often staying up until midnight to pore over texts and write.

In 1625, at the age of sixteen, Milton continued his formal education by attending Christ's College, Cambridge, where he continued his study of classical literature and languages, earning his bachelor's degree in 1629 and his master's, cum laude, in 1632. Following his master's degree, Milton devoted the next six years to full-time private study. In 1638, he traveled on the Continent, where he met a number of notable figures, including Grotius and Galileo.

Milton was what Ray Flannigan calls an "omnivorous reader." As Flannigan states, "There is no one that I know of, living or dead, who

2. . Harris Francis Fletcher, "Preface" to *The Intellectual Development of John Milton*, vol. 1 (Urbana: University of Illinois Press, 1956), 2 vols., n.p.

3. . John Milton, *The Reason of Church Government*, as quoted in Marjorie Hope Nicolson, *John Milton: A Reader's Guide to His Poetry* (New York: Noonday Press, 1966), 6. Hereinafter Nicolson, *Milton: A Reader's Guide.*

has read all of the books that we know Milton read in his lifetime. . . . No modern scholar, indeed, no scholar . . . from any time after Milton, would have the combined linguistic skills and historical scope to be able to read and comprehend all of what Milton seems to have studied with pleasure and understanding."[4]

Milton established himself early as a poet of considerable talent, writing his first major poem, "On the Morning of Christ's Nativity," at age twenty in 1629, followed by "L'Allegro" and "Il Penseroso" in 1631, "Comus" in 1634 (at about twenty-four, the same age Joseph Smith was when he published the Book of Mormon), and "Lycidus" in 1637. Milton published his first collection of poetry in 1645, which ran "the gamut of various genres: psalm paraphrase, sonnet, canzone, masque, pastoral elegy, verse letter, English ode, epigram, obituary poem, companion poem, and occasional verse."[5] In other words, Milton, began writing mature verse in a variety of genres in his twenties and continued doing so (with an interruption at midcentury when he was occupied primarily with governmental affairs) until in his fifties and early sixties he produced his masterpiece, *Paradise Lost.*

Milton was also a gifted and prolific writer of prose (which he referred to as "the work of his left hand") who composed tracts and other polemical writings in this genre, primarily during the middle decades of the seventeenth century when he was heavily engaged in supporting and defending Cromwell's government, including serving as Secretary of Foreign Tongues, which included being responsible for diplomatic correspondence. *Areopagetica* (1644), considered his most famous prose work, is an impassioned defense of freedom of the press. Other major prose works include *The Reason of Church Government* (1641), *The Doctrine of Discipline and Divorce* (1643), and *The Tenure of Kings and Magistrates* (1649).

---

4. Ray Flannigan, *John Milton: A Short Introduction* (Oxford: Blackwell, 2002), 10. Hereinafter Flannigan, *John Milton.*

5. "John Milton," http://www.poetryfoundation.org/bio/john-milton.

This is not the place to discuss Milton's personal life, which included three marriages, the deaths of two wives and a son and daughter, and imprisonment (for his political convictions and publications), among other challenges, perhaps none of which was as significant as his blindness in 1652 at the age of forty-four. For so intense an intellectual and ambitious writer as Milton, this affliction affected his life profoundly. His most famous sonnet addresses it:

> When I consider how my light is spent,
>> Ere half my days in this dark world and wide,
>> And that one talent which is death to hide
>> Lodged with me useless, though my soul more bent
> To serve therewith my Maker, and present
>> My true account, lest He returning chide; . . .
>>>>> . . . who best
>> Bear His mild yoke, they serve Him best.

The poem confirms Milton's Puritan stoicism in accepting his fate while remaining faithful to his calling as a Christian poet. From this point on, he was dependent on the eyes and voices of readers and the pens of those who took dictation from his tongue for his compositions, including the culminating work of his great epic poem.

There is ample evidence that Milton had been preparing to write an epic tragedy of one kind or another since his days at Cambridge. Marjorie Nicolson speculates that from his youth, "Milton aspired to write an epic" and that his "Latin exercise [at Cambridge] vaguely foreshadows *Paradise Lost*, in that its main character is Satan."[6] Ray Flannigan argues, "Milton undoubtedly began outlining the tragedy that would become the epic *Paradise Lost* long before he became completely blind."[7] In the absence of evidence from the historical record, Nicolson speculates that Milton's plan to write a drama on the subject of the Fall, "Adam Unparadised," took form as early as the 1640s (in

---

6. Nicolson, *Milton: A Reader's Guide*, 177.
7. Flannigan, *John* Milton, 75.

his early thirties, fifteen years before he began dictating it and approx-imately twenty-five years before its publication). One could argue that in a way Milton had been preparing almost his entire life for his mas-terwork. Many of the elements of his early poetry and even some of his prose writings were his "try-works" for his epic poem. I believe it is accurate to state that Milton's muse was (or muses were) both Christian and Classical. That is, as a devout believer deeply rooted in the Christian tradition and immersed in the Bible, he was fully aware of the process by which inspiration and revelation come through the ministry of the Holy Spirit, but he was also aware of the appeal of Greek and other writers to the Muses, including Calliope, the muse of epic and heroic poetry. In his Prologue to *Paradise Lost*, he invokes the muses of both traditions:

> Sing Heav'nly Muse, that on the secret top
> Of Oreb, or of Sinai, didst inspire . . .

> . . . What in me is dark
> Illumin, what is low raise and support . . . (ll 7-8, 22-23)

This darkness, one imagines, was at least partly an allusion to Milton's blindness. Apparently, his muse responded with illumination even in his dreams, for upon awakening Milton often felt an urgency to dictate what had come to him by way of nocturnal inspiration and was impatient for friends and family to assist him in getting the words and images down on paper. According to Barbara Lewalski's biography of Milton, "The report of Cyriack Skinner who sometimes served Milton as an amanuensis, corroborates . . . his 'nightly visitations' indicating Milton's habit of composing poetry on first awakening and his urgent need to get his verses set down: 'The time friendly to the Muses fell to his Poetry; And hee waking early (as is the use of temperate men) had commonly a good stock of Verses ready against his Amanuensis came; which if it happened to bee later than ordinary, hee would complain,

Saying *hee wanted to be* milkd.'"[8] That is, like a cow with an urgent udder, Milton wanted immediate help in getting the words swirling around in his mind down on paper

Milton began dictating *Paradise Lost* in 1656 with his two daughters alternating as scribes. His dictation was then transcribed and read back to him for any changes, revisions, or corrections. It was an arduous, time-consuming process that took more than a decade to complete the first ten books, which were published in 1667. In 1671 he published *Paradise Regained* and *Samson Agonisties*, both of which he had also dictated. The expanded version of *Paradise Lost* (in twelve books) was published in 1674 when Milton was sixty-three. He died later that year.

By any measure, *Paradise Lost* is one of the great accomplishments in the history of world literature, taking its rightful place alongside Homer's *Iliad* and *Odyssey,* Virgil's *Aeneid*, and Dante's *Paradisio*. That it was dictated by a blind poet makes it an even more astonishing accomplishment. Fortunately, we can trace its development over the course of Milton's entire life, showing how his family circumstances, religious training, education, public service, foreign travels, personal history, and especially his voluminous reading and extensive writing prepared him to dictate a poetic composition of such majestic proportions.

In comparison with Milton and the writers of the American Renaissance, each of whom had a clear record of evolving through a long apprenticeship to become a mature major writer, as noted before, we actually have very little history of Joseph Smith's intellectual or compositional development prior to the publication of the Book of Mormon. In other words, there is no evidence of Joseph spending hours in libraries or even reading on his own. To the contrary, as reported earlier, according to his mother, "he seemed much less inclined to the perusal of books than any of the rest of our children."[9] There is also no

---

8. Barbara Kiefer Lewalski, *The Life of John Milton: A Critical Biography* (Oxford, U.K., Blackwell: 2003), 448.
9. *Lavina Fielding Andersen*, ed., *Lucy's Book: A Critical Edition of Lucy Mack Smith's Memoir* (Salt Lake City: Signature Books, 2001), 344. Hereinafter *Lucy's Book*.

evidence that he was keeping a journal or developing his writing style; no record of his writing sketches or short stories, or really anything of substance; no indication that he was creating the major characters of the Nephite history, planning its plots, creating its characters, or working out the major themes and ideas found in its pages; nor is there any evidence that he was consciously developing an authorial voice or cultivating a personal writing style (or that he even understood what this would have entailed). Neither did he exhibit any proclivity for composing large narrative forms or differential styles or anything at all like the complex, interwoven, episodic components of the Book of Mormon. At this point in his life one could argue that Joseph Smith was more a "mute inglorious Milton"[10] than anything like the real Milton.

An article titled "Could Joseph Smith Have Written the Book of Mormon?" on MormonThink is representative not only the lack of seriousness by some scholars on this subject but their occasional downright silliness, as exemplified by the assertion that the imaginative stories about the inhabitants of ancient America his mother recalls Joseph telling his family reveal a "vivid, constructive imagination . . . [that] was as strong and varied as Shakespeare's and no more to be accounted for than the English Bard's."[11] That's about as uninformed an opinion as one could imagine. The same article argues that Smith's "lack of education does not mean lack of intelligence or imagination." Perhaps so, but neither does it substantiate the notion that Smith had the ability to produce anything like the Book of Mormon. The article so frequently resorts to the hypothetical as to be a parody of responsible scholarship.

Some argue that the only substantive preparation Joseph Smith needed to write the Book of Mormon was a knowledge of the Bible. The MormonThink article also makes this argument: "Young Joseph was able to read and ponder scriptures. [He] also attended many protestant

10. Thomas Gray (1716–1771), "Elegy Written in a Country Churchyard" https://www.bartleby.com/101/453.html

11. See http://mormonthink.com/josephweb.htm#full.

church services and studied the Bible in depth."[12] As evidence the author cites Joseph's assertion, "I can take my Bible, and go into the woods, and learn more in two hours, than you can learn at meetings in two years, if you should go all the time."[13] Instead of seeing this as an example of youthful boasting and typical frontier exaggeration, the writer takes it as fact, ignoring Lucy Smith's assertion that her son "had never read the Bible through . . . in his life."[14] Thus, although there is ample evidence, according to Philip Barlow, that Joseph's "mind was demonstrably saturated in biblical language, images, and themes,"[15] the same and more could be said of many of his contemporaries (including most of the clerics and others more educated and scholarly than Joseph Smith) who failed to produce anything comparable to the Book of Mormon.

The contours of Smith's life as a creator of narratives is rather simple and essentially undisputed, at least by those whose scholarship is based on fact rather than speculation. That he was bright and had a far-reaching mind and imagination is agreed upon by his defenders and critics alike. Nevertheless, like many who came of age on the American frontier, Smith had only the rudiments of a formal education. As pointed out earlier, according to his own brief history, he attended elementary school for several years, which consisted of being "instructid in reading and writing and the ground [rules] of arithmatic which constuted my whole literary acquirements"[16] (spelling and punctuation in the original). Beyond this, according to school teacher William McLellin, Joseph attended "high school during the winter of 1834" (when he was twenty-nine, five years after the publication of the Book of Mormon) where, although entering "without scientific knowledge or attainments," he

---

12. *Ibid.*

13. *Lucy's Book*, 357.

14. *Ibid.*, 344.

15. Philip L. Barlow, *Mormons and the Bible: The Place of the Latter-day Saints in American Religion* (New York: Oxford University Press, 1991), 220.

16. The Personal Writings of Joseph Smith, ed., Dean C. Jessee (Salt Lake City: Deseret Book, 1984), 4.

"learned science"[17]—whatever that consisted of. Richard Bushman observes, "Few clues about Joseph's reading, other than the Bible, remain to explain how he came to think of himself as a prophet. Books of all kinds were in circulation in his immediate environment, but he was not bookish; Joseph was no Abraham Lincoln borrowing books and reading when he finished plowing a furrow. No minister reported conversations about religious writings."[18]

As in many families in America's nineteenth-century small towns and rural areas, Joseph's parents attempted to provide their children as much education as limited time and resources allowed. Although his educational and reading materials were limited, Joseph was, according to his mother, often "given to meditation and deep study."[19] What this actually amounted to is difficult to tell, but those who take historical tidbits as evidence that Joseph was capable of composing the Book of Mormon simply do not understand either the preparation or the process required to write so complex and lengthy a work, even if it were fiction. Martin Harris recalled, "I was Joseph Smith's scribe, and wrote for him a great deal; for he was such a poor writer, and could not even draw up a note of hand [a promissory note] as his education was so limited."[20]

As pointed out in earlier chapters, according to his wife, Emma, by the time he was translating and dictating the Book of Mormon, Joseph "could neither write nor dictate a coherent and well-worded letter; let alone dictating a book like the *Book of Mormon*."[21] As Brant Gardner says, "The Book of Mormon is a translation that shouldn't have happened.

---

17. Michael De Groote, "Inside the Lost McLellin Notebook," *Deseret News*, January 28, 2009, http://www.deseretnews.com/article/705280695/Inside-the-lost-McLellin-notebook.html?pg=all.

18. Richard Lyman Bushman, *Joseph Smith: Rough Stone Rolling* (New York: Vintage, 2005), 128.

19. *Lucy's Book*, 344.

20. Simon Smith to the editor, April 30, 1884, *Saints' Herald* 31 (May 24, 1884): 324; http://scottwoodward.org/bookofmormon_translationprocess_accounts.html.

21. Interview of Emma Smith by her son, Joseph Smith III, February 4–10, 1879, published in *The Saints' Herald*, 26:19 (October 1, 1879), 289–90.

Joseph Smith Jr. should not have been able to translate anything."[22] Or, as Richard Bushman asks, "Why would Joseph Smith think that he could translate when he lacked all of the necessary qualifications?"[23]

As noted in the last chapter, when Walt Whitman sent Emerson his first edition of *Leaves of Grass*, Emerson immediately recognized it as a great work of imagination, telling his fellow poet that his great poem "must have had *a long foreground somewhere* for such a start"[24] (emphasis added). Emerson was right, of course. There was a long foreground, including Whitman's education, journalistic career, early fiction, and extensive reading, which included Emerson's own poetry and essays. Milton's daughters, whose father schooled them in literature and languages, did not consider his dictation of *Paradise Lost* as somehow supernatural or even miraculous. They knew that the words that flowed from their father's lips as well as his monumental creativity and voluminous memory had their foreground in both his lengthy study and his extensive writing. On the other hand, Emma Smith, who knew her husband better than anyone, including during the years preceding the translation and dictation of the Book of Mormon, considered the process by which her husband produced the record of the Nephites truly miraculous. Previous chapters have snatched a sentence or two from Emma's 1879 interview with her son, Joseph Smith III. Her testimonial is even more powerful recounted at length:

> Joseph Smith could neither write nor dictate a coherent and well-worded letter; let alone dictating a book like the Book of Mormon. And, though I was an active participant in the scenes that transpired, and was

---

22. . Brant Gardner, *The Gift and Power: Translating the Book of Mormon* (Salt Lake City: Kofford Books, 2011), 3.

23. . Richard Lyman Bushman, "Joseph Smith as Translator," in *Believing History: Latter-day Saint Essays*, ed. Reid L. Neilson and Jed Woodworth (New York: Columbia University Press, 2004), 189–212.

24. . "Ralph Waldo Emerson (1803–1882) to Walt Whitman (1819–1892)," Library of Congress, http://www.loc.gov/exhibits/treasures/ww0017-trans.html, emphasis added.

present during the translation of the plates, and had cognizance of things as they transpired, it is marvelous to me, 'a marvel and a wonder,' as much so as to any one else,. . . . My belief is that the Book of Mormon is of divine authenticity—I have not the slightest doubt of it. I am satisfied that no man could have dictated the writing of the manuscripts unless he was inspired; for, when acting as his scribe, your father would dictate to me hour after hour; and when returning after meals, or after interruptions, he would at once begin where he had left off, without either seeing the manuscript or having any portion of it read to him. [Imagine the prodigious skill in memorization and recall this would have taken!] This was a usual thing for him to do. It would have been improbable that a learned man could do this; and, for one so ignorant and unlearned as he was, it was simply impossible.[25]

By way of summary, one can trace almost everything in *Paradise Lost* to the "long foreground" of its composition. As stated above, Milton had been planning and preparing to write his epic poem for decades before its actual composition. One can trace specific elements of the epic to Milton's actual sources, experiences, and previous writings. Everything could be considered Milton's "try-works" for dictating his masterpiece. In addition, he had many people to assist him in checking his sources, correcting, and rewriting his own dictation as it was read back to him, and helping him through all the stages of composition and publication.

By contrast, Joseph from all we can tell had none of these advantages. Certainly there was no decades-long history of study, planning,

---

25. . "Last Testimony of Sister Emma," *The Saints' Herald*, 26: 9 (October 1879), 299, in Dan Vogel, ed. *Early Mormon Documents*, 5 vols. (Salt Lake City: Signature Books, 1996–2003), 1:538–39.

or "working out" of rhetoric and content that preceded and prepared the young prophet to dictate what we find within the pages of the Book of Mormon. Further, as pointed out in earlier chapters, there is no evidence in any of Joseph's writing before 1830 (and scarcely any thereafter) of the sophisticated use of such things as irony, multiple narrative styles, differential authorial voices, use of imagery and symbolism, and the array of rhetorical devices that we find in the Book of Mormon. Also, when one looks at the years immediately preceding the production and publication of the book, Joseph was anything but a person with abundant leisure and freedom to devote to the work of composition and translation.

Of course, the Book of Mormon is no *Paradise Lost*, but 150 million copies of it have been published since 1830, and it is read today by many more people than read Milton's great epic poem about our lost Edenic paradise.

12

The Midrashic Imagination

> *"We learn from what we know [scripture],*
> *that which we should want to find out*
> *[Midrash]."*
> —*Jacob Neusner*[1]

> *"Midrash invites us to be attuned to the*
> *many sounds that the text makes in our*
> *souls."*
> —*Sandy Eisenberg Sasso*[2]

With the Babylonian destruction of the First Temple in 587 BCE, it became necessary for the Jewish Fathers to create, as it were, a "synagogue in exile," in which the emphasis shifted from the temple to the Torah as the locus of worship. (Scholarly consensus places the

---

1. Jacob Neusner, *The Midrash: An Introduction* (Northvale, New Jersey: Jason Aronson, 1994), xi. Hereinafter, Neusner.
2. Sandy Eiseberg Sasso, *God's Echo: Exploring Scripture with Midrash* (Brewster, MA: Paraclete Press, 2007), 27. Hereinafter, Sasso.

compilation of the Torah during the 6th–5th centuries BCE). With the destruction of the Second Temple in 70 CE, the Jewish rabbis once again emphasized the Torah as their temple. During these periods and after, the text of God's revelation became the focus not only of the Jewish heart and mind but also of its imagination. These sages considered every jot and tittle, every caesura and metaphor as God's design and, further, that God intended—even commanded—the rabbis to search out not only all possible interpretations of the text and everything that lay hidden in the text, but more than this, to create all possible inventions and imaginative explorations that lay embedded in or suggested by the text.

Thus the Jewish Midrash, which runs to some twenty volumes (composed from the 1st to the 3rd century CE and beyond), is a treasure house of "rabbinical exegeses, extrapolations, interpretations and expansions on the Torah."[3] Traditional midrashim, based on both oral and written tradition, constitute an extensive library of Jewish insight into the *possible* interpretations of scripture. For clarification, *Midrash* (capitalized) refers to the library or collection of midrashic writings, whereas *midrash* (lower case) refers to an individual midrashic composition. It is important to distinguish between the two types or categories of Midrashim—*Halakhic or Tannaitic Midrashim*, which focus on the laws derived from scripture and *Aggadic Midrashim*, which focus on edification derived from imaginative readings of scriptural text.[4]

---

3. Robert A. Rees, "Toward a Feminist Mormon Midrash" *Sunstone* 166 (March 2012), 55–61. In his study, *Beholding the Tree of Life: A Rabbinic Approach to the Book of Mormon* (Greg Kofford Books, 2014), Bradley J. Kramer encourages readers to take time to dive deep into the text, "using interpretive techniques developed by Talmudic and post-Talmudic rabbis." Specifically, Kramer shows how to read the Book of Mormon closely, paying attention to the details of its expression as well as to its overall connection to the Hebrew Scriptures—all in order to better appreciate the beauty of the Book of Mormon and its limitless capacity to convey divine meaning." An overview of Bradley Kramer's main argument can be found in his Preface, located at https://www.amazon.com/Beholding-Tree-Life-Rabbinic-Approach/dp/1589587022.
4. *Halakhic or Tannaitic Midrashim* is a much more legalistic approach and focuses on extremely close readings of the Torah in order to ascertain the minute

The word "midrash" comes from the Hebrew root *daled-resh-shin* which means "interpretive retelling"[5] with the specific intent: "to examine," "to investigate,"[6] to "search" and interpret. Midrash has been defined variously as:

- "creative interpretation," "a means of extracting meaning" *from* as well as "a way of reading meaning *into* the text," and "a passionate and active grappling with God's living word";[7]
- a way to "derive homiletical meaning from [a] passage" of scripture, a process that gives "the narrative new life and make[s] it meaningful for another generation"[8];
- "reconsideration and reinterpretation," "narrative retellings"[9];

---

and esoteric aspects of the law. In the second category of Midrashim, *Aggadic Midrashim*, "The historical themes of the Scriptures are midrashically interpreted in such a way that the entire story of Yisrael becomes a continuous revelation of G-d's love and justice." ("What is Midrash?" http://www.headcoverings-by-devorah.com/WhatIsMidrash.htm) An example of the more legalistic Halakhic Midrash is seen in the attempt to "discover the law that the Shabbat can be profaned in order to save life (e.g., where the doctors say that hot food must be served to a dangerously sick person and no hot food is available . . . so one is allowed to cook) derives this from the verse: '*You shall keep My decrees and My laws, which man shall carry out and by which he shall live—I am Hashem*' (VaYikra 18:5) Since the verse states 'shall live', it is implied that where death may result from the observance of the laws, the laws may be set aside." (Ibid.)

"A Aggadic Midrash is the comment on the verse: '*. . . G-d did not lead them by way of the land of the Pelishtim, . . .*' (Shemot 13:17), that is, His providence over the Yisralim in the Wilderness was not through natural process ('the way of the land'). In natural order bread comes from the ground and water from the sky, whereas in the Wilderness the Manna came from heaven and water from the flinty rock." (Ibid.)

5. David C. Jacobson, *Modern Midrash: The Retelling of Traditional Jewish Narratives by Twentieth Century Hebrew Writers* (Albany: State University of New York Press, 1997), 1. Hereinafter, Jacobson.

6. Naomi M, Hyman, *Biblical Women in the Midrash: A Sourcebook* (London: Jason Aronson, 1998), xxvii. Hereinafter, Hyman

7. Ibid., xxix.

8. Sasso, 30, 69–70.

9. Leila Leah Bronner, From *Eve to Esther: Rabbinic Reconstructions of Biblical Women* (Louisville, KY: Westminster John Knox Press 1994), xxi, 185.

- a process by which the "human imagination" illuminates "the hidden, holy meanings of scripture"; and
- "to find, in the liquid, living language of Torah, a new way to meet God."[10]

In short, creating midrash requires creative engagement with holy writ. As Emerson noted, "There is . . . creative reading as well as creative writing. When the mind is braced by labor and invention, the page of whatever book we read becomes luminous with manifold allusion. Every sentence is doubly significant, and the sense of our author is as broad as the world."[11]

It is important to make a distinction between textual exegesis or commentary and midrash. In his *The Midrash: An Introduction*, Jewish scholar Jacob Neusner observes, "For the sages wrote *with* scripture, by which I mean that the received Scriptures formed an instrumentality for the expression of a writing bearing its own integrity and cogency, appealing to its own conventions of intelligibility, and, above all, making its own points. . . . They did not write *about* scripture, they wrote *with* Scripture, for Scripture supplied the syntax and the grammar of their thoughts."[12] Neusner makes a distinction between "exegetical" writing ("getting meanings *out of* the text") and "eisegetical" writing ("reading meaning *into* the text"). He clarifies, "But when our sages of blessed memory proposed to compose their statements, and while they, of course, appealed to Scripture, it was an appeal to serve a purpose defined not by Scripture but by a faith under construction and subject to articulation."[13] Thus, as we will see later with the story of Abraham's sacrifice of Isaac, various interpreters/extrapolators of the text over the generations have seen the story differently because of the

---

10. Judith M. Kunst, *The Burning Word: A Christian Encounter with Jewish Midrash* (Brewester, Mass.: Paraclete Press, 2006), 5, 30, 87. Hereinafter Kunst.

11. "The American Scholar," *Ralph Waldo Emerson: Essays and Lectures* (New York: The Library of America, 1983), 59.

12. Neusner, x–xi, emphasis added.

13. Ibid.

particular circumstances under which their "faith [was] under construction and subject to articulation."

This is why every generation has the opportunity (and responsibility) to read scripture with new eyes, minds, and hearts and why sacred texts are always open and never exhausted. As the distinguished rabbi and theologian Abraham Joshua Heschel says of the Bible, "It is a book that can never die. . . . In fact, the full meaning of its content [has] hardly touched the threshold of our minds. Like the ocean at the bottom of which countless pearls lie, waiting to be discovered, its spirit is still to be unfolded. Though its words seem plain and its idioms translucent, unnoticed meanings, undreamed-of intimations break forth constantly. More than two thousand years of reading and research have not succeeded in exploring its full meaning. Today it is still as if it had never been touched, never been seen, as if we had not even begun to read it."[14]

According to the rabbis, "What Moses delivered amidst the thunder and lightning of Sinai was not a final product but rather the beginning of a conversation between God and the people of Israel. Revelation did not end with Moses but began with him . . . ; the rabbis highlight Torah as a continuing revelation."[15] Since it sees scripture not as the ending but rather the beginning place in the search for meaning, midrashic composition is foreign to many and even forbidden to some Christians (including perhaps some Latter-day Saints) because of their tendency to see sacred texts as fixed, inerrant, immutable, even closed.

The collected midrash contains not only imaginative retellings, but also alternative and even contradictory versions of traditional biblical narratives. For example, with one of the Bible's most powerful and perplexing stories—namely, Abraham's attempted sacrifice of Isaac (Genesis 22:1–24), referred to as the Akedah—Jewish writers (ancient and modern) have reimagined the story a number of different ways,

---

14. *God In Search of Man: A Philosophy of Judaism* (New York: Farrar, Straus and Giroux, 1976), 242.
15. Sasso, 11.

some of which respond to questions raised by the text (e.g., Why is Sarah left out of the story? What is the impact on Isaac of what seems like his father's duplicity and incipient violence? How does this experience affect their relationship afterward? And more . . .).

As David C. Jacobson in his introduction fo *Modern Midrash* observes, "From a literary point of view, the rabbinic, medieval, and modern authors of these retold versions of the story of the binding of Isaac created new works out of the biblical text in significantly different ways that reflect each period's literary norms and its attitude toward the Bible. Nevertheless, these authors share a common midrashic impulse to use the Bible as a source of characters, plots, images, and themes that represent the respective issues and concerns of the composers. For authors of midrash, the way that a biblical text can serve as a meaningful vehicle for the representation of contemporary reality is by transforming it, sometimes even to the point of turning it on its head."[16]

Modern and contemporary Jewish writers, not content to let the ancient rabbinical sages be the only writers of midrash, have tried their hand at this inventive form. Some have been anthologized in such collections as David C. Jacobson's *Modern Midrash* (1987), Naomi M. Hyman's *Biblical Women in the Midrash: A Sourcebook* (1998), and Jill Hammer's *Sisters at Sinai: New Tales of Biblical Women* (2001). See also the website of the Institute for Contemporary Midrash (www. icmidrash.org/).

In *The Burning Word: A Christian Encounter with Jewish Midrash*, Edith M. Kunst presents a persuasive argument for Christian-composed midrashim. She argues that in both traditions there is an invitation from God to be passionately engaged not only in reading and understanding scripture, but in imaginatively exploring its deeper, subtle, and even hidden meanings. Indeed, one could argue that much of the New Testament consists of midrashic readings of the Old Testament.

Creating midrash involves risk, just as Peter stepping out of the boat at Galilee did. As Kunst observes, "This is what imaginative

---

16. Jacobson, 3.

reading ultimately requires: a willingness to step completely out of the boat and dive into the waters with a God who has declared from the beginning that we will not drown."[17] Speaking of her own Christian upbringing, Kunst makes a distinction between her tradition's emphasis on *information* in scripture and the Jewish emphasis on *conversation* with scripture[18]—conversation with oneself, with others, and with God about the meaning of sacred texts.

All this is a prelude to my argument that Latter-day Saints should consider writing midrashim in conversation with Restoration scriptures, especially the Book of Mormon. Given the Latter-day Saint belief that the Book of Mormon was written by Israelites who began their long exiled history in the New World with the Law and the Prophets up to and including Jeremiah on the brass plates, it seems inviting to consider the Book of Mormon a source, as the rabbis did the Torah during their exile, not only for interpretation but for invention, expansion, and imagination. Latter-day Saint scholar Bradley Kramer argues, "Given that the rabbis took seriously the words of Hebrew Scripture; assumed that these scriptures formed a coherent and inspired whole; and devoted themselves to scrutinizing every aspect of that whole in order to uncover subtle, sometimes hidden messages from God, why wouldn't their approach not work well with other scriptures?"[19]

Writing Book of Mormon midrash is likely to take some adjustment in our attitude toward scripture, given our tendency toward literalistic interpretation of scripture and greater focus on answers than on questions, and yet questioning is at the heart of a rabbi's encounter with sacred writ. The Israeli author Amos Oz emphasizes this difference: "Fundamentalists live life with an exclamation point. I prefer to live my life with a question mark."[20] As Susan Eisenberg Sasso observes, "The rabbis turned the text and turned it again. They

---

17. Kunst, 86.
18. Kunst, 128.
19. *Beholding the Tree of Life*, xii.
20. As quoted in Sasso, 17.

delighted in reading the Bible with question marks to discover not just what the Bible meant but what it continues to mean. They entered into dialogue with the text and added another voice in the room. And it was from these voices and question marks that they wrote midrashim."[21]

Actually, Latter-day Saints should be comfortable with the idea of midrashic writing, especially since much of Restoration scripture could be so categorized. That is, it is possible to consider parts of the books of Abraham and Moses as midrashic extrapolations of or extensions on Old Testament or other ancient texts, passages in the Doctrine and Covenants as midrashic revisions of certain Old and New Testament scriptures, and Joseph Smith's inspired revision of the Bible as midrashic refinements of certain biblical passages. One might even argue that Joseph Smith was modeling midrash for Latter-day Saints to imitate!

So, how does one begin to approach the Book of Mormon as the rabbis did the Torah and as many contemporary Jewish writers currently do in carrying on the tradition? To begin with, I think we need to remember that the Book of Mormon was written for us—for our times. As Moroni, the concluding prophet of the book, states, "The Lord hath shown unto me great and marvelous things concerning that which must shortly come, at that day when these things shall come forth among you. Behold, I speak unto you as if ye were present, and yet ye are not. But behold, Jesus Christ hath shown you unto me, and I know your doing" (Mormon 8:34–35). Ezra Taft Benson said, "The Book of Mormon was written for us today. God is the author of the book. It is a record of a fallen people, compiled by inspired men for our blessing today. Those people never had the book—it was meant for us. Mormon, the ancient prophet after whom the book is named, abridged centuries of records. God, who knows the end from the beginning, told him what to include in his abridgment that we would need for our day."[22]

It was with the idea that the Torah was written for each generation that Jewish writers keep coming back to it to see what fresh meaning,

21. Ibid.
22. "The Book of Mormon is the Word of God," Ensign (May 1975), 63.

what new readings it might yield. Commenting on Deuteronomy 5:3 ("Not with our fathers did the Lord seal the covenant but with us—we who are here today, all of us alive."), biblical scholar Robert Alter states, "The heavy emphasis of Moses's language, in which, exceptionally, 'us' in the accusative is followed by 'we' in the nominative and then the triple language of spatial and temporal presence, 'here,' 'today,' and 'alive,' powerfully dramatizes the logic of reenactment at the heart of Deuteronomy."[23]

One of the reasons to keep open minds and imaginations to the possible meanings of the text and the possible explorations of what is only hinted at in the text (or what may not be there at all but nevertheless relevant) is that each generation has not only the readings and inventions of the past, but new tools—both technical and critical—at its disposal. Also, both our expanded understanding of human and divine nature and the continual unfolding of history open new vistas to us. As Jewish scholar Jill Hammer argues, "The Torah grows by reinterpretation."[24] For example, a generation ago, there was very little feminist midrashic literature. Today, as Hammer point out, it is one of the richest veins of the tradition as a new generation of women scholars and writers hold sacred texts up to the light to see what new meanings shine through them.[25]

In "Toward a Feminist Mormon Midrash," an article published elsewhere, I outline a number of ways in which contemporary Mormon women could begin exploring the midrashic possibilities, not only of the central texts of the Judeo-Christian tradition but of Restoration

---

23. *The Five Books of Moses: A Translation with Commentary* (New York: W. W. Norton, 2004), 905.

24. *Sisters at Sinai: New Tales of Biblical Women* (Philadelphia: The Jewish Publication Society, 2001), xiii.

25. See for example, Alice Ogden Bellis, *Helpmates, Harlots, and Heroes: Women's Stories in the Hebrew Bible* (Louisville, KY: Westminster John Knox Press, 2007) and Avivah Gottlieb Zornberg, *The Beginning of Desire: Reflections on Genesis* (New York: Doubleday, 1996).

texts as well, especially the Book of Mormon.[26] I suggest, for example, that Latter-day Saint women, like their Jewish and Christian counterparts, could name, clothe, and create lives for the many anonymous female characters in the Book of Mormon who are referred to only by their generic identities: wife/wives (80 times), daughter/daughters (76), woman/women (55), mother/mothers (17), concubine/harlot/harlots (15), widow/widows (7), female (5), and maidservant/maid/mistress (3).[27] Consider how generations of Latter-day Saint girls and women have been coming to the Book of Mormon looking for mirrors of their own lives in the livers of these ancient peoples, but finding very little by way of female models.

While it is true that all readers have Nephi, Alma, Abinadi, King Benjamin, Mormon, and Moroni as spiritual models, it is important for girls and women, as well as their male counterparts, to have faithful, courageous, and heroic models of their own gender. Hopefully, Latter-day Saint women, like their Jewish and Christian counterparts, will awaken their imaginations to the possibilities that lie hidden in the record of Lehi and Sariah's people.[28]

Contemporary Mormonism is blessed to have a number of Latter-day Saint women scholars and textual commentators who have opened our scriptures in wonderful ways. Such women may well be following President Spencer W. Kimball's invitation to women in his 1979 address, "The Role of Righteous Women," which was read at the General Conference women's fireside by his wife, Camilla Kimball. He emphatically stated, "I stress again the deep need each woman has to study the scriptures. We want our homes to be blessed with sister

---

26. *Sunstone*, 166 (March 2012), 55–61.

27. See "Charting the Book of Mormon," http://byustudies.byu.edu/januarybom-charts/charts/108.html. See also J. Gregory Welch and John W. Welch, *Charting the Book of Mormon* (Provo, UT: FARMS/Maxwell Center, 1999).

28. I have written a midrash imagining the story of the Prodigal Son told from the point of view of a mother with two daughters: "The Prodigal Daughter," which can be found in *Parables for Our Time*, ed. Kenny Kemp (Salt Lake City: Alta Publishing, 2012).

scriptorians—whether you are single or married, young or old, widowed or living in a family."[29]

It is interesting to contemplate whether the Nephites took with them from Jerusalem not only the brass plates, but also some concept of midrash. Even though the earliest collections of midrashic literature as we know them date from the middle to late third century CE, as one Midrash scholar Steven F. Faade speculates, "They contain interpretive traditions, whether attributed or anonymous, that might be significantly older."[30] Indeed, as Michael Katz and Gershon Schwartz in *Searching for Meaning in the Midrash* observe, "In one sense the process of midrash began the very first time the Torah was read."[31]

What midrashic possibilities does the Book of Mormon present? To answer that question, I have considered how both the sages and modern Jewish readers familiar with their rich tradition of mining the text and all that lies within, beneath, and beyond it might begin approaching this New World scripture. I am not an expert on the Midrash, but I have immersed myself in enough midrashic writing to offer some tentative ideas and directions.

To begin with, it would be enlightening to imaginatively reconstruct the lives of the first Book of Mormon family before they begin their perilous journey into the wilderness, across the Arabian Peninsula and finally to the New World. We know that Lehi was a prominent man and that his family enjoyed both status and wealth in Jerusalem. What more can we imagine that would add to the scant information we are provided in the first chapters of the book? What, for example, are the "many great and marvelous things" Nephi says his father read in the book given to him by an angel (or the Lord)? What can our imaginations

---

29. https://www.churchofjesuschrist.org/study/general-conference/1979/10/the-role-of-righteous-women.

30. "Rabbinic *Midrash* and Ancient Jewish Biblical Interpretation," *Cambridge Companion to the Talmud and Rabbinic Literature*, ed. Charlotte Elisheva Fonrobert and Martin S. Jaffee (Cambridge: Cambridge University Press, 2007), 99.

31. *Searching for Meaning in Midrash* (Philadelphia: The Jewish Publication Society, 2002), 9.

reconstruct of Lehi and Sariah's family—especially of the sibling rivalry that is already fully developed by the time the family leaves Jerusalem? What explains Laman's and Lemuel's antagonism toward their younger brother? Was it akin to other biblical sibling rivalries, such as Cain and Abel, Jacob and Esau, Joseph and his brothers? Certainly, the older brothers have murderous intent toward Nephi similar to that which Joseph's brothers have toward him. It is difficult to understand Laman's and Lemuel's spiritual schizophrenia because it is so extreme (and so predictable). Yet as pointed out in earlier chapters, nothing determines or defines the family's journey to the Promised Land more directly and dramatically than their behavior, with the exception of Nephi's steadfast spiritual leadership. What could have happened back in Jerusalem to have created two such malcontents? (It is clear that they have family riches more on their mind than anything spiritual.)

Sometimes the writers of midrash tell the story from another point of view. Since Nephi is the lone narrator of the odyssey from Jerusalem to the New World, we need to keep in mind that, as Wayne Booth and other textual critics argue, first-person narrators (including even narrators of sacred texts) can be unreliable, or at least limited in the way they see and report events.[32] In some ways, in the beginning Nephi seems like an insufferably righteous younger brother. That's certainly the way his two older brothers experience him. What if the story were told from the point of view of Laman or Lemuel or Zoram? What if it were told by Nephi's wife? How would another point of view change the way we see the drama unfold? How do Ishmael and his family experience their journey from Jerusalem, across the desert, and to the New World?

One of the things that marks the Hebrew Bible as great literature is its willingness to present both individuals and families with honesty, to position them within the full range of psychological and social

---

32. Wayne C. Booth, "Telling as Showing: Dramatized Narrators, Reliable and Unreliable," Chapter 8, *The Rhetoric of Fiction* (Chicago: University of Chicago Press, 1983). See also "The Unreliable Narrator," Wikipedia, http://en.wikipedia. org/wiki/Unreliable_narrator.

complexity. Thus, we are presented with a range of characters who not only are courageous, faithful, and heroic, but also jealous, lustful, and murderous. It is, in fact, such unflinching portrayals that allow us to position ourselves within the real world of sacred literature. If God can take a man like Abraham or a woman like Sarah who doubt that God can bless them with a child in their old age and through the refining process of faith and sacrifice make them among the most venerable figures of human history, through whom "all families of the earth [would] be blessed" (Genesis 12:3, 1 Nephi 22:9), then we may have hope that we too can rise above our sins and weaknesses and be transformed when God touches our souls.

Regarding the Nephites, there are many relational matters to consider. What, for example, was the family's relationship with Ishmael and his family before the brothers returned to persuade them to join the exodus? Had the romantic relationships that blossomed in the desert already begun? Were the pairings determined by their parents? Was everyone content with his or her chosen or assigned spouse? How did the wives and the children of the brothers get along? Imagine how wrenching the internecine conflicts must have been for the children of these families. The bonds that would have been forged among the brothers' wives and children, from Jerusalem to Bountiful and across the seas, would have been particularly painful to sever when the tribes split shortly after arriving in the New World. Could we imagine one of Ishmael's daughters continuing a clandestine relationship with one of her sisters after the families separate into warring tribes?

And what of the episode of building the ship? It is such an audacious undertaking for desert dwellers to suddenly be told that they are to build a ship and that they are actually going to board it and set sail on what must have seemed an endless sea to a far, unknown country. Who could blame some of the party for being incredulous? Who among us under similar circumstances might not have said, "Our brother is a fool, for he thinketh that he can build a ship; yea, and he also thinketh that he can cross these great waters" (1 Nephi 17:17)?

The Midrash contains commentary on such enterprises undertaken by the people of the Bible, including Noah's neighbors mocking him for undertaking to build so fantastic a vessel as the Ark. One legend tells how God, as with his turning stones into lights for the Brother of Jared (Ether 3:6), "showed Noah with His finger how to make the ark," and according to another legend, "Noah learned how to build [the ark] and mastered as well the various sciences, from the *Sefer Razi'el* (the book from which the angel Raziel taught Adam all the sciences), which had been brought to him by the angel Raphael."[33] Another Midrashic story telling about the building of the Tower of Babel makes me think of Laman and Lemuel's misplaced priorities: when one of the builders "fell and was killed, no one noticed. But if a brick fell and was broken, they sat down and wept."[34]

The voyages of both the Jaredites and the Nephites offer wonderful opportunities to explore the dynamics of the first Book of Mormon immigrant families. As Steve Walker wryly notes, the construction of the Jaredite's sea-going vessels (Ether 2:20) might have made for a particularly interesting and perilous voyage: "'Behold, thou shalt make a hole in the top, and also in the bottom; and when thou shalt suffer for air thou shalt unstop the hole and receive air. And if it be so that the water come in upon thee, behold'—I'll bet they beheld with rapt attention, as ocean came pouring in on them—'ye shall stop the hole, that ye may not perish in the flood.' If the plug lets in the ocean, Mahonri, consider the possibility you may have opened the wrong end!"[35] Finding humor in such episodes, as Walker does, is also characteristic of some midrashim. Chuckling over another detail of the Jaredites' long voyage

---

33. *"Sefer haYashar (midrash), Wikipedia; http://en.wikipedia.org/wiki/Sefer_haYashar_(midrash.*
34. Batnadiv HaKarmi, "Hubris, Language, and Oppression: Recreating Babel in Primo Levi's *If This is a Man* and the Midrash." See also, *Midrash Pirkei De Rabbi Eliezer 24:176*, en.wikipedia.org/wiki/Midrash.
35. "Last Words: 4 Nephi-Moroni," in *The Reader's Book of Mormon*, ed. Robert A. Rees and Eugene England (Salt Lake City: Signature Books, 2008), vol. 7, xviii. Hereafter, *Reader's Book of Mormon.*

to the Promised Land, Walker observes, "Consider, for instance, the slapstick inconvenience of how the Jaredites in their claustrophobically close-quarter boats 'did carry with them swarms of bees' (Ether 2:3)."[36]

Claudia Bushman, like most readers of the Book of Mormon, yearns both for more narrative and more detail. Speaking of the abbreviated history kept by such scribes as Enos, Jarom, and Omni, she writes, "The years pass quickly in these little books. Fifty-five years after settlement, Jacob, the brother of Nephi born in the wilderness, begins his charge to engrave entries on the small plates. Jacob is told to hand his records down to his seed, from generation to generation. But, at the end of this period, his line has died out, and the records have moved to another lineage. Just twenty-six pages later, the space occupied by these five short books, we have traversed more than four hundred years."[37] Bushman, in the spirit of midrash, writes, "If I were Jacob and I were writing a short book, I would make it a narrative history of my time. But Jacob gives us very little narrative history. . . . More of an anthologist than an historian, Jacob seems to lack the drive to keep the record."[38]

Out of what I consider a nearly inexhaustible source for a Book of Mormon Midrash, let me suggest several possible especially fruitful narratives to consider:

- The excursion to the New World by the Mulekites as revealed in Omni (1:12–14). These are people without a book and therefore with a fading historical memory until they meet and then join up with King Mosiah's people. Coming, as both groups did, from the same location and historic period, it must have been fascinating for them to compare remembered stories of Jerusalem, the changing political scene following Lehi's departure, their voyages

36. Ibid.
37. "Big Lessons from Little Books (2 Nephi 5 Through the Words of Mormon)," *Reader's Book of Mormon*, vol. 2: vii-viii. Hereinafter, "Big Lessons."
38. Ibid., viii.

to a new continent, and their experiences after arriving. Once they became assimilated, one wonders how much of their language, customs, and tribal memory the Mulekites retained.

- The Mulekites inform Mosiah that they had discovered Coriantumr, the lone survivor of the Jaredite mutual annihilation, and that he had lived among them for "nine moons," during which Coriantumr "spake a few words concerning his fathers. And his first parents came out from the tower [i.e., The Tower of Babel]" (Omni 1:20–22). How strange this meeting must have been and, assuming they could communicate with one another intelligibly, what stories must Coriantmur have told, both about the violent end-game of his civilization and about his experience of wandering alone in such a wide world. Imagine what it must have been like for him to have human companionship once more.

- In Alma 63 we are told of Hagoth, "an exceedingly curious man" who built ships and inspired a major northward Nephite migration, consisting of 5,400 men and their families (vv. 4–5). After reaching his destination, Hagoth returned to build more ships for additional immigrants and supplies and departed with a second group, including Alma's son Corianton, but we are told they "were never heard of more." The remaining Nephites concluded that these people may have "drowned in the depths of the sea," but offer no proof of this presumption (v.8). These people offer additional fruit to sample for midrashic composition.

- When the prophet Abinadi is pursued by the murderous agents of King Noah (Mosiah 11–12), we are told that he was gone "for the space of two years," after which "he came among them in disguise, that they knew him not" and began to prophesy. What can we imagine Abinadi doing during his two-year exile in which he invents a disguise so he will not be detected? We could certainly portray him so full of anxiety that he immediately gives himself away, telling those assembled, "Behold, . . . Thus has the Lord commanded me, saying—Abinadi, go and prophesy" (11:20, 12:1).[39]

- The story of the Nephites, like that of the Jaredites before them, ends darkly, with Moroni, the remaining righteous survivor, witnessing his people's barbarism. As he speaks of the destruction of his people and the death of his father, Mormon, his words are heartbreaking: "And I even remain alone to write the sad tale of the destruction of my people. But behold, they are gone, and I fulfil the commandment of my father. And whether they will slay me, I know not. . . . and whither I go it mattereth not. . . . And behold, I would write [more] also if I had room upon the plates, but I have not; and ore I have none, for I am alone. My father hath been slain in battle, and all my kinsfolk, and I have not friends nor whither to go; and how long the Lord will suffer that I may live I know not" (Mormon 8:3–6). Referring to Moroni's lament in these verses, Reid Bankhead, one of my religion teachers at BYU, called him "Sad-sack Moroni," but I hear genuine heartache and loneliness, not self-pity in these verses. Moroni's situation calls out for compassion: to be all alone for sixteen years, to be constantly in danger of falling into the hands of his enemies without a single person to befriend him must have been extremely trying for Moroni. It might be instructive for modern readers, faced as we are by the threat of terrorist attacks, weapons of mass destruction, and the specter of unending war, to identify with Moroni, to imagine his life during these lonely, dangerous years of exile.

---

39. I cite this as a particularly amusing example of irony in Chapter 7.

There are, of course, many other stories, episodes, incidences, puzzling references, and provocative allusions that might awaken our spiritual and narrational imaginations were we to undertake the composition of what might constitute a Book of Mormon Midrash. (See for one example, "Imaging Peace," Chapter 6.) In fact, every page of the Book of Mormon might call forth what one midrashic scholar has called "secular scripture,"[40] by which he likely means scripture written by other than prophets or other God-ordained writers.

For nearly two hundred years, Latter-day Saints have been yearning for the time when the sealed portion of the Book of Mormon would be opened to them. According to Joseph Smith's contemporaries, that which is sealed could be as large as or larger than the translated portion.[41] Nephi described the untranslated text as containing "a revelation from God, from the beginning of the world to the end thereof" (2 Nephi 27:7). From the time the Book of Mormon was first published considerable speculation has flourished as to when and under what conditions the remainder of the Jaredite and Nephite records would become available. As individual readers, we may not have control or influence over the timing of new revelations or the unveiling of old revelations, but we do have influence and control over how we might imaginatively engage with the record we do have. That is, while we may not have access to the sealed portion of the Book of Mormon, using our spiritual imaginations, we could unseal more of the possibilities of the portion we do have.

Of course, such imaginative "unsealing" is not meant to be a substitute for close and careful readings of the Book of Mormon that might help us reconstruct some of what has been abridged—plus enable us to uncover depths of meaning by pursuing explicit comments and connecting intentional scriptural allusions within the text. In other words,

---

40. Jacobson, *Modern Midrash*, 15.
41. Alexander L. Baugh, "Sealed Portion of the Gold Plates," *Book of Mormon Reference Companion*, ed., Dennis L. Largey (Salt Lake City: Deseret Book, 2003), 707.

creating midrash is *not* a substitute for serious penetrating reading of scripture.

I recognize that what I propose might be seen as arrogating to individual members a privilege that some would say should be reserved for prophets or other ecclesiastical leaders, but in reality it is simply a call to extend and deepen that discipline which as Latter-day Saints we have already been called to do: ponder, expound, and interpret scripture, even to imaginatively stretch the boundaries of sacred texts to make them more relevant to the challenges of our everyday lives. One could argue that this is precisely what the new Come Follow Me family scripture study curriculum invites members to do.

Speakers in General Conference as well as in many sacrament meetings participate in something akin to midrash. That is, Latter-day Saints believe in what might be called the democratization of scripture—not that scripture might mean anything or that it means whatever we want it to, but that each person is encouraged to engage with scripture with his/her heart, mind, and even imagination. As long as such ponderings do not counter or challenge doctrine, they might be seen as part of our spiritual work and an appropriate response to the Savior's challenge to "Search the scriptures" (John 5:39). If the purpose of reading scripture is to understand how we might be better disciples, then anything that furthers that objective should be deemed acceptable. In other words, the Holy Ghost might enlighten our imaginations as much as our minds, were we to be open to that possibility.

Perhaps the judgment of Mormon midrashic writing could be measured against at least some of Lowell Bennion's criteria for judging interpretation of scripture. As Philip Barlow summarizes, "Bennion gauges a scriptural interpretation as worthy if it (1) is consistent with gospel fundamentals . . . , (2) is confirmed by the promptings of the Holy Spirit, (3) appeals to thoughtful ethical judgment, (4) has won wide agreement among informed and rational persons of good will,

(5) allows for the human as well as the divine in revelation, and (6) is primarily concerned with scripture's religious intent."[42]

It could be, as the rabbis themselves argued consistently, that such imaginative encounters with sacred literature is what God intends, that rather than his wanting our attention focused on fixed, immutable texts, rather than our seeing the human story as closed, he has been inviting us all along to open our hearts and minds to their imaginative possibilities. In fact, according to one bold suggestion, attributed to rabbis, the Torah is also continually open to God's heart and mind. That is, the rabbis viewed even God as continuing to read and wrestle with his own scriptures: "The Talmud says that God himself studies the Torah every day. It says God is sitting in the *bet midrash*, the study house, wearing a round black cap and holding an open Bible, arguing and wrestling his own text right along with learned rabbis throughout the ages."[43]

While we may tend to be suspicious of the imagination, to think of imaginative impulses as "vain," it is important to recognize that everything, including the creation of the world itself, was, and first had to be, imagined. As humanistic scholar Ihab Hassan states, "Perhaps the imagination is the true teleological organ in our evolution, directing all change."[44] I believe that the Book of Mormon awaits a new generation

---

42. *Mormons and the Bible: The Place of the Latter-day Saints in American Religion* (Oxford: Oxford University Press, 1991), 203–04.

43. Kunst, 4.

44. *Liberations: New Essays on the Humanities in Revolution* ed. Ihab Hassan (Middletown, Conn.: Wesleyan University Press, 1971), 179. In regard to the topic of "vain imaginations" mentioned in scripture (see Moses 8:22; Genesis 8:21; Romans 1:21; 1 Nephi 12:18; and elsewhere), the always denounced "vain imaginations of a man's heart" clearly refers to untruths springing from self-gratifying and self-aggrandizing beliefs. The KJV of Romans 1:21 (" Because that, when they knew God, they glorified him not as God, neither were thankful; but became vain in their imaginations, and their foolish heart was darkened") is translated in the NRSV as follows: "For though they knew God, they did not honor him as God or give thanks to him, but they became futile in their thinking, and their senseless minds were darkened"; https://www.biblegateway.com/.

of bold, thoughtful, and imaginative readers, those who, to borrow a phrase from B.H. Roberts, "will not be content with merely repeating some of [the Book of Mormon's] truths, but will develop its truths; and enlarge it by that development." Roberts calls not only for more dedicated discipleship but what I like to think of as more imaginative discipleship:

> Not half—not one-hundredth part—not a thousandth part of that which Joseph Smith revealed to the Church has yet been unfolded, either to the Church or to the world. The work of the expounder has scarcely begun. The Prophet planted by teaching the germ-truths of the great dispensation of the fullness of times. The watering and the weeding is going on, and God is giving the increase, and will give it more abundantly in the future as more intelligent discipleship shall obtain. The disciples of "Mormonism," growing discontented with the necessarily primitive methods which have hitherto prevailed in sustaining the doctrine, will yet take profounder and broader views of the great doctrines committed to the Church; and, departing from mere repetition, will cast them in new formulas; cooperating in the works of the Spirit, until they help to give to the truths received a more forceful expression and carry it beyond the earlier and cruder stages of its development."[45]

I contend that one of the ways in which Latter-day Saints can cooperate in works of the spirit is, as Roberts urges, to "cast [Restoration scriptures] in new formulas," including perhaps the creation of a body of midrashic readings of our sacred texts. As pointed out earlier, Rabbi Sandy Sasso speaks of the rabbis' unfolding of Torah as "continuing

---

45. B. H. Roberts, *The Improvement Era* 9 (1906),712–13; also found in B.H. Roberts, *The Seventy's Course in Theology,* vol. 5 (1912), pp. iv–ix.

revelation,"[46] a concept central to Mormon experience. Thus, Latter-day Saints should be open to continuing imaginative revelation through both ancient and modern scriptures. As the rabbis said of their study of Torah, "Turn it and turn it again, for everything is contained therein."[47]

---

46. Sasso, 11.
47. Kunst, 58.

13

The Figure of Love:
The Ultimate Message
of the Book of Mormon

*"I have beheld his glory. And I am encircled
about eternally in the arms of his love."*
—2 Nephi 1:15

*"The Figure a poem makes . . . is the same
as for love."*
—Robert Frost[1]

Although it may not be apparent on casual reading, the primary message of the Book of Mormon from beginning to end is the importance
of love—the love of God for all his children, the love of Jesus Christ for

---

1. *Selected Prose of Robert Frost* (New York: Holt, Rinehart & Winston, 1966), 18.
Hereinafter *Selected Prose.*

humanity, and our love for ourselves and for one another, including our enemies. I did not see, nor did I understand this important message when as a young adult I first started reading the Book of Mormon seriously. In fact, the various homes in which I grew up were so dysfunctional and chaotic that I was more familiar with the absence and failure of love than its presence and success. The alcoholism, abandonment, and abuse I experienced from the adults in my life led me to distrust the possibility of love, although I yearned for it intensely. Not being raised in a religious environment during my first decade, I did not know God. In fact, because I saw the failure of love all around me in these years when I first became aware of God, I was more afraid of than drawn to him. Years later when I read Annie Dillard's essay, "God in the Doorway," her words expressed how I felt as a young man: "[God], I ran from you. . . . you meant only love, and love, and I felt only fear, and pain."[2]

In an essay called "The Turning Point of My Life," Mark Twain recounts several significant events in his youth that pointed his life in a new direction, including reading a travel narrative about the Amazon when he was a teenager living in Hannibal, Missouri, that motivated him to catch a steamboat to New Orleans where he planned to sail to South America and take a boat up the Amazon. Twain never made it to the Amazon, but "lighting out" for it was an important turning point in his life because the voyage down the Mississippi led to his becoming a steamboat captain and eventually to writing *Life on the Mississippi* and other classics of American literature.

One of the important turning points of my life was receiving my patriarchal blessing when I was fifteen. This happened at a time when I felt absolutely lost and alone. My father had just divorced his second wife and our family of seven was split apart. At this time I was the only active person in my family and so a friend drove me from the small

2. In *Teaching A Stone to Talk: Expeditions and Encounters* (Harper and Row: New York, 1982), 141.

Arizona town in which we lived to Mesa, where Patriarch Alma Davis laid his hands on my head and spoke the following words:

> The Lord has blessed you with very sensitive feelings. Be thankful for these sensitive feelings, dear brother, and at times when you have been sorely hurt, and have wished you were not so easily touched and hurt in your feelings, be thankful for them for these feelings will lead you into paths of truth and righteousness. In seeking after the finer and better things of life, great will be your joy and happiness.

Sensitive feelings, yes, I could relate to that, but in truth, his last words did not have much meaning for me at the time because I had had no exposure to or experience with "the finer and better things of life." I didn't really know to what he was referring.

Fortunately, he became more specific, pointing me in an unthought-of direction,

> As yet you have not fully developed the beautiful talents with which the Lord has blessed you. . . . Dear brother, develop these beautiful gifts and talents with which he has blessed you, the beautiful in music, the beautiful in thought, the beautiful in literature and the higher and finer things of life. Seek after these things and you will be led into paths of truth and righteousness.

Several years later when I entered college, I began my quest for the beautiful, although at the outset I had little awareness of what that really meant or that my life would unfold in this pursuit. Neither of my parents graduated from high school, and although they wanted me to get an education, like many parents of children born during the Great Depression, they hoped (if they had any such hope at all) I would choose a prestigious profession like law or medicine.

There was, in the various homes and family environments in which I came of age, no literature except for the token Bible and, after I joined the Church at age ten, the Book of Mormon, also unread much beyond the first chapters. Until I went to high school (and even then) my reading consisted almost entirely of comic books. While it is likely I read other books in high school, I can't recall a single specific author or title, although I have a vague memory of our teacher helping us fumble through *Hamlet* when I was a junior.

I entered college with no great ambition, certainly not one that involved advanced study or a profession in the humanities and university teaching. In the beginning I wanted to be a high school counselor, but each time I took a class in an interesting subject with a good teacher, I thought I might choose that discipline and profession. So, for a time I considered majoring in geology and later in psychology and education.

It wasn't until I took Robert Thomas's "Introduction to Literature" course during my sophomore year that I came alive. As I recounted earlier in this book, Bob was the most gifted teacher I had the privilege of studying under. I took every class he taught and went to hear him speak every chance I got. In Bob's classes I fell in love with literature and with teaching, which lead me to seek for the beautiful in thought, in music, and in the other arts. Apparently, Bob saw something in me that I had no idea was there, and he befriended and mentored me in ways that I now see shaped not only my intellectual and professional life but also my personal and spiritual life, what I have come to understand a great teacher does, whether or not he or she intends it.

Learning to Read

> *"There is an art of reading, as well as an art of thinking, and an art of writing."*
> —Isaac Disraeli[3]

What I learned from Bob and other teachers, albeit it haltingly and slowly, was that I too could learn to read a poem, short story, play, novel,

---

3. As quoted in *The Literary Character; or the History of Men of Genius Drawn from Their Own Feelings and Confessions*, (Edward Moxton:, London, 1839), 177.

and sacred text—and could read them closely and carefully enough so that I could see not only what others saw, but, beyond that, have intuitive perceptions and insights that were unique to me. I remember precisely when this happened: Bob had assigned Anton Chekov's short story, "On the Road," over Thanksgiving holiday during that semester. On a trip home to California, I read the story but had no clue as to what it meant. I concluded, as I had on previous assignments, that I was incapable of understanding complex, multi-layered works of literature. Listening to their comments in class, I felt my fellow students had a special gift for "sounding" a poem or work of fiction that I simply did not have—and would never have.

Since I had to find *something* to say about Chekov's story, I paid what I considered in those days the ultimate price—I read the story a second time! That didn't seem to help much, so I kept reading and re-reading. Suddenly, on one of these readings, I saw this incredible structure, saw the way imagery, symbolism, plot, setting, and character all came together to reveal not only meaning but astonishing artistry. "Reveal" is the right word, in the sense that H. D. Lewis intends when he says, "The wonder and mystery of art, as indeed of religion in the last resort, is the revelation of something 'wholly other' by which the inexpressible loneliness of thinking is broken and enriched."[4] That "wholly other" exhilarated me. As I write these words, I feel it again all over my skin.

What I came to understand is that Bob Thomas as my professor was trying to do for me and with me—and what I have tried for the past fifty-five plus years to do for and with my students—was to get me to see on my own, to see further and deeper than I had seen before, to learn enough to discriminate among the things I saw (and learned from others) and, ultimately, to come to trust my intellect, imagination, and intuition so that I could make informed judgments on my own and share them with others.

---

4. H. D. Lewis, "On Poetic Truth," Philosophy 21 (1946) (79):147–166. This quote has been misattributed to Wallace Stevens. See George S. Lensing, *Wallace Stevens and the Seasons* (Baton Rouge: Louisiana State University, 2001), 130.

Because of Bob's influence and the maturing influence of a two-year mission between my sophomore and junior years, I went from being a mediocre student to a good one, from getting B's and C's to getting A's. I was starting to awaken, and it felt good. I also realized that somehow opening my heart and mind to literature and the other arts also opened me to love. That opening was most evident in my evolving engagement with sacred literature, which was enhanced by my taking Bob's "Bible as Literature" and "Book of Mormon" classes.

It was in these classes that I learned how to read and respect sacred texts and began to understand their messages about love. As I read, it was as if I were reading some of the words for the first time. For example, although I had read about Nephi's dream of the tree on previous readings, suddenly it was as if I were witnessing the dream myself. I was struck by the way the angel kept directing Nephi's attention with his repeated instructions to "Look!" and then asking Nephi to say what he saw. It was as if the angel were inviting *me* to look and think about the unfolding scene. When the angel asks Nephi if he knows the meaning of the tree, I thrilled at Nephi's response: "Yea, it is the love of God, which sheddeth itself abroad in the hearts of the children of men; wherefoere, it is the most desirable above all things." At that moment, I felt the truth of the angel's response, "Yea, and the most joyous to the soul." (1 Nephi 11:21–23)

On another reading, as I recounted in the chapter on Alma's great Sermon at Zarahemla, I felt challenged by Alma's ultimate questions:

> "Have ye spiritually been born of God?
> Have ye received his image in your countenances?
> Have ye experienced this mighty change of heart?" . . .
> "If ye have experienced a change of heart,
>   and if ye have felt to sing the song of redeeming love,
> I woud ask, can ye feel so now?"
>
> (Alma 5:14, 26)

Those questions continue to reverberate in my life.

Learning to See

It was because of Bob's guidance that I received a prestigious Woodrow Wilson Fellowship and was a finalist for a Danforth Fellowship for graduate study. I had other great teachers at BYU (Parley Christensen, Hugh Nibley, Truman Madsen, to name just three of many) and at the University of Wisconsin (Madeline Doran, Helen White, Ricardo Quintana, Henry Pochmann, and others), but I never had a teacher who influenced my life as Bob did. More than sixty years after having taken his classes, I often find myself telling stories he told, teaching literature the way he taught, and, I hope, seeing sacred texts the way he saw them.[5]

When I got to graduate school, I had many opportunities to read texts, as we were fond of saying, "from Beowulf to Virginia Woolf—and beyond." Reading Shakespeare, Milton, George Eliot, Emerson and Emily Dickinson, as well as a host of other writers, combined with the real-life experiences of being a husband and father, helped me to read the Book of Mormon more intelligently; my understanding of love as well as literature expanded and deepened—as it has continued to do over the decades.

As I read and studied the Book of Mormon and my understanding grew, I felt like the blind man in Mark's gospel whom Jesus heals. After Jesus anoints his eyes and touches them, he asks, "Do you see anything?" The blind man replies, "I see men as trees, walking." In other

---

5. Bob was even instrumental in guiding me in love, for when I found the woman I hoped to marry, I feared that I might follow the ruinous examples of my parents in their wrecked marriages and multiple divorces. When I took my dilemma to Bob, he gave me what he called his A-I-R test: "She needs to be attractive because you are going to look at her the rest of your life. She needs to be intelligent because you are going to talk with her the rest of your life. And she needs to be religious because you will want to share with her those things, including sacred things, that are of most value to you. If she has all those things–and has a sparkle in her eye–there is a good chance it will work out." And it did for the fifty-one years of our married life until she passed away in 2012. When I remarried two years ago, the formula still worked!

words, his vision is unclear. Jesus then touches his eyes again, after which we are told that Jesus "made him look up and he saw every man clearly" (Mark 8:24). Seeing sacred texts clearly takes skill and practice as well as diligence and patience. No one sees everything, although some are gifted to see things that others do not. Sharing what we see awakens us not only to the delights of God's revelations and to one another's insights but to a fellowship of meaning and beauty that deepens our love for one another.

Learning to Think

If I first started thinking seriously about the Book of Mormon in Bob Thomas's classes, it was in other classes and conversations with people like Hugh Nibley and Truman Madsen that I sensed the book's power to touch people's hearts and to lead them to Christ. It is that combination of thinking and feeling, of heart and mind, of imagination and revelation that has made the Book of Mormon such a powerful text in my own life. In his course on literary criticism, Bob used the term "ontological density" for the depth of meaning and rhetorical richness that characterize great literary texts. It is that density I have sought and found in my study of this New World text.

It was in graduate school and in my first years of teaching literature at UCLA that my study of the Book of Mormon broadened and deepened. As I studied, I often saw things that had entirely escaped my previous readings. The more I read from both the Book of Mormon and other sacred texts (as well as history, poetry, drama, fiction, and non-fiction), and the more I experienced the rich artistic creations of the human mind and imagination in music, art, architecture, and the other arts, the more the lights came on and the more I was able to discern the presence in the Book of Mormon of what Henry James speaks of metaphorically as the "complex figure in a Persian carpet."[6]

---

6. Henry James, *The Figure in the Carpet* (Boston: Le Roy Phillips, 1890), 32–33.

Reading and teaching the Book of Mormon and studying scholarly writing related to it over the years has helped me to see some of that complex figure, although I hasten to add that there is much that I have yet to see. Seeing that figure is enhanced through the critical insights of others. As in previous chapters, I call particular attention to Grant Hardy's magnificent *Understanding the Book of Mormon* (2010). Reading Hardy, I feel as Keats felt when he read George Chapman's English translation of Homer's great epic poems, *The Iliad* and *The Odyssey*. In his poem, "On First Looking into Chapman's Homer," Keats speaks of his personal knowledge of the Greek world through his own travels and the views of others, then adds,

> Yet did I never breathe its pure serene
> Till I heard Chapman speak out loud and bold:
> Then felt I like some watcher of the skies
> When a new planet swims into his ken;
> Or like stout Cortez when with eagle eyes
> He star'd at the Pacific—and all his men
> Look'd at each other with a wild surmise—
> Silent, upon a peak in Darien.

Surmise and surprise, and on occasion awe, await the careful reader of any rich text. What Keats is suggesting by his metaphors is that sometimes an insight comes unexpectedly, like a meteor or star shooting across the night sky. Other times it comes by revelation as when, after reaching a promontory overlooking the Pacific, "stout Cortez" (actually, it was Balboa) stands astonished, the blue expanse of the Pacific stretching endlessly before him mirroring the heavens. That ocean and sky constitute a powerful metaphor for the seemingly limitless possibilities that great literature and art in all their expressive forms engender and inspire. I have had more than one such moment in writing this book.

How one sees and reads the Book of Mormon depends not only on one's intent but also on one's world view and epistemological approach—that is, one's way of seeing and knowing, one's way of making meaning and organizing the world, one's way of being open to and discovering truth, and one's openness to love. If, as Oliver Wendell Holmes said, "Every man [and woman] is an omnibus in which his [or her] ancestors ride," a literary critic is an omnibus in which his or her teachers, fellow critics and students, and loved ones ride, as well as do the wide range of persons, real and imagined, who inhabit the worlds of one's reading. And, if the reader is a good critic, where the discovered mysteries of consciousness and understandings of love ride.

Several years ago, Adam Gopnik published an article in *The New Yorker* titled, "1 Nephi," in which he said the following about the Book of Mormon: "Scholarly opinion on Smith now tends to divide between those who think that he knew he was making it up and those who think that he sincerely believed in his own visions"[7] (as if, somehow, prophets are not inclined to believe their own visions!). Gopnik then alludes to Mark Twain's satire of the Book of Mormon.

Since I did my Ph.D. dissertation on Mark Twain and the Bible, I am well acquainted with Twain's humorous quips on the Book of Mormon, which are like his at times delightful mockery of the Bible. Of the Mormon scripture, Twain said, as related in an earlier chapter, "If Joseph Smith composed this book, the act was a miracle—keeping awake while he did it was, at any rate. If he . . . merely translated it from certain ancient and mysteriously engraved plates . . . the work of translating was equally a miracle, for the same reason." Twain also said that the entire book should have been named "Ether" because he found it "chloroform in print."[8] Twain's comments, like those of many modern readers, reveal that he never took the book seriously.

In his *New Yorker* article, Gopnik states, "The reader who sits down to read the Book of Mormon today may find it even harder going than Twain suggests. . . . Smith mimicked the endless, generation-counting longueurs of the Old Testament so skillfully that he rendered the book

---

7. *The New Yorker* (10 Sept. 2012); https://www.newyorker.com/magazine/2012/09/10/mail-53.
8. Mark Twain, *Roughing It* (New York: Harper and Brothers, 1899), Chapter 16.

dead as literature while giving it credibility as a sacred text: a book as boring as this could have been inspired only by the breath of God."

In a response to Gopnik published in the Letters to the Editor section of the *New Yorker*, I wrote:

> After a lifetime of serious study of the Book of Mormon, as a textual and literary critic, I can come to no other conclusion than that it is an amazingly complex, deep, and sophisticated book—one that contains important and, in places, even profound spiritual messages. Like many critics, Gopnik reads the book through the biography of its assumed author, Joseph Smith, and thus sees it as a product of a deluded visionary. In addition to alluding to Mark Twain's witticisms about the book, Gopnik faults it for being "compulsively biblical," a strange charge for a book claiming, in fact, to be biblical—written by Israelites who emigrated to the New World during the time of Jeremiah, and who brought the Hebrew scriptures with them as both heritage and model. Whether one sees the Book of Mormon as an ancient or a modern text, as history or fiction, like all sacred books, it deserves to be read with both an open heart and an open mind.[9]

An open heart because, as Pascal famously observed, "The heart has its reasons which reason knows nothing of. . . . We know the truth not only by the reason, but also by the heart."[10] An open mind because God is also a God of reason who speaks to our minds by appealing to our cognitive capabilities and our rational inquisitiveness. As Paul

---

9. "The Mail," *The New Yorker* (10 Sept. 2012); https://www.newyorker.com/magazine/2012/09/10/mail-53.
10. "Le coeur a ses raisons dont la raison ne sait rien." Blaise Pascal, *Pascal's Pensées* (New York: E. P. Dutton, 1958), 277. 282.

wrote, "And from one blood he made the whole world of humanity . . . So that they would be seeking and inquiring after God; and they may find him by his creation, because also he is not far from every one of us" (Acts 17:26–27, Aramaic Bible in Plain English). This is how I have tried to think and hope to continue thinking about the Book of Mormon—paying attention to beginnings and endings, to imagery and symbolism, to point of view and setting, to plot and pattern; looking for repetition, tropes, and figures; listening for consonance and assonance as well as rhythm and rhyme; looking for poetry and prophesy as well as logic and love.

As I mention in the "Preamble" to this book, over the course of a lifetime, I have taught the Book of Mormon in gospel doctrine classes as well as in seminary, institute, and university courses; written about it in scholarly journals and anthologies; and lectured about it at scholarly conferences, symposia, and firesides. In addition, I have read extensively in the secondary literature relating to it, both that which supports Joseph Smith's claims about its origins and that which postulates that it is a product of nineteenth-century imagination. Much of my interest in and approach to the Book of Mormon lies in its text, but it isn't just the vibrant, fecund landscape for intellectual inquiry and scholarly exploration that draws me to the book; it is also the vivid movement of narrative, the complexity of plot, the variety of story, the array of characters who inhabit the world of the text, and the premise that the book is about ultimate matters—God's dealings with his children in the New World and beyond, in the ancient world and today.

Learning to Love

One of the primary reasons to read scripture is that in seeing how God acts in the lives of others, we feel emboldened to invite him to act in similar ways in ours. When we see him acting in history, we believe that the ultimate fate of the world is in his hands. When we believe he truly sent his Son to die for our sins, we are inspired to change our hearts, our minds, and our lives and, in the words of the Lamanite ruler, King Lamoni, to give away all our sins to know him (Alma 22:18). While fictional characters, especially if they are artfully drawn, can also inspire us, ultimately, once beyond the narrative, we are distanced from them. We suspend our disbelief for a time, but in the end, it is still disbelief. This is not the way we are asked to engage with scripture. We are to enter the narrative with eyes of faith, believing in the truth of what we are reading, not suspending disbelief in it.

In truth, the Book of Mormon is an astonishing book, more so than most readers realize. It is not a book whose depths can be plumbed by casual or indifferent or even simply devotional reading. I believe the Book of Mormon invites our thoughtful, inquisitive, imaginative, and intelligent reading and contemplation—and I believe that in giving ourselves to it in these ways, not as fiction but as Truth, it reveals not only new depths of knowledge and understanding but also new levels of enlightenment and even of love. In his essay, "The Figure A Poem Makes," Robert Frost says a poem "begins in delight and ends in wisdom."[11] My experience in a lifetime of reading the Book of Mormon is that at times and in places, it also begins in delight and ends in wisdom, and sometimes it is the other way—it begins in wisdom and ends in delight. In both ways it is like what I have come to know of love.

To continue, in the same essay Frost says that a poem "ends in a clarification of life," which is what I also find true of certain passages, verses, and chapters in the Book of Mormon, especially those that share some of the characteristics of poetry, which in another place Frost refers to as a "thought-felt thing."[12] In another essay, "The Constant Symbol," he jokes, "[A] poem is the emotion of having a thought while the reader waits a little anxiously for the success of dawn."[13] This is also true of some sacred texts, which awaken and then, with the dawn, harmonize those two often disjointed aspects of our selves, thinking and feeling.

---

11. *Selected Prose*, 18.
12. Frost and Nature, www.frostfriends.org.
13. *Selected Prose*, 26.

Returning to Frost, we read, "The Figure a poem makes . . . is the same as for love,"[14] which I argue is also the case with some sacred texts, including the Book of Mormon. As mentioned earlier, when the angel who guides Nephi in his dream asks if he knows the meaning of the tree, Nephi responds, "It is the love of God, which sheddeth itself abroad in the hearts of the children of men; wherefore, it is the most desirable above all things" (1 Nephi 11:21–23). The importance of partaking of that fruit is affirmed by the last writer in the book, Moroni, who admonishes his readers to "come unto Christ, and be perfected in him, . . . and love God with all your might, mind and strength" (Moroni 10:32). Finding love in any book is a gift. If we don't find love in the pages of the Book of Mormon, we have not read it deeply or carefully enough.

---

14. *Ibid.,* 18.

Original Publication of
Articles and Essays Included in this Study

Prelude "It Has Opened My Heart Wide to Experience His Love," in *Converted to Christ through the Book of Mormon,* ed. Eugene England (Deseret Book, 1989), 192–98.

Chapter 2 "To Sing the Song of Redeeming Love, Alma 1–19," in *The Reader's Book of Mormon* (2008).

Chapter 3 "Ammon," in *The Book of Mormon: It Begins with A Family* (Salt Lake City: Deseret Book, 1983), 79–89.

Chapter 4 "Alma the Younger's Seminal Sermon at Zarahemla," *Bountiful Harvest: Essays in Honor of Kent Brown* (Provo, UT: Maxwell Institute, 2011), 329–344.

Chapter 5 The Heart of and In Alma 12 and 13," *A Preparatory Redemption: Reading Alma 12–13,* ed. Matthew Bowman and Rosemary Demos (Provo, UT: Maxwell Institute, 2018), 44–53.

Chapter 6 "Imagining Peace: The Example of the Nephites Following Christ's Visit to the New World," *War and Peace in Our Time: Mormon Perspectives*, ed. Patrick Q. Mason, J. David Pulsipher & Richard L. Bushman (Salt Lake City: Kofford Books, 2012), 41–55.

"Children of Light: How the Nephites Sustained Two Centuries of Peace," in *Third Nephi: An Incomparable Scripture*, ed. Andrew C. Skinner and Gaye Strathearn (Provo, UT: Maxwell Center, BYU, 2012), 309–328.

Chapter 7 "Irony in the Book of Mormon," *Journal of Book of Mormon Studies* (fall 2003), 20–31.

Chapter 8 "The Book of Mormon and Automatic Writing," *Journal of Book of Mormon Studies* 15:1 (2006), 4–17, 68–70.

Chapter 9 "Joseph Smith, the Book of Mormon and the American Renaissance," *Dialogue* 35:3 (Fall 2002), 83–112.

Chapter 10 "Joseph Smith and the American Renaissance, an Update," *Interpreter: A Journal of Mormon Scripture* 19 (2016), 1–16. See also the conversation that follows the article: http://www.mormoninterpreter. com/joseph-smith-the-book-of-mormon-and-the-american-renais- sance-an-update/#comments

Chapter 11 "John Milton, Joseph Smith and the Book of Mormon," *BYU Studies* 54:3 (2015), 6–18.

Chapter 12 "The Midrashic Imagination and the Book of Mormon," *Dialogue: A Journal of Mormon Thought* (Fall 2011), 44–66.

Permissions for publish each of the above granted by the respective authority, where required.

Robert A. Rees, Ph.D., is a scholar, university professor, poet, and humanitarian. He has taught at a number of universities including the University of Wisconsin, UCLA, UC Santa Cruz, UC Berkeley, and Vytautas Magnus University in Lithuania, where he was a Fulbright Professor (1995–96). He served as Assistant Dean of the UCLA College of Fine Arts, Director of Continuing Education in the Arts and Humanities at UCLA, Director of the UCLA-Cambridge Program, Director of the UCLA-Royal Colleges of Art and Music Programs, and Director of Education and Humanities at the Institute of HeartMath. Since 2010 he has been a Visiting Professor of Religion at Graduate Theological Union in Berkeley where he also serves as Director of Mormon Studies. Rees has published widely in the arts, humanities, education, and religious studies. He is the editor or author of numerous studies, including *Proving Contraries: Essays in Honor of Eugene England* (2005); *The Reader's Book of Mormon* (2008); *Why I Stay: The Challenges of Discipleship for Contemporary Mormons* (vol. 1. 2011; vol. 2, 2021); and a collection of poetry, *Waiting for Morning* (2017).

Rees is the co-founder and current vice-president of the Bountiful Children's Foundation, which addresses malnutrition among Latter-day Saint children in the developing world. He has served as a seminary and institute teacher, bishop, high counselor, and member of the Baltic States Mission Presidency (1994–96).

Made in the USA
Middletown, DE
19 September 2021